5/12

DAN SAVAGE is the author of the syndicated column "Savage Love" and the editorial director of Seattle's weekly newspaper *The Stranger*. TERRY MILLER is an event promoter, musician, and DJ. They were married in Canada and live in Seattle with their son, DJ.

Praise for *It Gets Better*

"An offshoot of Savage's online movement to reach out to bullied gay teens, this collection gathers inspiring essays from the likes of Ellen DeGeneres, Tim Gunn, and Barack Obama."
—*Entertainment Weekly*'s "Must List"

"Handpicked and heartfelt essays from contributors famous and obscure, gay and straight."
—*Chicago Sun-Times*

"If a copy of *It Gets Better* could find a home in every school library in America, think how many teachers, administrators, and parents would have the tools they need to improve their school's climate."
—*The Huffington Post*

"Brand-new and expanded essays, a section devoted to resources for LGBT teens, and an introduction from Savage that looks back at the project's meteoric rise to viral fame. It's chicken soup for the gay teenage soul."
—*Salon*

"The book's success springs from the variety of voices represented, both famous and unknown. . . . In addition to the narratives, the book is rich with resources for youth, parents, and teachers. . . . This is a must for all public libraries and high school libraries."
—*GBLT Reviews*

"*It Gets Better* is one of those books that slams you from emotion to emotion in six pages or less. Readers will get teary, they'll laugh, nod their heads, gasp, and want to scream. And this book isn't just for teens: adults who need it and read it will find comfort here, too."
—*The Bookworm Sez*

"We now ⌐ ⌐ ⌐ ⌐ ⌐ ⌐ ⌐ ⌐ ⌐ ⌐ ⌐ ⌐ ⌐ ⌐ ⌐ ⌐ real people overcomi⌐ ⌐ ⌐ ⌐ ⌐ ⌐ ⌐ ⌐ ⌐ ⌐ ⌐ ⌐ ⌐ ⌐ , for *RedEye*

Also by Dan Savage

*Savage Love: Straight Answers from America's
Most Popular Sex Columnist*

*The Kid: What Happened After My Boyfriend
and I Decided to Go Get Pregnant*

*Skipping Towards Gomorrah: The Seven Deadly Sins
and the Pursuit of Happiness in America*

The Commitment: Love, Sex, Marriage, and My Family

IT GETS BETTER

Coming Out, Overcoming Bullying,
and Creating a Life Worth Living

**Edited by DAN SAVAGE
and TERRY MILLER**

A PLUME BOOK

PLUME
Published by the Penguin Group
Penguin Group (USA) Inc., 375 Hudson Street, New York, New York 10014, U.S.A; Penguin
Group (Canada), 90 Eglinton Avenue East, Suite 700, Toronto, Ontario, Canada M4P
2Y3 (a division of Pearson Penguin Canada Inc.); Penguin Books Ltd., 80 Strand, London
WC2R 0RL, England; Penguin Ireland, 25 St. Stephen's Green, Dublin 2, Ireland (a division
of Penguin Books Ltd.); Penguin Group (Australia), 250 Camberwell Road, Camberwell,
Victoria 3124, Australia (a division of Pearson Australia Group Pty. Ltd.); Penguin Books
India Pvt. Ltd., 11 Community Centre, Panchsheel Park, New Delhi – 110 017, India;
Penguin Group (NZ), 67 Apollo Drive, Rosedale, Auckland 0632, New Zealand (a division of
Pearson New Zealand Ltd.); Penguin Books (South Africa) (Pty.) Ltd., 24 Sturdee Avenue,
Rosebank, Johannesburg 2196, South Africa

Penguin Books Ltd., Registered Offices: 80 Strand, London WC2R 0RL, England

Published by Plume, a member of Penguin Group (USA) Inc. Previously published in a
Dutton edition.

First Plume Printing, March 2012
10 9 8 7 6 5 4 3 2 1

Ⓟ REGISTERED TRADEMARK—MARCA REGISTRADA

CIP data is available.

ISBN 978-0-525-95233-6 (hc.)
ISBN 978-0-452-29761-6 (pbk.)

Printed in the United States of America
Original hardcover design by Daniel Lagin

ALWAYS LEARNING   PEARSON

For all the LGBT kids . . .

CONTENTS

. . . .

"You gotta give 'em hope."

—HARVEY MILK

STAY WITH US

• • • • • • • • • • • • • • • • • • •

by Jules Skloot
BROOKLYN, NY

Okay. Listen up, people.

It gets better. You being here makes this world a more blessed place. There's art to be made. And there are songs to be sung. There's so much to learn about yourself. There are sexy people to make out with. Yeah.

There's joy coming for you. So stay with us. It gets better.

• •

Jules Skloot is a performer, choreographer, and educator working to make things better every day in Brooklyn, New York.

INTRODUCTION

· ·

One hundred videos.

That was the goal, and it seemed ambitious: one hundred videos—best-case scenario: two hundred videos—made by lesbian, gay, bisexual, and transgender adults for lesbian, gay, bisexual, and transgender youth.

I was sitting in a hotel room in Bloomington, Indiana, when I began to suspect that we were going to see a lot more than one hundred videos. The video that I had made with my husband, Terry, a week earlier, the very first It Gets Better video, had been live on YouTube for just a few hours when e-mails and likes and friend requests started coming in so fast that my computer crashed. The second It Gets Better video arrived within twenty-four hours. Three days later we hit one hundred videos. Before the end of the first week, we hit one thousand videos.

Terry and I were relieved to learn that we weren't the only people out there who wanted to reach out to LGBT kids in crisis.

Justin Aaberg was just fifteen when he killed himself in the summer of 2010. He came out at thirteen, and endured years of bullying at the hands of classmates in a suburban Minnesota high school. Justin hanged himself in his bedroom; his mother found his body.

Billy Lucas, also fifteen, wasn't gay-identified but he was perceived to be gay by his classmates in Greensburg, Indiana. His tormentors threatened him, called him a fag, and urged him to kill himself. Billy hanged himself in a barn on his grandmother's property in early September of 2010. His mother found his body.

Reading about Justin and Billy was emotionally crushing—I was particularly outraged to learn that "Christian" parents were blocking efforts to address the rampant anti-gay bullying at Justin's school, claiming that doing so would somehow infringe upon the "religious freedom" of their straight children—and I began to think about the problem of anti-gay bullying.

I was aware of anti-gay bullying, of course. I had been bullied in the Catholic schools my parents sent me to; my husband endured years of much more intense bullying—it's amazing he survived—at the public high school he attended; I knew that many of my LGBT friends had been bullied. But it wasn't something we talked about or dwelt on.

I was stewing in my anger about what had been done to Justin and Billy when I read this comment, left on a blog post I wrote about Billy: "My heart breaks for the pain and torment you went through, Billy Lucas. I wish I could have told you that things get better."

What a simple and powerful truth. Things get better—things *have* gotten better, things *keep* getting better—for lesbian, gay, bisexual, and transgender people.

I knew that to be true because things had certainly gotten better for me.

I came to fully understand that I was gay—that I had always been gay—when I was a thirteen-year-old boy being bullied at a Catholic school on the north side of Chicago. I became increasingly estranged from my parents at a time when I needed them most because I was working so hard to hide who I was from them. Five years later, I found the courage to start coming out. Coming out is a long process, not a single event, and I tested the waters by telling my eldest brother, Billy, before telling my mom or dad. Billy was supportive and it helped me decide to tell my mother, which would be the hardest thing I had yet done in my life. Because coming out in 1982 didn't just mean telling my mother that I was gay. It meant telling her that I would never get married, that I would never be a parent, that my professional life would be forever limited by my sexuality.

Eight years after coming out, I would stumble into a rewarding and unlikely career as a sex-advice columnist, of all things, and somehow leverage that into a side gig as a potty-mouthed political pundit. And fifteen years after coming out, I would adopt a son with the love of my life—the man I would marry—and, with him at my side, present my parents with a new grandchild, my siblings with a new nephew.

Things didn't just get better for me. All of the gay, lesbian, bisexual, and transgender adults I knew were leading rich and rewarding lives. We weren't the same people and we didn't have or want the same things— gay or straight, not everyone wants kids or marriage; people pursue happiness in different ways—but we all had so much to be thankful for, and so much to look forward to. Our lives weren't perfect; there was pain, heartbreak, and struggle. But our lives were better. Our lives were joyful.

What was to be gained by looking backward? Why dwell on the past?

There wasn't anything we could do about the bullying we had endured in school and, for too many of us, at the hands of our families. And it didn't seem like there was anything we could do about or for all the LGBT kids who were currently being bullied.

A bullied gay teenager who ends his life is saying that he can't picture a future with enough joy in it to compensate for the pain he's in now. Justin and Billy—and, as that terrible September ground on, Seth and Asher and Tyler and Raymond and Cody—couldn't see how their own lives might get better. Without gay role models to mentor and support them, without the examples our lives represent, they couldn't see how they might get from bullied gay teenager to safe and happy gay adult. And the people gay teenagers need most—their own parents—often believe that they can somehow prevent their children from growing up to be gay—or from ever coming out—by depriving them of information, resources, support, and positive role models. (Justin Aaberg's parents knew he was gay, and were supportive.)

That fall, as I thought about Justin and Billy, I reflected on how frequently I'm invited to speak at colleges and universities. I address audiences of gay and straight students, and I frequently talk about homophobia and gay rights and tolerance. But I don't get invited to speak at high schools or middle schools, the places where homophobia does the most damage. Gay kids trapped in middle and high schools would benefit from hearing from LGBT adults—lives could be saved—but very few middle or high schools would ever invite gay adults to address their student bodies. Acknowledging the existence of LGBT people, even in sex-ed curriculums, is hugely controversial. A school administrator who invited a gay adult to address an assembly before there was a crisis—before a bullied gay teenager took his own life—would quickly find herself in the crosshairs of homophobic parents and bigoted "Christian" organizations.

It couldn't happen—schools would never invite gay adults to talk to kids; we would never get permission.

I was riding a train to JFK Airport when it occurred to me that I was waiting for permission that I no longer needed. In the era of social media—in a world with YouTube and Twitter and Facebook—I could speak directly to LGBT kids right now. I didn't need permission from parents or an invitation from a school. I could look into a camera, share my story, and let LGBT kids know that it got better for me and it would get better for them too. I could give 'em hope.

But I didn't want to do it alone. I called Terry from the airport and tentatively explained my idea for a video outreach campaign. I wanted to encourage other LGBT adults to make videos for LGBT kids and post them to YouTube. I wanted to call it: The It Gets Better Project. And I wanted us to make the first video together, to talk about our lives together, to share our joy.

This was a big ask. Terry doesn't do interviews, he doesn't allow cameras in our home, he has no desire to go on television. But he said yes. My husband was the first person to recognize the power of this idea.

The second person to recognize it was our good friend Kelly O, a straight friend and a supremely talented photographer and filmmaker.

She had just one question after I explained what we wanted to do: "When can we shoot it?"

We did two takes. The first was a long, depressing video that we shot against a bare wall in our dining room. It looked like a hostage video and we both talked too much about the bullying we'd endured in high school. We watched the video and shook our heads. Kids who are currently being bullied don't need to be told what bullying looks and feels like. Kelly packed up her camera and we went to a friend's bar and tried again. This time Kelly peppered us with questions: Share a happy memory. How did you two meet? What would you tell your teenage self? Are you happy to be alive?

Kelly edited the video, created a YouTube account, and called me when it was live.

Four weeks later I got a call from the White House. They wanted me to know that the President's It Gets Better video had just been uploaded to YouTube.

My computer crashed a second time.

The It Gets Better Project didn't just crash my computer. It brought the old order crashing down. By giving ourselves permission to speak directly to LGBT youth, Terry and I gave permission to all LGBT adults everywhere to speak to LGBT youth. It forced straight people—politicians, teachers, preachers, and parents—to decide whose side they were on. Were they going to come to the defense of bullied LGBT teenagers? Or were they going to remain silent and, by so doing, give aid and comfort to the young anti-gay bullies who attack LGBT children in schools and the adult anti-gay bullies at conservative "family" organizations who attack LGBT people for a living?

The culture used to offer this deal to lesbian, gay, bisexual, and transgender people: You're ours to torture until you're eighteen. You will be bullied and tormented at school, at home, at church—until you're eighteen. Then, you can do what you want. You can come out, you can move away, and maybe, if the damage we've done isn't too severe, you can recover and build a life for yourself. There's just one thing you can't do after you turn eighteen: You can't talk to the kids we're still torturing, the LGBT teenagers being assaulted emotionally, physically, and spiritually in the same cities, schools, and churches you escaped from. And, if you do attempt to talk to the kids we're still torturing, we'll impugn your motives, we'll accuse you of being a pedophile or pederast, we'll claim you're trying to recruit children into "the gay lifestyle."

That it was the old order and it fell apart when the It Gets Better Project went viral. Suddenly gay, lesbian, bisexual, and transgender adults all over the country—*all over the world*—were speaking to LGBT youth. We weren't waiting for anyone's permission anymore. We found our voices. And LGBT adults who made videos for the project weren't just talking *at* LGBT youth. The kids who watched videos sent e-mails, via YouTube, to the adults posting them. Thousands of LGBT adults who thought they were just going to contribute a video found themselves talking with LGBT youth, offering them not just hope but advice, insight, and something too many LGBT youth lack: the ear of a supportive adult who understands what they're going through.

Soon straight people—politicians and celebrities—were talking to LGBT youth, too, delivering the same message: It gets better, there's nothing wrong with you, and we're working to make it better. LGBT kids could see that the world was full of people like our friend Kelly—loving, supportive, progressive straight people. And as a capstone—living proof—that things were indeed getting better, Don't Ask/Don't Tell was finally repealed. Days later Joe Biden, who also made an It Gets Better video, would go on television and describe marriage equality—marriage rights for lesbian and gay couples—as an inevitability.

Things are getting better before our very eyes.

I do want to acknowledge what the It Gets Better Project can't do, though.

It can't do the impossible. It won't solve the problem of anti-gay bullying, everywhere, all at once, forever, overnight. The point of the project is to give despairing LGBT kids *hope*. The point is to let them know that things *do* get better, using the examples of our own lives. For some people things get better once they get out of high school, for others things get better while they're still in high school. And there are brave, out LGBT kids in high schools and middle schools all over the country who are helping to make things better—for themselves and their peers—in their schools today.

Nothing about letting LGBT kids know that it gets better excuses or precludes us from pressing for the passage of the Student Non-Discrimination Act; demanding anti-bullying programs in all schools; confronting bigots who are making things worse for all kinds of kids; and supporting the work of the Trevor Project, GLSEN, and the American Civil Liberties Union's LGBT Project's Youth & Schools program. (Indeed, the It Gets Better Project has raised tens of thousands of dollars for these organizations.) But we're not going to get legislation passed this instant and it will be years before we get anti-bullying programs and GSAs (Gay-Straight Alliances) into all public schools, and we may never get them into the private evangelical schools where they're needed most.

In the meantime, while we work to make our schools safer, we can and should use the tools we have at our disposal right now—social media and YouTube and digital video and this book—to get messages of hope to kids who are suffering *right now* in schools that do not have GSAs and to kids whose parents bully and reject them for being lesbian, gay, bisexual, or transgender. There's nothing about the It Gets Better Project—nothing about making a video or sharing one—that prevents people from doing more. Indeed, we've heard from thousands of people who were inspired to do more after making or watching a video.

A few weeks after we launched the It Gets Better Project, this letter arrived for me and my husband:

Thank you for the It Gets Better Project. My son is 14 and a sophomore in high school in rural Kentucky. He isn't athletic. He isn't religious. He isn't in ROTC. He is constantly being called "gay" or "faggot," oftentimes by the people he thought were his friends. . . . So far, it hasn't gone beyond name-calling, but I worry. I showed him your site the day it went live. He sat down and watched the video that you and Terry put up. Since then, I have seen him checking the site out on his own. I don't know if he is gay, but I do know that your message has touched him. Although he does confide that four years is still a long time to wait for things to get better. I think that seeing so many other people say the same thing holds much more weight than having his mother tell him. So thank you again for sharing.

Four years *is* a long time to wait. So let's all commit to making things better right now, let's all do what we can to create a world where no child, gay or straight, is bullied for being different.

We don't live in that world yet. There are children out there who are being bullied every day, and while gay, lesbian, bisexual, or transgender children aren't the only kids dealing with this harassment, they are often more isolated, more alone, and more at risk.

Nine out of ten LGBT students report experiencing bullying in their schools; LGBT teenagers are four to seven times likelier to attempt suicide. LGBT children who are rejected by their families are eight times likelier to attempt suicide and at much higher risk of winding up homeless and living on the streets.

If you know a child who's being bullied for being gay or perceived to be gay—particularly if you know a child who isn't lucky enough to have a mother like the one who wrote to us—you can help that child find hope by helping them find their way to this book and the It Gets Better Project's website (itgetsbetter.org), with more than ten thousand videos and counting.

Do your part. Give 'em hope.

DAN SAVAGE
SEATTLE, WA

PRESIDENT OBAMA
SHARES HIS MESSAGE OF HOPE AND SUPPORT FOR LGBT YOUTH WHO ARE STRUGGLING WITH BEING BULLIED

∙∙∙∙∙∙∙∙∙∙∙∙∙∙∙∙∙∙∙∙∙∙∙∙∙∙∙∙∙∙∙∙∙

WASHINGTON, DC

Like all of you, I was shocked and saddened by the deaths of several young people who were bullied and taunted for being gay, and who ultimately took their own lives. As a parent of two daughters, it breaks my heart. It's something that just shouldn't happen in this country.

We've got to dispel the myth that bullying is just a normal rite of passage—that it's some inevitable part of growing up. It's not. We have an obligation to ensure that our schools are safe for all of our kids. And to every young person out there, you need to know that if you're in trouble, there are caring adults who can help.

I don't know what it's like to be picked on for being gay. But I do know what it's like to grow up feeling that sometimes you don't belong. It's tough. And for a lot of kids, the sense of being alone or apart—I know can just wear on you. And when you're teased or bullied, it can seem like somehow you brought it on yourself for being different, or for not fitting in with everybody else.

But what I want to say is this. You are not alone. You didn't do anything wrong. You didn't do anything to deserve being bullied. And there is a whole world waiting for you, filled with possibilities. There are people out there who love you and care about you just the way you are. And so, if you ever feel like because of bullying, because of what people are saying, that you're getting down on yourself, you've got to make sure to reach out to people you trust. Whether it's your parents, teachers, folks that you know care about you just the way you are, you've got to reach out to them; don't feel like you're in this by yourself.

The other thing you need to know is: Things will get better. And more than that, with time you're going to see that your differences are a source of pride and a source of strength. You'll look back on the struggles you've faced with compassion and wisdom. And that's not just going to serve you, but it will help you get involved and make this country a better place.

It will mean that you'll be more likely to help fight discrimination—not just against LGBT Americans, but discrimination in all its forms. It means you'll be more likely to understand personally and deeply why it's so important that as adults we set an example in our own lives and that we treat everybody with respect. That we are able to see the world through other people's eyes and stand in their shoes—that we never lose sight of what binds us together.

As a nation we're founded on the belief that all of us are equal and each of us deserves the freedom to pursue our own version of happiness; to make the most of our talents; to speak our minds; to not fit in; most of all, to be true to ourselves. That's the freedom that enriches all of us. That's what America is all about. And every day, it gets better.

Barack H. Obama was elected the forty-fourth President of the United States on November 4, 2008, and sworn in on January 20, 2009. He and his wife, Michelle, are the proud parents of two daughters, Malia, twelve, and Sasha, nine. President Obama has published three books: *Dreams of My Father: A Story of Race and Inheritance, The Audacity of Hope: Thoughts on Reclaiming the American Dream,* and *Of Thee I Sing: A Letter to My Daughters.*

YOU WILL FIND YOUR PEOPLE

● ●

by Laurel Slongwhite

BALTIMORE, MD

When I was ten, my family moved to a suburb of Boston, Massachusetts, and, for the first time, my sister and I were put into Seventh-Day Adventist schools. My family's very conservative Christian. These schools were really small. There were only a hundred kids, total, in grades K through 8. And the high school had only fifty students altogether.

I did not fit in.

When I started at these schools, I was only ten and I didn't know I was gay. I knew I didn't like boys, and I knew I was different. But I didn't quite understand what that meant yet. The other kids knew I was different, too, and they picked on me. I was actually afraid to go to school because I got made fun of all the time. And once I got there, on any given day, I was afraid to move. Because if I moved, they'd see me, they'd notice me. And every time somebody noticed me, they would make fun of me. They said terrible things. I remember getting a note from one student saying, "If you're too stupid to know how to kill yourself, I can offer you some suggestions." I went to the principal when it got bad enough. I actually cried myself to sleep in her office.

She told me, "Don't take it personally. Your class has always had a scapegoat." Which, I've got to tell you, did not help a hell of a lot. I tried running away from school. I tried to kill myself. I just didn't believe it would ever get better. I didn't think it was possible. I tried to kill myself when I was ten years old. And again when I was twelve. And again when I was thirteen.

High school was both better and worse. The other students weren't as cruel but, because I had been dealing with this for so long, by the time I got there I was pretty mad and was acting out. The teachers decided that I was a bad kid and told me that all the time. I had to stand in front of a church tribunal, where I was told to beg God for forgiveness for my anger. I remember getting a letter from a church elder telling me that my parents were ashamed of me.

As soon as I graduated, it got better. It got better immediately. I lived at home for a few years after high school and went to a community college. And, even though I was staying with my parents while I was doing that, it was still better. I came out while I was living with my parents. They weren't happy about it. After all, they were very conservative Christians. They said some things that were pretty mean, and some things that were kind of silly. My mom said at one point, "You're just doing this because you're used to rejection." And, "You're just doing this because you're desperate to be *accepted*." They told me that I couldn't bring home any girlfriends and that I wasn't allowed to do this while I was in their house or under their roof.

A year after graduating from the community college, I went away to a four-year college and moved out of the house. And then my life got amazing. If I had managed to kill myself when I was ten or twelve or thirteen, then I would have missed out on meeting my people. On finding friends. And that would have been terrible. I would have missed out on learning another language. I would have missed out on going to Ecuador and Denmark. I would have missed out on this amazing trip I took a couple of years ago with a couple of my friends. Just for a weekend we rented this crappy hotel room in Savannah and spent all of our money on expensive restaurants and amazing food. It was fantastic and I would have missed that.

If I had killed myself, I would have missed out on having a horribly awkward first date with a girl. She was *way* too hot for me, and I was way too excited and incredibly intimidated. Just going out with her was amazing. I would have missed having a first kiss. I would have missed falling in love. I would have missed breaking up. I know, that's the crappy part. Who likes that? But I'm glad I didn't miss it.

I am glad I did not miss out on having an amazing relationship with my family. I really thought they were ashamed of me, that I was hurting them somehow by being gay. And it's just not true. I believed all that crap I was told when I was young. I believed that I was going to hell and that I was a bad kid and that I was hurting my parents. And none of it was true.

My parents tell me all the time now how proud they are of me; how much they love me. They're proud that I've worked so hard to go back to school. They're proud that I've moved to a city and have all these friends. They are so proud of me, period. And it's not even that they're proud despite the fact that I am gay. My mom tells me all the time that the day I left the church is the day she knew she succeeded as a parent. She tells me she is proud to have a gay daughter—somebody who is brave enough to choose her own way. It is amazing to hear that, and to believe it. To know without question that my whole family—my grandparents, my sister, my aunts and uncles and cousins—they all love me and are proud of me. I would have missed knowing that. And I'm glad I didn't. I'm glad I didn't miss that.

I'm glad that I got to the good part. And you will, too. Your people are out there, whoever you are. If you're a geek, like I am. If you're a queer theater kid. If you're a jock. If you're a loner. It does not matter who you are. It might feel like nobody can understand you, and nobody will ever like you, but your people are out there. You will find friends and you'll find love and you'll find happiness. You will get to the good part. You just have to slog through a little bit of crap first. And that sucks. I'm really sorry about that.

If you start feeling bad, just look at these amazing people who are part of this project. It's not just me. It got better for all of us. We're not all the same. We grew up at different times; we grew up in different places; we have different families. And we have different problems that we faced along the way. But it still got better for all of us. And it will get better for you, too. I promise. Your life will be amazing; you just have to get there.

The good parts—they're totally out there waiting for you. Don't give up.

Laurel Slongwhite is addicted to higher education and helping people. She recently started medical school, living the dream of becoming Mother Teresa in comfortable shoes. In her free time, she helps run an LGBT youth group near Baltimore, Maryland.

THE LIFE ALMOST LOST

by Bruce Ortiz

CHICAGO, IL

The beginning of high school wasn't actually that bad. I went to a fairly culturally diverse school. My sister attended the same school two years ahead of me, so as a freshman I already had this built-in support system. Since she already had a group of friends, I was able to fit into that crowd, in addition to making my own friends and finding my own way.

By the middle of my sophomore year, I began to question my sexuality, a process that really rocked my self-esteem and confidence. And, while I still had the support of my sister and friends during that time, it started to feel more like a curse than a blessing. I could lean on them to try and forget what I was dealing with, but at the same time, I felt I had to hide myself. I felt I had no one that I could fully confide in and that I couldn't fully explore who I was discovering myself to be. Despite being surrounded by all of these people, I felt I had no one I could really talk to.

By the end of my junior year, my family moved, and I had to go to a different high school, one very different from the first. This school was not culturally diverse, and within the first week a decision I made would set the tone for the rest of my time there. I was sitting next to someone who started making fun of another student, making homophobic jabs at him. I don't know if maybe I was feeling brave at the time or feeling that since I was at a new school I could make a new start, or what, but I defended him. And within a day, I was marked as the new gay guy, "the fag." Even then, I wasn't all that sure about my sexuality. I was even dating a woman. Regardless, I experienced a lot of bullying from that point on. I got pushed into lockers, got called names, and was generally made to feel like an outcast. It was a really rough time, and all I kept thinking was, "I need to graduate; I need to get out of this school." I knew I needed to get out of that town and go someplace else where I could be more accepted. I thought college would be the answer.

Fast-forward to my freshman year of college and a hospital ICU, where I found myself after an attempted overdose—things had clearly not gotten better after leaving high school. Instead, I was in a new environment where I felt I had no support, and I had no coping skills at all. I just wanted to be done with it. I really didn't know any other way to deal with it.

While I was in the hospital, the doctor told my family that they should probably start calling other family members because it looked like I wasn't going to make it. It looked like I was going to pass away. But I was given a second chance; I pulled through. It took a long time after that for me to find peace—to make peace with myself, with the issues I was struggling with. It also took me some time to make peace with my family. It was pretty hard on them. They felt helpless; they didn't understand why I hadn't gone to them for support. And yet, I hadn't really known I could.

In those months after I left the hospital, there was a lot of communication with my family. We became a lot more open, sharing thoughts and feelings in a way we hadn't before. I'm so thankful that I was given this second chance. My family is great. My parents, the people I wasn't sure would love me if they knew who I really was, are my number one supporters now.

It's been ten years now, and I have a really wonderful partner who loves me. We've been together for more than five years and just recently bought a home to share together. We've begun talking about having a family of our own, too. My parents love him. My whole family loves him. My partner recently told me a story about my dad. We were at an engagement party for my sister, and my dad and my partner were outside together, and my father looked at him and asked, "When are you and my son getting married?" That's a really remarkable moment, you know? I certainly did not give my father, or my family, enough credit.

I just didn't give them enough credit.

Life is so much better now than it was in high school or college. I have a wonderful family and an amazing support system. And while I went through a lot of struggles, life definitely did get better. I didn't think it would while I was in high school and college. I felt like nothing could get better—I felt like I was very alone. I'm so glad that I was given that second chance after my suicide attempt, but not everyone's so lucky. It's not worth trying it. It's not worth the attempt. Just go out there, find your support system, find that support system within yourself because life does get better. It's going to be rough; and you may be surrounded with people who don't understand you, or you may feel like you're alone, but you're going to find that support system. I had that support with me all along. I was just too scared to recognize it. I was too blinded by the fear of rejection to give my family the opportunity to get to know me. I wasn't giving them enough credit, and sometimes you have to trust and give people more credit to learn who you are and still love you for you. You have to give yourself credit, too. Trust that even with rejection, you have strength within yourself to pick yourself back up and carry on. You're going to find the people who love and support you. You're going to learn how to love and support yourself. And you're going to live a very happy life.

Bruce Ortiz lives in Chicago, Illinois, with his partner and their dog, where he works full-time in the marketing industry and part-time in the creative arts as a professional dancer. He actively advocates on behalf of LGBTQ rights and equality and is very humbled to have participated in this important project.

IN THE EARLY MORNING RAIN

•••••••••••••••••••••••••••••••

by Jennifer Finney Boylan

BELGRADE, ME

When I was young there was a time when I figured, the hell with it. I'd never even said the word *transgender* out loud. I couldn't imagine saying it, ever. I mean, please.

So instead, one day a few years after I got out of college, I loaded all my things into the Volkswagen and started driving. I wasn't sure where I was going, but I knew I wanted to get away from the Maryland spring, with its cherry blossoms and its bursting tulips and all its bullshit. I figured I'd keep driving farther and farther north until there weren't any people. I wasn't sure what I was going to do then, but I was certain something would occur to me that would end this transgender business once and for all.

I set my sights on Nova Scotia. I drove to Maine and took a ferry out of Bar Harbor. I drove onto the SS *Bluenose* and stood on the deck and watched America drift away behind me, which as far as I was concerned was just fine.

There was someone walking around in a rabbit costume on the ship. He'd pose with you and they'd snap your picture and an hour or so later you could purchase the photo of yourself with the rabbit as a memento of your trip to Nova Scotia. I purchased mine. It showed a sad-looking boy—*I think that's a boy*—with long hair reading a book of poetry as a moth-eaten rabbit bends over him.

In Nova Scotia I drove the car east and north for a few days. When dusk came, I'd eat in a diner, and then I'd sleep either in the car or in a small tent that I had in the back. There were scattered patches of snow up there, even in May. I kept going north until I got to Cape Breton, which is about as far away as you can get from Baltimore and still be on dry land.

In Cape Breton I hiked around the cliffs, looked at the ocean. At night I lay in my sleeping bag by the sea as breezes shook the tent. I wrote in my journal, or read the poetry of Robert Frost, or grazed around in the Modern Library's *Great Tales of Terror and the Supernatural*. I read one up there called *Oh, Whistle, and I'll Come to You, My Lad*.

In the car I listened to the Warlocks sing "In the Early Morning Rain" on the tape deck. I thought about this girl I knew, Grace Finney. I thought about my parents. I thought about the clear, inescapable fact that I was female in spirit and how, in order to be whole, I would have to give up on every dream I'd had, save one.

I stayed in a motel one night that was officially closed for the season, but which the operator let me stay in for half price. I opened my suitcase and put on my bra and some jeans and a blue knit top. I combed my hair out and looked in the mirror and saw a perfectly normal-looking young woman. *This is so wrong?* I said to myself in the mirror. *This is the cause of all the trouble?*

I thought about settling in one of the little villages around here, just starting life over as a woman. I'd tell everyone I was Canadian.

Then I lay on my back and sobbed. Nobody would ever believe I was Canadian.

The next morning I climbed a mountain at the far northern edge of Cape Breton Island. I climbed up to the top, trying to clear my head, but it wouldn't clear. I kept going up and up, past the tree line, past the shrub line, until at last there was just moss.

There I stood, looking out at the cold ocean, a thousand miles below me, totally cut off from the world.

A fierce wind blew in from the Atlantic. I leaned into it. I saw the waves crashing against the cliff below. I stood right at the edge. My heart pounded.

I leaned over the edge of the precipice, but the gale blowing into my body kept me from falling. When the wind died down, I'd start to fall, then it would blow me back up again. I played a little game with the wind, leaning a little farther over the edge each time.

Then I leaned off the edge of the cliff at a sharp angle, my arms held outward like wings, my body sustained only by the fierce wind, and I thought, *Well all right. Is this what you came here to do?*

Let's do it then.

Then a huge blast of wind blew me backward and I landed on the moss. It was soft. I stared straight up at the blue sky, and I felt a presence.

Are you all right, son? said the voice. *You're going to be all right. You're going to be all right.*

Looking back now, I am still not sure whose voice that was. My guardian angel? The ghost of my father? I don't know. Does it really change things all that much, to give a name to the spirits that are watching out for us?

Still, from this vantage point—over twenty-five years later—my heart tells me that was the voice of my future self, the woman that I eventually became, a woman who, all these years later, looks more or less like the one I saw in the mirror in the motel. Looking back on the sad, desperate young man I was, I am trying to tell him something. *It will get better. It will not always hurt the way it hurts now. The thing that right now you feel is your greatest curse will someday, against all odds, turn out to be your greatest gift.*

It's hard to be gay, or lesbian. To be trans can be even harder. There have been plenty of times when I've lost hope.

But in the years since I heard that voice—*Are you all right, son? You're going to be all right*—I've found, to my surprise, that most people have treated me with love. Some of the people I most expected to lose, when I came out as trans, turned out to be loving, and compassionate, and kind.

I can't tell you how to get here from there. You have to figure that out for yourself. But I do know that instead of going off that cliff, I walked back down the mountain that morning and instead began the long, long journey toward home.

••

Jennifer Finney Boylan is the author of eleven books, including *She's Not There,* which was the first bestselling book by a transgender American. Professor of English at Colby College in Maine and Ursinus College in Pennsylvania, she is a frequent contributor to the op/ed page of *The New York Times* and *Condé Nast Traveler* magazine. She lives in Belgrade Lakes, Maine, with her spouse, Deirdre, and their children, Zach and Sean.

SOMETHING HAS CHANGED WITHIN ME

by Gregory Maguire

CONCORD, MA

I always wrote. Took my cue from *Harriet the Spy* in fifth grade and never looked back. But like many kids, I wasn't introspective. Didn't question my own identity. I came of age in a liberal time (early '70s), in a progressive Catholic environment (not always an oxymoron), among good people who were tolerant of many things as long as they went unnamed. So I remained basically clueless about myself.

For a while, in high school, a cadre of friends caught my writing habit. We scribbled approximations of our real feelings in the safety and pretend anonymity of our journals. Then we circulated these notebooks for peer review, scrawling appreciative comments or jokes in the margins. A way of sharing private apprehensions and affections in a safe environment. A pre-electronic community blog, you could call it. Nixon-era Facebook.

I'd always gone about my own business, a cheery isolate of sorts, enjoying female friends who were never, somehow, girlfriends. I'd never been part of a sports team or a male mob. Junior year, this seemed to change; I started hanging out with three musicians, teenage guys. One February afternoon, after a basement jam session, we took some hot chocolate into the parlor. One of the boys—one I later realized I'd had a crush on—closed the doors. They cleared their throats and the spokesfellow said, as kindly as possible, "We've been thinking about it, and we've decided that guys writing in journals is a faggy thing to do. We're going to stop and we think you should too."

What happened next? I suspect I left the house with a polite excuse, masking my shame and the pain of rejection. Except for pausing to rinse out my mug, I didn't hesitate, though. If to be a writer meant to be a loner, I would be a loner. I cried all the way home.

Years later, I would hear Elphaba sing on Broadway, "Something has changed within me. Something is not the same. I'm through with playing by the rules of someone else's game." Sing it, sister. Now, I realize I committed myself to becoming a writer that awful afternoon.

Of course, it wasn't just a writer I was choosing to be. I was choosing to be myself.

Gregory Maguire is a novelist best known for *Wicked*, which inspired the blockbuster Broadway musical of the same name. He has written plays, essays, picture books, science fiction, novels for children and adults, and performed original work on National Public Radio's *All Things Considered* and *Selected Shorts.* With his husband, the painter Andy Newman, and their three children, he lives in New England and in France.

This piece originally appeared in *The Boston Globe*.

ACTION MAKES IT BETTER

· ·

by Urvashi Vaid

NEW YORK, NY

Despite the title of this book, there is nothing inevitable about change for the better. The only reason big changes happen is when people like you and me decide to fight for things to change, when we take action to make things different.

Gandhi organized for decades in India to get rid of the British. In 1947 (only sixty-four years ago!), the movement he created overthrew one of the biggest colonial empires using nonviolent resistance.

Your grandmothers and great-grandmothers could not vote in the United States—it only changed in 1921 (ninety years ago!).

Black people did not have full voting rights in this country until 1965 (forty-six years ago!).

And lesbian, gay, bisexual, and transgender people did not have the right to have sexual relationships without violating criminal laws until 2003 (only eight years ago!). Or think about India: The LGBT movement just got a court to overturn the laws criminalizing same-sex/same-gender behavior in 2009 (two years ago!).

All of these changes—for women, for African Americans, for LGBT folks—took a massive social movement to make happen.

This is my story of how it's gotten better for me. I'm Indian

American, born there, and grew up here since I was eight. Like all Asian kids, my family's expectations—their dreams for me, their demands on me—weighed heavily on me, and never heavier than when I realized I was a lesbian.

But you know what? Activism saved my life. I got involved with a feminist group (of men and women working to really transform gender roles and patriarchy into a more just system). I got involved with a movement trying to end the racist Apartheid system in South Africa (you guys, it only ended in 1994!). I got involved with queer activism, with lefty groups, with all the rabble-rousers and radicals working to end the AIDS epidemic, to create a fairer economy, to win rights for immigrants, to end wars, and make the world more fun and sexy!

What I found in social movements was a whole life that has given me hope, inspiration, friendships, and my lover, Kate (of twenty-three years), whom I met at a queer conference. Social activism is all about optimism, even when you lose. The process of doing something about it all generates lots of adrenaline and serotonin that just make you feel better, like a sweaty dance to music you love.

But truthfully, social change is not always fun—just like life. There's a lot of wacky people, nut-bucket opponents, and powerful forces that want to maintain things just the way they are—so defeat, occasional despair, loss, and discomfort are all part of the process of social action.

What keeps me going, though, is a combination of stubbornness (I'll be damned if they are going to knock me around and get away with it), cold-blooded anger (don't get mad, get even), faith (social-justice activism is an act of belief in the possibility of something you do not know will ever happen), and pleasure (in the people I have met along the way, the incredible change I have been a small part of making, and the massive amounts of fun I have had along the way).

The great news is that there is a global queer movement today. And it is full of young and old people fighting to make space for us to live and love and breathe and be who we are and create the lives we imagine. You can join it; in fact you can lead it. It's all being made right before your eyes.

So make it better—get active.

• •

Urvashi Vaid is an organizer and writer who works in the progressive and LGBT movements.

YOU ARE A RUBBER BAND, MY FRIEND

••••••••••••••••••••••••••••••••••••

by Brinae Lois Gaudet

WEST BEND, WI

H igh school sucks.

It's even worse if you're lesbian, gay, bisexual, or transgender. There's the whole getting comfortable with your sexuality thing. There's the straight-girl crushes. Oh, the frustration of the straight-girl crushes! There's the school administration that can sometimes make you feel like they don't really care about you. They can seem purposefully obtuse, like they're out to make your life miserable. Sometimes your administration *is* homophobic and *is* purposefully making things hard for you, even though they're the people who are supposed to be there to help you. And then there are the other students. They're just so . . .

Yeah, we're not even going to talk about them.

I grew up in small-town, conservative Wisconsin. The town is very sheltered, and the ignorance and silence of the majority really encouraged the homophobic minority. There were many incidents of homophobia in my school and community. The one that had the biggest effect on me personally was when a member of my community forced the removal of all "safe zone" posters from classrooms. These posters stated that harassment based on race, religion, *sexual orientation*, et cetera, would not be tolerated by the teacher in that classroom.

It was these same posters that had made me feel a bit more comfortable in high school as a freshman, and knowing that future freshmen will not have that same comfort still upsets me today.

Overall, the atmosphere in my hometown was not exactly the best environment for a young gay girl. I know that many other people have had worse experiences, but that doesn't mean it didn't affect me. I struggled with depression and suicidal thoughts while coming to terms with my identity.

The cool thing about high school, however, is it doesn't last forever. It is not the rest of your life. It will end. Once you get out of high school you are free. You are no longer trapped in those prisonlike walls for seven hours a day. You can go see the world. You can go do things; you can get an education; you can make something of your life.

I am a freshman in college now. I haven't even been out of high school for a year and already I can see how awesome life is beyond high school. I know it gets tough and sometimes you feel like there's no way to possibly go on. But now I am here in an awesome, much better place for me, and it's wonderful. The most astounding thing to me was seeing a "safe zone" poster outside my RA's door. This poster, which had been so controversial in my high school, is now something to be taken for granted every time I come home after class.

Once you're out of high school you can find an environment that will support you. You can find an environment where you can be happy, where you'll find people that will be there for you and accept you and love you the way you are. And you can meet cute girls! Or boys, I guess, I don't know. I haven't really been paying attention to them, but . . . I guess they're around here.

Think about it this way: Imagine you are a rubber band and right now you are pulled taut. You have all this potential energy building up and you are going to go so far once your potential is unleashed on the world. I know that sometimes the stretching hurts, it feels like you're going to break, but please just hold on. You can make it through this, and once you're let go you're going to fly so far.

The important thing to keep in mind now is that there is an end in sight. It is there. A better life is in your future and you can make it there. I believe in you. You have the power to be happy in your life and you are going to do amazing things. So please, please, please remember: It will end. It will get better.

And I love you.

....

Brinae Lois Gaudet is a first-year student at the University of Wisconsin majoring in "undeclared." She likes alphabetizing, British actors, Finnish metal bands, grammar, Harry Potter, the Internet, nerdfighteria, *Star Trek,* and your face. It's freaking gorgeous.

GOD BELIEVES IN *YOU*

• •

by Bishop Gene Robinson

CONCORD, NH

I know that many of you might be feeling in a dark place right now because religion and religious people are telling you that you are an abomination before God. Maybe you're growing up in a Roman Catholic household and you hear from your Church that you are intrinsically disordered. Or maybe you're growing up in a Mormon household or a Southern Baptist household and you're told that somehow your life is not acceptable to God.

Well, I want to tell you, as a religious person, that they are flat-out wrong. God loves you beyond anything you can imagine. And God loves you the way you are. I am an out and proud gay man, who is also the bishop of New Hampshire. A bishop in the Episcopal Church. I am living proof that it gets better. And that it *is* getting better.

Growing up in a fundamentalist congregation, I heard and believed that God found me unworthy of His love, even unworthy of the same respect accorded other human beings. Yet I became the first openly gay and partnered man ever to be elected to the office of bishop in the worldwide Anglican Communion. That is astounding proof that it is not only getting better for LGBT people in the world, but also in the Church.

You can have the life that you hope for because God hopes for that kind of life for you, a better life. If you want a partner, or when marriage equality comes—and it will come—you can have a husband or wife and live together and make a life together. If you want children, you can have children. And you can be a great mom or dad.

God loves you the way you are. God doesn't want you to change. God doesn't want you to be cured or healed, because there's nothing to be healed from. You are the way you are, the way God made you. And the way God loves you.

It gets better, I promise. And it is getting better all the time. Things are changing. So if you're considering hurting yourself, please don't. God wants you to live in the light of God's love and that light will take away all of this darkness. So hang in there. Be strong. And know that despite the messages you get from religious people, God loves you beyond your wildest imagining and only wants the best for you.

• •

In 2003, the Episcopal Diocese of New Hampshire elected **Gene Robinson** to be its ninth bishop of New Hampshire. In addition to leading his diocese, Bishop Robinson has been a leading advocate, nationally and internationally, for LGBT rights. In January 2009, he was asked by Barack Obama to pray the invocation for the opening inaugural event at the Lincoln Memorial in Washington, DC.

LA PERSONA POR LA QUE VALE LA PENA LUCHAR, ERES TU

de Alex R. Orue

Sé lo difícil que puede ser de crecer en un lugar con mentalidad cerrada. Soy un chavo latino y gay de diecinueve años, vengo de la Ciudad de México. Y aunque vengo de una de las ciudades más progresivas en Latinoamérica (en el sentido legal), estos valores no aplican a la sociedad como un todo. No hay duda de que México ha progresado mucho en asuntos de derechos humanos en años recientes, como al legalizar el matrimonio gay y las adopciones homo-parentales. Aún así, a pesar de los avances, la religión y los valores tradicionales aún influyen enormemente en la sociedad Mexicana, especialmente en las generaciones anteriores.

Crecí en una familia políticamente diversa. La familia de mi mamá es muy liberal y la de mi papá es muy conservadora y muy católica. Por esta polaridad, nunca tuve el valor de decirle a mi familia que era gay. En la escuela, las cosas eran muy diferentes. Desde la primaria, la gente parecía que sabía que yo era gay mucho antes de que yo mismo lo supiera. Y como resultado, la escuela fué muy difícil. Cuando los niños encuentran algo con que burlarse de alguien, molestan y abusan una y otra vez.

La Secundaria y la Preparatoria, fueron mejores etapas para mi, aunque no por razones de las que este orgulloso. Como dice el dicho: "Si no puedes con el enemigo, únetele." Y eso fué lo que hice. Aprendía ser duro. Le entré al juego, y sí, fuí cruel con la gente, aunque nunca un gandaya. Me burlaba de la gente pero nunca por lo que eran, solo por lo que decían o hacían. Aún así no estoy orgulloso de eso. Supongo que muchos de ustedes entenderán. Si uno no le entraba al juego, era suicidio social. Y muchos de los gandayas no se detenían en los insultos; incluso suelen llegar a la violencia física.

Después de la graduación, me mudé a Canadá, para estudiar la carrera y he estado viviendo en Vancouver por casi dos años. Es totalmente diferente aquí. Viviendo en México casi toda mi vida, siempre recibí el mensaje de que ser gay estaba mal. Que era malo. Que era una enfermedad. Que ser gay significaba que eventualmente me enfermaría de SIDA. Que significaba que era un pervertido.

Pero viviendo en Canadá, es totalmente distinto. Recuerdo que la primera vez que fui a la calle Davie (el área gay del centro de Vancouver) ví a gente, parejas gay, tomadas de la mano y besandose en público. Simples gestos como cosas que heterosexuales dan por hecho. Cosas normales. Viviendo aquí he aprendido de yo mismo y a dejar ir todos esos tabúes, todos esos miedos que he cargado conmigo desde muy niño.Y ahora, afortunadamente, soy abiertamente gay. Mi familia lo sabe y las cosas han mejorado desde entonces.

Me imagino que muchas otras personas tienen historias más difíciles y otras más fáciles. El punto es que no podemos dejarnos llevar por las cosas y personas negativas en nuestras vidas. Hay mucha gente retrograda en el mundo, y desafortunadamente, algunos de nosotros tenemos que dejar nuestros lugares de origen en orden para vivir abierta y honestamente. Tenemos que viajar lejos, como yo lo hice. Pero las cosas mejoraran eventualmente en todos lados, y a nivel individual, las cosas mejoran una vez que uno es capaz de vivir honestamente con uno mismo y con aquellos nuestro alrededor. La familia eventualmente te aceptará y al final verás quienes son tus verdaderos amigos, aunque termines contándolos con los dedos de una sola mano.

Para ver las maravillas que esta vida te tiene preparado, tienes que vivir. Y a veces la mejor venganza contra aquellos que te insultaron y te hicieron sentir mal, es vivir bien.

Eventualmente encontrarás a esa persona que te hará feliz y a quien harás feliz.

Pero para que eso pase. Tienes que aguantar.

THE PERSON WORTH FIGHTING FOR IS YOU

∙∙

English Translation by Alex R. Orue

VANCOUVER, BC

I know how difficult it can be to grow up in a narrow-minded place. I'm a nineteen-year-old, Latino gay guy from Mexico City. And although I come from one of the most progressive cities in Latin America (in a legal sense), these values do not run through the society as a whole. There's no doubt that Mexico has made a lot of progress on human rights issues in recent years, like legalizing gay marriage and adoption by gay couples. Yet despite these advances, religion and traditional values still have an enormous influence on Mexican society, especially among older generations.

I grew up in a politically diverse family. My mother's family was very liberal and my father's was very conservative and very Catholic. Because of this polarity, I never had the courage tell my family I was gay. At school, things were totally different. Even in elementary school, people seemed to know that I was gay before I did. And as a result, school was really difficult. When kids find something about you to make fun of, they will tease and bully you over and over.

Junior high and high school were better for me, though not for reasons I am necessarily proud of. As the saying goes, "If you can't defeat your enemy, join them." And that's what I did. I learned to be tough,

I played the game, and yes, I was cruel to other people, though never a real bully. I would mock people but never for what they were, just for something they had said or done. Still, I'm not proud of it. I suspect many of you might understand. If you didn't join in and play by their rules, it was social suicide, and a lot of the bullies didn't stop at insults and name-calling; they resorted to physical violence.

After graduation, I moved to Canada to attend college and have been living in Vancouver for nearly two years now. It's totally different here. Living in Mexico most of my life, I'd always gotten the message that being gay was wrong. That it was evil. That it was an illness. That being gay meant that I would eventually get infected with the AIDS virus. That it meant I was a pervert.

But here in Canada it's totally different. I remember the first time I went to Davie Street (the unofficial gay Village of downtown Vancouver). I saw people, gay couples, holding hands on the street and kissing in public. Simple gestures like that, things that straight people take for granted. Normal things. Living here I've come to learn about myself and let go of all those taboos, all those fears, I've carried around since I was a kid. And now, fortunately, I am openly gay. My family knows and things have gotten better ever since.

I imagine lots of other people have stories that are more difficult, and others that are easier. The point is we cannot let ourselves be dragged down by negative events and negative people in our lives. There're so many bigoted people in the world, and unfortunately, some of us have to leave the places we are from in order to live openly and honestly. We have to travel away, like I did. Eventually things will get better everywhere, and on an individual level, things do get better once you are able to be open with yourself and those around you. Your family will eventually accept you, and in the end you'll see who your real friends are, even if you can count them all on one hand.

To see the wonders this life has prepared for you, you gotta live. And sometimes the best revenge against all of those people who insulted you and made you feel bad is to live well.

Eventually you'll find that person that will make you happy and whom you'll make happy, too.

But for that to happen, you gotta hold on.

. . . .

Born in Texcoco (just outside Mexico City) in 1990, **Alex R. Orue** grew up as the first of three sons of a successful entrepreneur/ businessman and a dedicated mother. With a little incentive from both parents (and a personal interest in travel), he moved to Vancouver, Canada, after high school. He is currently studies at Langara College in the psychology department and he also volunteers at Friends For Life Society.

A MESSAGE FROM
ELLEN DEGENERES

• •

LOS ANGELES, CA

I was devastated over the death of eighteen-year-old Tyler Clementi. Tyler was a bright student at Rutgers University whose life was senselessly cut short. He was outed as being gay on the Internet and he killed himself.

Something must be done. There have been a shocking number of news stories about teens who have been teased and bullied and then committed suicide, like thirteen-year-old Seth Walsh in Tehachapi, California; thirteen-year-old Asher Brown in Cypress, Texas; and fifteen-year-old Billy Lucas in Greensburg, Indiana. This needs to be a wake-up call to everyone that teenage bullying and teasing is an epidemic in this country, and the death rate is climbing.

One life lost in this senseless way is tragic. Four lives lost is a crisis. And these are just the stories we hear about. How many other teens have we lost? How many others are suffering in silence? Being a teenager and figuring out who you are is hard enough without someone attacking you.

My heart is breaking for their families, their friends, and for our society that continues to let this happen. These kids needed us. We have an obligation to change this. There are messages everywhere that validate this kind of bullying and taunting and we have to make it stop. We can't let intolerance and ignorance take another kid's life.

I want anyone out there who feels different and alone to know that I know how you feel. There is help out there. You can find support in your community. If you need someone to talk to or if you want to get involved, here are some organizations doing great work: The Trevor Project (at 866-4U-TREVOR) is a twenty-four-hour national help line for gay and questioning teens. And Angels and Doves is a nationwide anti-bullying nonprofit organization (www.angelsanddoves.com).

Things will get easier, people's minds will change, and you should be alive to see it.

Ellen DeGeneres's distinctive comic voice has resonated with audiences from her first stand-up comedy appearances through her hit syndicated talk show, *The Ellen DeGeneres Show*. The show, now entering its eighth season, has recently won the Daytime Emmy® for Outstanding Talk Show. In 1997, DeGeneres was the recipient of the coveted Peabody Award and earned an Emmy® for writing the critically acclaimed "Puppy Episode" for the sitcom *Ellen*, when her character came out as a gay woman to a record 46 million viewers. In 2008, DeGeneres became the newest face for CoverGirl and had the honor of hosting the highly rated seventy-ninth Annual Academy Awards. She is the author of two bestselling books, *The Funny Thing Is . . .* and *My Point . . . And I Do Have One*.

LIFE UNFOLDS EXACTLY AS IT SHOULD (BUT NOT AS YOU PLANNED)

by Sean Blane and David Rosen

OTTAWA, ON

Sean: David and I are gay. And while we're in our forties now, we were teenagers once, and we know that it's not that easy to be gay. Role models can be hard to come by, especially in very small town like the one I came from. The only gay people I saw were on 1970s TV sitcoms. (*Three's Company*, really?) I didn't even know that being gay and having a normal, fantastic life was an option then. I just figured that this was a phase I'd grow out of, you know, like my '80s hair products. Well, *Jack Tripper* got canceled and now my hair is a lot shorter. Somewhere along the line I knew it was going to get better. The first sign was probably when David and I met each other when we were about twenty-five years old. We've been together for almost twenty years now. We've both got good jobs; I'm a diplomat with the Canadian government and David's a doctor, and we've been lucky enough to have traveled all over the world. It's sometimes hard to see when you're in high school that you are as good as everyone else. Today, I think being gay's a gift. You might not realize it at the moment but it makes you special, it makes you adaptable. It gives you the ability to be successful because you have developed a lot of skills most people never acquire at such an early age. You learn how to read people; how to be an observer; how to be empathetic. But first, you've got to get through some tough parts.

David: High school can be pretty tough. It's hard having to pretend you're something that you're not. And it can feel like it's never going to end. But it does. Once you leave high school and move on to the next phase, you will come in contact with all sorts of cool people who are just like you, people who will accept you for who you are. Sean and I were both worried about telling our families we were gay. We couldn't have been more wrong! Our parents joke that we need to get married. So far we've put them off, but we did give them grandchildren. We have two children, now six and ten, whom we adopted when they were babies. Never did either of us imagine in high school that we would be gay *and* parents. It's true, you have to weather some pretty difficult years but those experiences have their rewards. That's why there are so many creative, amazing gay people. They've all withstood the horrible stuff and made it through to the other side. The other side is pretty great.

....

David Rosen is an anesthesiologist, and his partner, **Sean Blane,** is a consul with the Canadian government. But their lives are really defined not by their jobs but their roles as dads to their two kids. They still pretend to be cool but carpooling and soccer practice are making the memories of circuit parties and fabulous dinners a little distant. Nevertheless, their kids have already declared they will elope with future spouses rather than dealing with their dads as wedding planners with a 1990s point of reference.

IT GETS BETTER FOR A BRITISH SOLDIER

by Lance Corporal James Wharton

LONDON, ENGLAND

'm twenty-three years old, and I'm an openly gay soldier in the British Army. Just over ten years ago, gay men and women were not allowed to serve in the armed forces. In fact, in 1998 alone, 298 people were discharged from the army simply because they were gay. This figure is greater than the losses sustained in the Falklands and the first Gulf War.

With the help of Stonewall, the ban on gay people serving in the military was lifted in 2000. For people like me, the progress that has been made in the last ten years has been truly life-changing. I can now be myself and be open about who I am, whilst doing the job I love.

This year I celebrated my civil partnership within the barracks of the Household Cavalry Mounted Regiment and was featured on the cover of the British army's official publication, *Solider Magazine*, as an openly gay man.

It was in 2005, at the age of eighteen, that I decided to come out. I had been in the army for two years at that point and felt ready, felt confident, to tell people the truth; I was gay. In 2007, I served in Iraq with my regiment for seven months, and whilst I was in Iraq I was able to operate more effectively because I could be myself. I didn't have to hide who I was. I didn't have to lie about who I was.

The army isn't perfect yet, and there is still room for improvement. But the British Armed Services is fully committed to making the military as gay friendly as possible, a place where everyone is able to be themselves. The Royal Navy, the British Army, and the Royal Air Force are all members of the Stonewall Diversity Champions program, where employers work with Stonewall, and each other, in order to improve the working environment for lesbian, gay, and bisexual service members.

My experience shows that a lot can change in a very short space of time. Things can get better today if we all work together to combat homophobia in our workplaces and in our schools. You, too, can make a difference by challenging homophobic bullying at school and by encouraging your school to do the same. If the army can do it, you can do it, too. It gets better today; we can make it happen.

Author Note: Stonewall is a lesbian, gay, and bisexual rights organization in the United Kingdom. Now the largest gay equality organization, not only in the UK but in Europe, it was formed in 1989 by political activists and others lobbying against Section 28 of the Local Government Act (an anti-gay amendment that has since been repealed). Although Stonewall is a lobbying organization rather than membership organization, it has diversified into policy development for the rights of lesbian, gay, and bisexual people.

• •

Lance Corporal James Wharton joined the British Army in 2003 at the age of sixteen, having just left secondary school. On completion of his phase 1 training (basic) in North Yorkshire, James decided to join the Blues and Royals, a regiment that makes up one-half of the Household Cavalry. In 2006, James began preparations for operations in the Middle East, and in 2007, deployed with the Household Cavalry to Southern Iraq on a seven-month tour of duty. In 2008, James spent four months in Alberta, Canada, assisting in the training of other soldiers facing operational deployments in Afghanistan and Iraq. The following year, James returned to central London, on promotion, to carry out further ceremonial duties. James and his partner, Thomas, were united by a civil partnership in 2010 and now live together in London with their dog, Pickle.

GETTING STRONGER AND STAYING ALIVE

by Gabrielle Rivera

BRONX, NY

As a gay woman of color, I just want to let the youth know that it kind of doesn't get better. All these straight, rich celebrities, I'm not even going to name them, they can tell you that it gets better because they've got money and people don't care what they do. They're comin' from a good place and stuff. And I appreciate that, but I'm gonna be real, because I live this life and I'm not rich and I'm brown and I probably look like most of you.

First of all, it doesn't get better but what does happen is this: You get stronger. You realize what's going on; you see how people are; you see how the world is. And as an adult, you learn how to deal with it. You learn how to love yourself. You learn to just take it for what it is. You learn that other people are just crazy and caught up in their own crap.

Like all the people that are religious that say that gay people are bad, and then you see them being caught up in gay scandals. I might be gay, but I don't have relationships with prostitutes—no disrespect to prostitutes—but I don't have illicit affairs with prostitutes and get caught up in drugs. I'm a normal person that lives her life as a gay individual, has a relationship, and just tries to make it in this world. And I would have been just like some of those other kids, and taken my own life, if it hadn't been for my strong family and my religious upbringing.

My parents raised us Pentecostal Protestant with a literal interpretation of the Bible as our guide to navigating life. Coming out to my parents was insane! I thought God was going to strike me dead as the words came out of my mouth. My dad was cool but my mom flipped like it was the end of her world; the world that had me as a straight woman that would give her grandkids. I also thought God would just turn His back on me. I asked Him through prayer every night to take my life, seeing as though I was a deviant homosexual. God never took my life and so I viewed that as a sign to carry on and find love anyway that I could. Even momma eventually came around but on her own terms. I didn't force an agenda. I was just always myself and as a loving mother she found herself with no choice other than to continue loving me as she always had. Damn, now she's practically a gay rights advocate and we've never been closer.

And as for me and God, I view our relationship as hella strong. God made all of us so God made me. Therefore, in my mind, God is cool with being gay. And if Jesus were alive today, he'd chill with us because everybody else hates us. I will say this: Don't give in to this myth that it's going to be fancy and amazing when you're older and that everything's gonna to be fine. Just know that you gotta get stronger. And the stronger you get the easier dealing with all this craziness will be. The stronger you get the more you hold on to your own life; the more you'll love yourself. And you'll be better able to be in relationships with other people. You'll be better able to deal with the fact that you are gay. And you'll realize that's not the problem. It's never a problem to be gay. The problem comes from everyone else giving you a hard time about it, making laws against you because they're afraid to be who you are.

So, do I say it gets easier? No, but you get stronger. And you get more beautiful. And you believe in yourself harder. And anything this messed up world throws at you, you'll be able to handle.

Don't take your own life. It's not worth it. If you take your own life, they win. And if you take your own life, that's one less gay person of color, or white, or disabled, or multi-abled, or whatever, that isn't here, able to show them the truth. So please love yourself. Please be strong. And you'll be all right. That, I do promise you.

· ·

Gabrielle Rivera is a Puerto Rican queer born and raised in the Bronx. She is a writer, poet, and director. Her short film, *Spanish Girls Are Beautiful,* details a night in the life of a group of queer Latinas navigating love and parties in an urban world. Her short stories have been pubished in *Hip Mama* magazine and *Portland Queer: Tales of the Rose City,* an anthology edited by Ariel Gore.

COMING OUT OF THE SHTETL: GAY ORTHODOX JEWS

by Marc Tannen, Chaim Levin, Ely Winkler, Justin Spiro, Moishie Rabinowitz, and Mordechai Levovitz

NEW YORK, NY

Chaim: Growing up, I always knew that there was something different about me. What you'd call queer or strange or what I felt was strange.

Ely: It's hard to explain when a person knows that they're gay. In general, I think it was just a feeling of being different from everyone else.

Justin: All my friends would always make jokes like, "That's so gay." Or, "What a fag." And I was so afraid that if I said I was gay, that people would make fun of me, taunt me, try to beat me up. So I didn't say anything.

Moishie: I always thought, growing up, that no one understood me.

Mordechai: The bullying never stopped in high school. It was always, "Why do you wear your hair like that? It's so girly?" Or, "Why do you talk like that? It's so high." Or, "Why do you sit like that and cross your legs? Boys don't cross their legs like that; girls cross their legs like that."

Chaim: Someone in school actually ridiculed me in public in front of fifteen other people. Not only did he embarrass me in front of all those people, but not one of those fifteen people said a word.

Mordechai: The only time I ever heard the word *gay*, was when I heard the rabbi speak about the "terrible gays" and "the gay agenda" and how they're an anathema against the Torah and Judaism.

Moishie: When I was about twelve years old, I went to an all-boys summer camp in the Catskills. It was the summer before my bar mitzvah, and my counselor took me to the side one day and said he had to speak to me about something very important. He wanted to tell me that most of the older kids in camp were talking about how Moishie Rabinowitz was a huge faggot.

Ely: As high school continued, I got more and more sad. I got more and more scared that I would never come out of it.

Mordechai: In high school, on yearbook picture day, I came to school and my hair was up in a chup [quiff] and I was wearing a colorful vest. I was just trying so hard to express myself. I was just trying to say, "This is who I am; this is Mordechai." The rabbi told me that there was no way I could be in the high school yearbook picture like that. He sent me home. My aunt happened to call the house and she sensed that something was very wrong. I think she also felt like an outsider when she went to high school. She said, "Mordechai, sometimes high school, sometimes day school, sometimes even college is just terrible. It's not fun. But I promise you that if you stick it out, it gets better. I promise you that there will be a time when you feel wanted in this world, when you feel like you can give something to this world, and when feel accepted and loved. But you just have to stick it out. You just have to live through this really hard time." And that was the exact thing that I needed to hear, someone in my family saying that they understood.

Ely: There were days where I didn't want to get out of bed because I felt that nobody wanted me in the world. I was too different. I wasn't going to fit with what my community wanted from me. I wasn't going to marry a woman and I wasn't going to have the traditional modern Orthodox family and life that I wanted for myself. And I did want it so badly.

Chaim: I didn't want to be gay. I didn't think being gay was an option. So I went to reparative therapy and I spent months of time and energy trying to change. And every day that went by that I didn't change, I blamed myself. I really thought that it was my fault that I wasn't working hard enough. I wasn't trying hard enough. And according to everyone around me at the time, it was possible to change. So I was constantly blaming myself. Then one day I just realized, it's not working. It just doesn't go away. I can't change. No matter how hard I try, no matter how hard I try to take my mind off these attractions, they're not going away. There was a time in my life where I actually tried ending my life. I swallowed a bunch of pills and ended up in the hospital. I wanted to die because things were so bad. I felt like I didn't want to live anymore. But afterward, lying in the hospital bed, I realized I had so much to live for. I had so many things that were good in my life. I'm smart. I'm a nice person. I'm a good person. I am a human being, and I want to live.

Mordechai: The greatest thing that happened to me was going to college and realizing that I really wasn't alone. Even in the Yeshiva, where I went to high school, I wasn't the only gay person. There were other gay people *in* the Yeshiva. I just didn't realize it at the time. In every camp that I went—where I felt bullied and felt like nobody could be like me, that nobody was going through the same thing that I was going through—I found out later that there were other gay people there, too.

Justin: When I moved to New York City, I met a lot of people through this great organization, JQY [Jewish Queer Youth]. I met people who grew up in the Hasidic world, in the ultra-Orthodox Yeshivish world, in the modern Orthodox world, and some who became more or less religious over the course of their lives. I realized that not only were there other people like me but there were dozens and dozens of people like me.

Chaim: They understood what it was like to be closeted, to be ashamed, to be embarrassed. And these people, they set an example for me because they were all just at peace with themselves. That's something I never had.

Moishie: Ultimately, it's about living your life. The more you live your life based on who you are, the better friend, the better son, the better brother, the better Jew you will be.

Chaim: With the help of good friends and a great support system, I started realizing that it's okay. I'm okay. I'm allowed to be the way I am.

Ely: Five years ago, when I was graduating from high school and was choosing which Yeshiva I would go to for a year in Israel, I never thought that I would be sitting here today so happy and so proud of who I am. Because it's hard to be proud of who you are when your community tells you not to be. When you feel that no one around you will accept you.

Mordechai: If you stick through it, if you live long enough, you'll find that not only do you grow older and more mature, but everyone around you also grows older and more mature. People do want to learn and understand, and, ultimately, accept you.

Ely: In my last year of high school, I told my rabbi—who I was very close with at the time and still am today—and he was one of the most supportive people I have ever spoken to.

Mordechai: There are many rabbis—Orthodox rabbis—who go out of their way to tell people to be nice, understanding, sympathetic, and to accept gay people in the Orthodox community.

Ely: I wish that I could have told myself this: The love and support is there. It's out there. Your friends are out there, your teachers are out there, and even, eventually, I learned that my family was out there.

Justin: If I could now, at twenty-six, speak to my fourteen-year-old self—or even my nineteen-year-old self in college—I would say don't worry about being gay. That's who you are. That's how God created you. He created me as a Jew, and he created me as a gay person.

Moishie: If you close your eyes right now and think about what it would feel like to lift that dark cloud off, lift that burden, lift that feeling of hopelessness and despair. Think about how awesome it would be to actually be able to live who you are and still have friends and still have ties to your community and still be respected. I can promise you that that feeling is a hundred times better in real life. I promise it gets better.

Chaim Levin was born and raised in the Crown Heights Lubavitch community. He spent two years in reparative therapy. It didn't work. Today he lives in New York City and speaks on panels supporting LGBT issues.

Mordechai Levovitz grew up in an Orthodox religious family in Lawrence, Long Island. In 2001, he cofounded JQYouth (Jewish Queer Youth), a support community for Orthodox LGBT youth. He is now the co-executive director of JQYouth, spearheading educational outreach into the Orthodox community about its LGBT population.

Moishie Rabinowitz grew up in an Orthodox Jewish community in Queens, New York. He is a founding member of JQYouth. Michael works in theater producing and is currently developing a television pilot based on his childhood.

Justin Spiro earned his master's degree in social work from New York University and he currently works as a psychotherapist in a Bronx middle school. Justin has spoken on numerous panels regarding Orthodox Judaism and homosexuality.

Marc Tannen (director/editor of video) was born in London, England, and raised in the Orthodox Jewish community of Hendon.

He moved to New York in 2002 and became a founding member of JQYouth. Marc is currently in production on a feature-length documentary film about the lives of gay Orthodox Jews.

• •

Ely Winkler is a twenty-three-year-old graduate student, studying for his master's in social work at Hunter School of Social Work in New York City, where he currently resides. Since coming out two years ago, Ely has been an activist for the gay Orthodox Jewish community through social media tools such as Blogger and Facebook.

For more information about JQYouth, please visit our website, www .jqyouth.org.

GOING BACK IN

by Michael Cunningham

NEW YORK, NY

Like so many gay kids, I had a secret childhood.

There was the conventional outward childhood: school and birthday parties, family trips, all that. And there was the darker inner childhood that started before I can remember. The sense that there was something deeply wrong about me. That I was impersonating someone. That I had to keep my strangeness to myself, or it would all come toppling down.

It was a little like having an unwholesome imaginary friend. A friend who hung around even though I detested his company.

Like so many gay kids, I grew adept at impersonation. I got fluent in normalese.

I grew so fluent that, by the time I got to high school, I had a crew of guy friends, a girlfriend, all that. There were times when I believed that the nasty imaginary friend, my own personal Gollum, had gone away. But he was always there.

I went to considerable lengths to keep him hidden. I became ultra-normal. I did well in school. I hung out. I hooted along with my friends about all the girls we wanted to do nasty things to. And, yes, I laughed at the gay jokes.

Here I am on an ordinary Saturday night, getting stoned with my friends. Their names were Craig, Peter, Bronson, and Rob.

Linda's tits got bigger over the summer. She bounces really nice now.
I'd like to bounce on her.
Dream on.
I've got a thing for Vicky's ass.
You're an ass man.
I'm Vicky's ass man.
Faggot!
You're a faggot.
Yeah, right.
Who brought it up first?
Eat me.
You'd like that.
I hereby vow I'm going to nail Linda by Thanksgiving.
Dream on, faggot.

It doesn't matter which of us said what. We were all working from the same script.

I was a spy in a hostile country. I had to be perfectly adept at its ways and customs, or my true identity would be revealed, and I'd be deported. I was nervous almost all the time.

I didn't come out until I went away to college. In college, it seemed I could be somebody new, and could befriend the outcasts and miscreants, the ones who loved David Bowie and who dressed extravagantly and went to the bars in San Francisco on the weekends.

It was, in a sense, the beginning of my real life.

But still. A beginning implies an end. I felt as if I couldn't go home anymore. I couldn't act like the high school boy I'd been, and I couldn't present myself in my new, mutated form, either. When I *had* to go back, over the holidays, I didn't see much of my old friends. They assumed it was snobbery. I'd gone off to a fancy college and left them behind.

What I wanted to leave behind, of course, was that perpetually frightened boy, that imposter.

I told myself it didn't matter. I had a new life, after all. My history started at the age of seventeen. Everything before that was more or less erased. The secret agent had gone to his true home.

Years passed. I published a novel, *A Home at the End of the World*, about a gay boy in love with his straight best friend.

I wasn't private anymore. I was taking it out into the world. Terry Gross, on NPR, asked me if I was a gay writer, and I told her I was.

I decided, after much debate, to send copies of the book to Craig, Peter, Bronson, and Rob. I didn't want an obliterated past anymore.

Craig called me a few weeks later.

Hey, buddy. I loved the book.
Did you really?
Yeah. Are you ever coming back to LA?
Yeah, for Christmas.
Let's have a drink when you're in town.
Okay. I'd like that

We did. The five of us. Here we are on that night, in a local bar festooned with garlands and blinking lights.

So. I'm gay. Ta-da.
We knew.
You did not.
We sort of did.
Hey, as long as you never hit on me.
You're ugly. I'd never hit on you.
It must have been a drag for you.
I don't do drag.
Ha-ha.

Does this mean we can't talk about women in front of you?

No. Talk about poontang all you want.

I like the cocktail waitress.

Dream on.

I like the guy sitting at the bar.

The one with the mustache?

Yeah, him.

That's your type?

I don't have a type. I just think he's cute.

Go talk to him.

I don't pick people up in bars.

No shit.

Well, sometimes I do. But he's straight.

How can you tell?

I just can. We call it gaydar.

Do you have a boyfriend?

Yeah. His name is Mark.

Bring him next time.

You want to meet him?

Man. Of course we do.

And on into the night.

I did bring Mark, the next time. Craig and Rob brought their girl-friends. Peter and Bronson were still shopping around.

Our friendship has dwindled over the years, as childhood friend-ships do. We call occasionally. I get Christmas cards with family photos inside.

I was lucky, luckier than many gay boys. But I still remember—I will always remember—that ongoing feeling of terror, that sense that my dark secret must remain forever concealed. Like many men who were once gay kids.

And I'll always know that I was more loved, and more clearly seen, than I'd ever dared to imagine.

Michael Cunningham is the author of the novels *A Home at the End of the World, Flesh and Blood, The Hours* (winner of the Pen/Faulkner Award and Pulitzer Prize), and *Specimen Days*. His latest novel is *By Nightfall*. He lives in New York.

AND THE EMMY GOES TO . . .

by Barbara Gaines

NEW YORK, NY

'm fifty-three-years old, and I'm a lesbian. I'm also an executive producer of the *Late Show with David Letterman*. I've got the kind of full life I never could have imagined would be mine when I was in my teens and twenties.

I grew up in the '60s and '70s in the suburbs of Long Island. I didn't find it easy. I looked, felt, and acted different from all the other kids. When I was ten years old, I was actually the only kid in my class who wore eyeglasses. I could never really play the clarinet but, of course, I was that kid who played the clarinet in the band. I had three good friends in my neighborhood, but I didn't fit in, wasn't interested in what other people were interested in, was more sensitive, and less able to handle school and navigate challenges.

I started doing drugs when I was twelve to feel better, but self-medicating never works. My high school guidance counselor said I wasn't college material but my parents wouldn't let me stay home. I was just as bewildered, lost, and unconnected in college.

There was a legend at my school that if a virgin graduated, the statue in the center of campus would fall down. I'm here to tell you that definitely isn't true, because at my graduation, the statue was still standing. But, in some ways, the miracle was that I graduated at all.

After college, and a short-lived job in Los Angeles, I tried to kill myself. I was in intensive care for three days. I was twenty-two years old.

But here's the thing: Just six months later, things started to get better. I met someone. I got a job.

Let me tell you, with all of my heart, if I had died in 1979, if I had left this earth then, I would have missed so many wonderful things: I never would have married my partner; I never would have seen the birth of my son; I would not have heard my mother, on her death bed, accept me for the gay person I am. And I would not have had the thrill and honor of receiving five Emmy Awards for the work I love to do.

In 1984, I started going to Congregation Beit Simchat Torah, the gay synagogue in New York City, where I found a community of Jewish gay people, something I didn't even know existed. In 1989, I started taking prescribed antidepressants. These are some of the things that worked for me. There are things that will work for you. Each person's path is different. Is my life perfect? No, it is not. But it's so much better now than it was or than I ever imagined it could be. And I want every bit of life that I can get. Please don't give up. Believe me, something better is around the corner.

Originally created as part of the Strength Through Community Project of Congregation Beit Simchat Torah in New York.

. . . .

Barbara Gaines has been an executive producer of the *Late Show with David Letterman* since May 2000, and has worked for David Letterman since starting as a receptionist on his morning show in 1980. In her fourteen years as a producer for the *Late Show*, Gaines has received thirteen Emmy nominations and won five consecutive Emmy Awards. She has also worked in production for the Orange Bowl Parade; *One of the Boys*, a comedy series starring Mickey Rooney, Nathan Lane, and Dana Carvey; and *The $50,000 Pyramid*. Gaines was raised in Hewlett, New York, where she began her career making home movies. She graduated in 1979 from Ithaca College with a BS in educational television. She lives in New York with her partner of twenty years, Aari Blake Ludvigsen, and four-year-old son, Simon Michael Ludvigsen Gaines.

A MESSAGE FROM
U.S. SECRETARY OF STATE
HILLARY RODHAM
CLINTON

• • • • • • • • • • • • • • • • •

WASHINGTON, DC

L ike millions of Americans, I was terribly saddened to learn of the recent suicides of several teenagers across our country after being bullied because they were gay or because people thought they were gay. Children are particularly vulnerable to the hurt caused by discrimination and prejudice and we have lost many young people over the years to suicide. These most recent deaths are a reminder that all Americans have to work harder to overcome bigotry and hatred.

I have a message for all the young people out there who are being bullied, or who feel alone and find it hard to imagine a better future: First of all, hang in there and ask for help. Your life is so important—to your family, your friends, and to your country. And there is so much waiting for you, both personally and professionally—there are so many opportunities for you to develop your talents and make your contributions.

And these opportunities will increase. Because the story of America is the story of people coming together to tear down barriers, stand up for rights, and insist on equality, not only for themselves but for all people. And in the process, they create a community of support and solidarity that endures. Just think of the progress made by women just during my lifetime, or ethnic, racial, and religious minorities over the course of our history—and by gays and lesbians, many of whom are now free to live their lives openly and proudly. Through the State Department, I am grateful every day for the work of our LGBT employees who are serving the United States as foreign service officers and civil servants here and around the world. It wasn't long ago that these men and women would not have been able to serve openly, but today they can—because it has gotten better. And it will get better for you.

So take heart, and have hope, and please remember that your life is valuable, and that you are not alone. Many people are standing with you and sending you their thoughts, their prayers, and their strength. Count me among them.

Take care of yourself.

On January 21, 2009, **Hillary Rodham Clinton** was sworn in as the sixty-seventh Secretary of State of the United States. Secretary Clinton joined the State Department after nearly four decades in public service as an advocate, attorney, first lady, and senator. Secretary Clinton is the author of bestselling books, including her memoir, *Living History*, and her groundbreaking book on children, *It Takes a Village*. She and President Bill Clinton reside in New York.

THIS I KNOW FOR SURE

by A. Y. Daring

WATERLOO, ON

egardless of what country you live in, regardless of where you're from, or what you look like, or who you are, once you are out of that phase called high school, it gets better. People stop treating you like a child. They start respecting your opinion. But even more than that, I think what happens, or at least what happened to me, is that I proved to myself that that wasn't as good as it gets. When I was in the tenth and the eleventh grade, right after I came out, I used to sit and cry all the time because I felt so alone. I thought I would never find anyone who got me or was like me. I'm black and I'm queer. Where the hell am I going to find people like me? You know what I mean? I was living in Burlington, Ontario, after all!

When I graduated, I moved to a bigger city and enrolled at a massive university, where our campus queer and questioning committee is about to celebrate their fortieth anniversary. It's the longest-running queer campus organization in the whole of Canada. So during all those years in high school, when I was sitting there wondering who would possibly understand me, and why I couldn't find them—turns out, they had been here the whole time, just waiting for me to get through high school and to get up the courage to leave that awful phase behind.

Everyone who has supported me, everyone who loves me for who I am—exactly the way I am—they have always been here, too. They weren't born the day I came out, or even the month before I came out. They've been here with open arms just waiting for me to come alive and realize my potential. And all the people who are going to be there for you on the other side, they're walking around right now wondering where you are. And they're waiting excitedly with open arms for the day you finally have that diploma and you can get out of there and go on to something better.

I can attest to the fact that I honestly, legitimately, literally do not know of a single queer adult who graduated from high school and went on to bigger cities and bigger schools—better, more accepting places— and didn't eventually find a place where they belonged . . . where they belong.

When you're young—and granted, I'm just a second-year student myself—everything feels like the end of the world because you haven't seen how good it can get. By the time you graduate from high school, four out of eighteen years feels like a pretty significant percentage of your life. But four out of forty years, or four out of fifty, or sixty years of amazing-ness is absolutely nothing.

So, in the meantime, you've got to hold your head up and you've got to look for the light at the end of your tunnel. Because it's there, even if you don't always recognize it or you can't always find it, it's there all the same, and always has been. And don't forget those people who are there to support you. They're so, so excited to finally get to meet you, they are waiting with open arms. Good luck, guys. See you on the better side!

Author's Note: I've started a project called Focus on the Love. (Like Focus on the Family, except not bat-shit crazy.) Focus on the Love is where you tell me what you love about yourself, and I write you back a love letter. I've got hundreds of envelopes and stamps waiting. The goal is to keep writing letters and various other super-exciting, still-in-development ideas until we've reach one million queer individuals and their allies with the message of self-love. Join in: www.piazzaroom .com/focus-on-the-love/.

. . . .

A. Y. Daring is a young, glamorous, and adventuresome jetsetter. When not gallivanting around the globe and putting out forest fires, she's a full-time university student with a major in philosophy and two minors in business and French. In her spare time, she writes about how to be fabulous and successful at www.aydaring .com and does choreography for Lady Gaga on the weekends.

IT GETS BETTER BROADWAY

. . . .

by Members of the Broadway and New York Theater Community

Michael Arnold (*Billy Elliot*): I grew up in a community where the only thing that mattered was sports, and anything else and everything else was gay. If you did anything else, you were a faggot. So when I started taking dance classes to improve my hockey game, I was a faggot.

I was bullied in high school, I was ridiculed, and I was made fun of. The thing that hurt the worst was that all the adults who were there to protect me . . . didn't protect me. Nobody stepped in.

J. R. Bruno (*West Side Story*): When I was getting changed for gym class one day, a bunch of kids stole my wallet and my watch and my glasses and my clothes. And the principal couldn't do anything about it because there was no proof.

Derek St. Pierre (*Rock of Ages*): I was called names all the time and bullied. People called me "faggot."

Tim McGarrigal (*High School Musical*): I remember distinctly having other kids call me "faggot" and "gay" and "homo." I didn't even know what that meant at the time but gradually I started feeling more and more isolated.

Brad Bradley (*Billy Elliot, Spamalot, Annie Get Your Gun*): Once I started taking ballet and wearing ballet tights, I was introduced to the word *faggot*. I was told I would make a really pretty girl if I wasn't a girl already, and my father even once referred to me as the "Sugar Plum Fairy."

Danny McNie (*Miss Saigon*): I was thrown against a fence and had my pants pulled down, just to prove to that group of guys—boys—that I was a boy.

Tony Gonzalez (*Mamma Mia!*): One morning when I was fifteen years old, a freshman in high school, I came outside to the entire side of my house spray-painted with terribly profane pictures and words.

Chris Nichols (New York talent agent): I would show up to high school and my locker would be Super Glued shut. People would kick me, people would beat me up.

Jeremy Leiner (*Bombay Dreams* and New York talent agent): This kid came up and pointed at me, stopping with his crowd, and said, "Fag." And they all just laughed and walked away. I remember how humiliated I felt; I wanted to just crawl in a hole and hide.

Raymond J. Lee (*Mamma Mia!*): Because of all this pressure from my parents, from my Christian friends, I actually attempted to take my life.

J. B. Wing (*High Fidelity*): I tried to take my own life. And I can't tell you how much I thank God that I was not successful in that attempt.

Corey West (*South Pacific*): I remember hearing so much in school and in church about praying. That if I just prayed, it would go away. So at night I would pray so hard, and I would cry, just asking for these feelings to go away.

Jose Llana (*Spelling Bee, The King and I, Rent*): I'm from a Filipino Catholic background. I was born in the Philippines and moved to the States when I was really young. At a certain point, as a kid, I knew I was gay but I didn't know how to tell my parents. As a Catholic, there were times I felt like I was the biggest failure to my family, my country, and my faith.

Ben Franklin: I grew up Southern Baptist, deeply immersed in my religious background, and as a young gay man, I was terrified. Fear was my bully. I was afraid I was going to lose my religion, my family, everything that I held dear to me. It ate me up inside.

Alex Quiroga (*Wicked*): It's a really different time, and I know that it's hard. And I am sure that you're sick of hearing everybody say, "I know how you feel. It gets better." And we don't really know how you feel because we're not you. But if you are feeling hopeless and you are thinking about doing something drastic, maybe hurting yourself or even suicide, don't, because then they win.

J.B. Wing: When I first came to New York to pursue my acting career, I got a survival job in an office. My first day walking in to that office I heard the soundtrack to Barbra Streisand's *Yentl* playing through the speakers, and the owner came out, wearing freedom rainbow rings in her ears, and shook my hand. I remember thinking, "Oh, my gay God. I'm home."

Ben Franklin: There are angels out there willing to lift you up and take care of you and give you wings to help you become the person you were meant to be, to help you discover the gifts you were born with.

Jose Llana: I've used that confidence and that self-assurance to help propel myself into a pretty happy career and a pretty happy life. I've got a partner I've been with for five years, and we're looking to buy an apartment together. And one day I hope to have kids, too.

David Beach (*Urinetown, Mamma Mia!*): I never expected to have such a beautiful baby girl or such a great husband. It gets so much better. Just think, you could grow up to have a boring life like me!

Jim Daly (*Altar Boyz* and New York talent agent): Today, I have a family with two wonderful women—two women I didn't even know were lesbians back then. They didn't even know, and now we have three beautiful kids together.

Brian Charles Rooney (*The Threepenny Opera*): I've been in a relationship with my partner for eleven years. And I can't imagine what his life would be like without me.

J.R. Bruno: Next month, I plan to propose to my boyfriend. I'm excited.

Kevin Crewell (*Jersey Boys, Spamalot*): Talk to somebody. That's what I kind of wish I'd done. I kept it all bottled up inside.

Danny McNie (*Miss Saigon*): If you're having a bad day, know that it gets better. Know that you have an army behind you. When you get a little bit older, you will find a home. And you will find a family of friends who will love the hell out of you.

Alex Quiroga: I'm surrounded by a lot of people who support me and love me for who I am. You'll get there. I promise.

Ben Sands (New York talent agent): I've created this incredible community of people around me—friends and family—that I absolutely love and treasure, which was hard to imagine when I was that little, scared fifteen-year-old boy coming out of the closet.

Chris Nichols: Call somebody. Look at these videos, there are thousands. Know that you are not the only one.

Steven Strafford (*Spamalot*): One of the greatest things about my life is the amount of people who know who I really am. Just live in truth and try to find people who will understand. It will free you.

Bryan Johnson (*Mamma Mia!*): You know why everybody's making videos and writing their stories for this project? Because you matter. *You* matter. Don't let anyone define you with their hateful words and actions. Believe in yourself, no matter what they say or do. Love yourself. Be good to yourself. Life is so wonderful with all its heartaches and joys. And the world is such an incredible, beautiful place. You deserve to be around to enjoy it. You deserve to have an amazing life.

ROCKIN' THE FLANNEL SHIRT

● ●

by Krissy Mahan

UPSTATE NEW YORK

If you follow the media, or pop culture, you might think that all gay people live in cities and have a lot of money. Well, as a person who lives in the country and doesn't have a lot of money, I can tell you that not all gay people are urban or rich. I've been really happy being a big rural dyke. So, if you want to live in the country, or just can't move away, you'll be fine. And, if you don't have a ton of money, you'll be fine, too. You'll get yourself a job. There are plenty of good jobs out there for people who want to work hard. You'll be a butch dyke and you'll be hot. Everyone will love it. It will be good.

Work hard and then go do something fun on Saturday night, like go look at girls . . . that's better.

One of the nice things about being in the country is you don't have to deal with people all the time. There's land out there, and you can just get away. Go build yourself a little fort in the woods. In the rural areas I've lived, people are more concerned with what I can do and what skills I have, rather than who I'm involved with. Competence and confidence are sexy. If you live in the country, you just "know" how to do stuff—the ladies love that. Also, there's a long tradition of support for unconventional people in rural areas. Even when people are mean, you don't have to go too far to be reminded about how great it is to be alive because nature is so beautiful. You can do things now that will feel good and will give you something to talk about with people when you're older.

Growing up I only knew one person who was gay. I took a lot of crap for being how I was, and honestly, I didn't even know that I was gay then. Everyone else seemed to think they knew that I was gay, which was kind of hard. There wasn't a lot of help either in those days. If I had wanted to talk with someone about all of it, it wouldn't have been very welcomed.

My grandparents had an outhouse and a hand pump we used to have to use to get water out of the ground. They grew and canned their own food, and kept chickens. I've had it much easier than they did, but the skills I learned from my family have served me well. Now I live on a farm in upstate New York. I build chicken coops. When there's a problem with a building or machine, I can fix it. My parents are not glad that I am gay but they are proud of raising a daughter who can take care of herself and build things. My girlfriend and I have both tried living in urban areas but we didn't really like it. We choose instead to live as an out lesbian couple with her parents on their family farm. Every day we are so happy. I think that things are getting better, for everybody, even in rural areas.

I still struggle with feeling okay. A while ago, I was even hospitalized. I got treatment in a psychiatric hospital after becoming really depressed. My friend killed herself, and I didn't handle it well. Psych facilities in rural counties are rough places. I don't ever want to go back. When I say that it gets better, I am not saying it will always be easy. You will just have more choices about how to handle tough times. That's a big improvement.

I know that maybe right now it feels like you don't have a lot of choices, and maybe you don't. But things will open up. You have to just ride it out. As someone who has been there, I can assure you, it gets better. If you're living in the country, I'm sure there are some things that are kind of frustrating for you, and you're probably rockin' the flannel shirt every now and then, but that is going to be totally hot to somebody someday. It's gonna get real better.

....

Krissy builds chicken coops and fixes things in upstate New York. Krissy is a member of the Austin Project, led by Dr. Omi Osun, Joni L. Jones, and Sharon Bridgforth.

HOW IT GOT BETTER FOR AN ORDAINED CHRISTIAN MINISTER

●●●

by Professor Stephen V. Sprinkle

FORT WORTH, TX

This year marks the fortieth anniversary of my high school graduation. As I look back across my life, I can remember times that weren't so good. I was a closeted gay man in a church setting that did not particularly congratulate young Christians for being gay or lesbian.

So when I received my call to the ministry, I was also living my way into what it meant to be gay. I remember very clearly making the decision that I would not be able to allow myself affection in this life if I were going to serve God in the church. It wasn't a very good decision. I was lonely for a lot of years.

I've served five churches as pastor, and every church I served grew. I was closeted all those years and always felt as though I had to look over my shoulder, fearing I would be discovered, or that I'd somehow slip up and give my secret away.

Carefully and slowly at first, I came out to a few selected friends and confidants where I lived and worked. While those moments of personal liberty were great, I found that partially coming out was not going to give me the freedom to be myself—not as long as the fear of exposure haunted me. A close friend of mine, to whom I had already come out, offered me some of the best advice I had have ever received.

He said, "Steve, if there are no longer any secrets, then there can be no ambushes."

I took what he said to heart, and made the decision to put secrets about my sexuality behind me. So twenty years ago, I came out—utterly, fully, and completely—and I wouldn't go back into the closet for anything in the world. I am able to tell you, person to person, that it does get better. Because now, as an ordained minister—and Baptist, at that—for the last thirty-three years, I've had a full, complete, and active religious life. I teach in a divinity school and I love what I do. I have the best job in the whole school, and wouldn't trade my job for any other job here. I love the students I teach; I respect the colleagues that I work with; I enjoy talking about God all day long; and I'm as out and free as I can be, partnered for the last eleven years with a wonderful man. We're even the proud parents of an English bulldog named Winston. He loves his two daddies, and we love him, too.

So, when it seems that things are about as bad as they can possibly be and the worries weigh upon you, like a murder of crows on top of your head, just tell yourself that Steve Sprinkle says it gets better. When I came out, I found out that I had a multitude of friends I just hadn't met yet—people who were willing to know me for exactly who I was. People in my church family loved and accepted me. Coworkers appreciated me even more than before I came out, because I had thought enough of them and myself to be honest about my personal life. And there were many friends and allies who just seemed to appear at my side out of nowhere, right when I needed their support and encouragement the most.

There were people who couldn't make the leap from the closeted person I had been to the open and honest gay man I became. I am sorry they could not accept the real me. But I can tell you that for each one of them who walked away from me because of my sexual orientation, scores of new friends arose in their place. I am so grateful that I have them all in my life.

I hope that if you are ever given to despair, you will take hold of hope with both hands. Never turn loose what gives you hope! Because you are going to find out that your life will get better. A lot better. And I hope down the road somewhere, I'll meet you in a divinity school classroom, and we can tell each other face to face, "You know what? It really did get better, for both of us."

Stephen V. Sprinkle is the director of field education and supervised ministry and an associate professor of practical theology at Brite Divinity School on the campus of Texas Christian University in Fort Worth, Texas. An ordained Baptist minister with the Alliance of Baptists, he is the first openly gay teacher and scholar in the history of his seminary, and the first out gay person to be tenured there. His most recent book is *Unfinished Lives: Reviving the Memory of LGBTQ Hate Crimes Victims*, published by Resource Publications of Eugene, Oregon.

OUT OF DARKNESS

• •

by Philip Deal

WINTHROP, MA

I grew up as a Jehovah's Witness. All my family and friends, and basically everyone I knew, were Jehovah's Witnesses. My parents are still devout followers. I know what it's like to live in that Witness bubble, and I'll bet there are a few gay kids reading this who are Jehovah's Witnesses, too. This story is for you.

When I was eight years old, I remember going to the Kingdom Hall and sitting down and opening up this book called *You Can Live Forever on a Paradise Earth*; you've probably heard of it. Turning through the pages, I stopped at one page that's burned into my mind to this day. It featured a collage of pictures depicting the horrible things in our world that God needs to destroy. There was a picture of an old lady getting her purse snatched, and one of a starving kid in Africa, and another of a junkie shooting up with heroin, and one of some guy who was shot in the head. All the images were very graphic and very scary. But right in the middle was a big picture of two guys dancing at a disco. Two guys embracing and dancing with one another in a disco. When I saw it, I remember thinking, *Oh my God, that's me.* And then I thought, *What if anybody finds out? What if they already know? What if they already know that I'm a big queer?*

I kept that a secret for a long time; I had to. You might have to, too.

Putting up with everybody else's bullshit is hard. Sometimes you have to put up with it for a long time. But the trick is not to give up until you get what you want.

Those kids who committed suicide had something to offer the world. Something special, something grand. They were unique and they had something to give. And they forfeited it; they let it go. They gave up too early before getting what they wanted out of life. I get it. I tried to commit suicide. I understand what they felt when they did it. Sometimes it feels like you just can't handle it anymore. But I am going to share a secret with you. I am going to tell you what helped me handle those feelings.

I love to dance. I love dancing, and I love teaching dance. I love ballet. And it's something I've done my entire life. When everything else is going wrong in my life I turn to that. I turn to the one thing that I love most. That is my recommendation to you: Whenever you get to that point where you feel you can't go on anymore, just remember that one thing that you love in the world more than anything else, and cling to it. Doesn't matter what it is. Whether it's watching television or listening to music, or putting on makeup, or singing, or doing karaoke, or whatever it is you love. Do it. Do the hell out of it, and try to remember that the bad times don't last forever. The good times don't last forever either, but that's okay.

And if you're one of those queer Jehovah's Witness kids out there, I am here for you. I know what it's like. But I guarantee things do get better.

Philip Deal is an internationally renowned classical and contemporary dancer. He is an award-winning choreographer and teacher and runs his own ballet instructional website and blog, www.philipdeal .com.

by Alison Bechdel

I drew this cartoon a long time ago, when I was in my thirties. But things had already gotten a lot better by then—I made it through the excruciating years of high school. I went on to make out with many delightful women, and dress like Fred Astaire when I felt like it. I did not take up boxing, but I did get my black belt in karate. Take *that*, Sylvester Stallone!

SOMETHING SPECIAL

by Sia Furler

NEW YORK, NY

grew up around wacky artists and knew from very early on that there was something special about me. I didn't really know what it was then, but it turns out it's a number of things. And one of them is that I was a queer-lord. Now I call myself a gay-lord, and art fag, a lezzie, a dyke, straight . . . all sorts of things because, the truth is, labels really shouldn't matter and don't essentially matter if you're lucky enough to come from an artistic background or a gay-friendly household. And I was lucky enough to come from that kind of household.

My story—I guess my queer story—starts from very early on. I really didn't mind if you were a girl or a boy, I just wanted you to love me. I had a very desperate energy about me. I feel sorry for my early self because I realize that I had a lot of shame about being different and special. So I overcompensated. I overcompensated by devaluing myself, putting myself down, sabotaging my success and my relationships with both men and women. I sabotaged it all.

It wasn't until maybe three years ago that I really, really realized that I am queer. And here. Even I'm getting used to it. I can now say that I'm queer and proud, and that I love you if you're having a hard time. I've always loved you. I just didn't know I loved me, too. And at some point, it gets better. It gets better, and you learn to love yourself and you learn to love your specialness.

Only you know when you're ready to come out. And if you're not ready to come out, that's okay too. A lot of us protect ourselves from danger. It's a matter of survival for many of us. But, I'm proud and I hope that one day we all are able to say, "I'm gay" or "I'm a lesbian" or "I'm transgender" or "I'm queer" and that it will be okay. I will tell you that for me, right now, I'm very comfortable with it. And you will be, too. It gets better.

• •

Australian-born singer and songwriter **Sia** has released four studio albums. The latest, *We Are Born*, has won critical accolades the world over as well as two 2010 ARIA Awards (the Australian Grammys) for Best Independent Release and Best Pop Release. Her last album, *Some People Have Real Problems,* won a 2009 ARIA Award for Best Music DVD for her distinctively visual videos. She is currently totally awesome.

THE DINNER PARTY

by Adam Roberts

NEW YORK, NY

When I told my friend Alex that I was cooking a dinner for my parents and Craig's parents, Alex (who knew me in college) said: "Did you ever think, ten years ago, that this would ever happen? That you'd cook a dinner one day for your parents and your boyfriend and his parents?" The answer to that question was most definitely: "No."

It's hard to get back into the headspace where that dinner would've seemed impossible. But there've been so many tragic gay suicides—thirteen-year-old Seth Walsh, fifteen-year-old Billy Lucas, thirteen-year-old Asher Brown and, perhaps the most publicized case, Rutgers student Tyler Clementi, who jumped off a bridge after his roommate broadcast his sexual encounter with another man online—that getting back into that headspace seems important. And so, I'd like to tell you how I got from that world of impossibility to the dinner I cooked one recent Friday night.

First, the dinner. As a passionate braiser, I decided to braise short ribs using a recipe from *The Babbo Cookbook*. I did this all the night before, browning the meat well, deglazing with red wine and filling the pot with herbs (rosemary, thyme, oregano), covering with foil, and braising in the oven for two hours until the meat came apart with a spoon. Then I cooled it to room temperature and placed in the refrigerator overnight.

I'm not sure if braising acts as a metaphor for the story I want to tell; perhaps in the way that something rigid and tough breaks down and becomes something tender and rich? Was I rigid and tough as a teen? Am I tender and rich now? The metaphor needs work.

But the idea is there: As a teenager, I was really repressed. Whereas some repressed teenagers become angst-ridden and sullen, I was the opposite: I was a manic sack of nervous energy. Fidgety, jokey, always hiding behind my humor, I sat mostly with girls at lunch. My freshman year, in PE class, I was bullied by this guy Nick and his friends who, strangely, called me "Alfredo" and harassed me in the locker room. Once one of those guys, Eric, who worked at the local grocery store, helped my mom to the car with her groceries. Unbeknownst to her, he was my bully. When she told me she met this nice boy from my PE class named Eric, I was mortified.

Needless to say, that was a tough year. And though high school got slightly better, I never truly felt like myself. It wasn't until college that things began to get clearer, that I began to realize that there was a truer me, within the me that everyone else knew.

But first, let's make some polenta. I bought my polenta at the farmer's market, and using a recipe from Lidia Bastianich, I started the polenta thirty minutes before our parents arrived, stirring it throughout the first hour or two until it thickened up, adding mascarpone and Parmesan cheese at the end to make it a little more intense.

And *intense* is a word that definitely describes my junior year of college.

By then, I'd found an incredible group of friends in Rathskellar, Emory's improvisational comedy troupe. It was in Rathskellar that I first learned I didn't have to be "on" all the time, that it was important to be introspective, and that being gay really wasn't that big of a deal. By my junior year of college, I'd made several gay friends. And it was at that point that I'd gotten tired of fielding questions from my family about why I didn't have a girlfriend and if I knew any nice Jewish girls and if any of them were marriable. Around this time of year (it was near Halloween), I came out to my closest college friends (I was so nervous, I couldn't say the word; I told my friend Travis I was a "h . . . h . . . hemophiliac!"). And then I told my parents.

Let's just say it didn't go very well. There were intense, emotional phone calls, awkward trips home, visits to a terrible therapist who tried to turn me straight, an explosive night at the dinner table where my grandmother said: "Why can't you just marry your friend Lisa?" To which I replied: "Because she doesn't have a penis!" It got ugly.

But then it got better. That's why Alex's comment was so on the nose; because things seemed so harrowing back then, I couldn't imagine that we'd ever turn a corner. But we did.

It happened when I met Craig.

This was years later, in 2006. By then, I'd gone to law school and hated it; I'd had my first boyfriend (a sweet guy named Michael, who I dated my senior year of college); I'd been to Atlanta's gay bars and gay pride parades, I'd lived with a lesbian and I'd taken classes on sexuality and the law. Then I moved to New York to go to dramatic writing school at NYU. And at my favorite coffee shop, Joe, I spied a cute guy who was there writing with his friend.

That guy ended up looking at my Friendster profile. Remember Friendster? You could tell who looked at your profile, so I wrote him an e-mail. Turned out he went to NYU, too, for film school. We decided to meet in the school lobby and to walk to dinner.

That first night we each tried to convince the other of where we should eat (I fought for Momofuku, he argued for something else) so we settled on a place neither of us had been to: Lucien, in the East Village. I ordered the cassoulet (note to future daters: don't eat beans on a first date). We went, afterward, to the Anyway Cafe, where they serve infused vodka. We had the black currant.

Things only got better from there. We saw plays, went to museums, we ate the flying saucer-sized chocolate chip cookies (possibly the best in New York) at the Levain Bakery.

And then I formally introduced him to my food blog readers when

I burned my mouth on a soup dumpling at a Chinatown restaurant, New Green Bo. I called him "the new man in my life," and my readers flipped out. Someone wrote: "Whee! You finally told us who you were kissing!" And someone else wrote: "Thank God you finally came out!"

That was almost five years ago. And so that brings us to the dinner.

My parents, over the past few years, have grown to really embrace Craig. How could they not? I think when being gay was an abstraction, it filled them with fear and dread, but when there was a concrete person there, it all made sense. And so now whenever I call home, they ask after Craig (my grandmother always ends her calls with: "Send my love to Craig!") and they always include Craig when they take me out to dinner or to see a Broadway show. When my parents went to Barcelona this summer, they bought both of us watches.

And so when I told them that Craig's parents were coming to town at the beginning of October and that I wanted my parents to meet them, my parents bought tickets to fly here just for that. And that's why I made this dinner.

There are no pictures in this book, but if there were, you'd see everyone in the first "getting to know you" moments. We're drinking champagne and even my cat Lolita's hanging out. (I call her "my cat" because Craig hates cats. It's his main character flaw.)

For the first course, I served my dad's favorite, Caesar salad. I went heavy with the garlic and the anchovies, because both my parents like it that way. They loved it.

For the entree, I plated the short rib on the polenta and topped it with a gremolata made of horseradish, lemon zest, and parsley. And for dessert, I served a flourless chocolate cake from an old issue of *Gourmet* magazine.

By the end of the night, the families had bonded and we made our plans for the next night, when we'd all journey to one of our favorite restaurants, Blue Hill Stone Barns.

That night with Craig and both of our families was proof that it gets better. If you're reading this and you're a gay teenager, take heart. It might seem like your life is a cold, depressing TV dinner, but I'm here to tell you that your future, if it's anything like mine, becomes a Michelin three-star restaurant. All you have to do is wait.

Trust me.

∙∙

Adam Roberts is the creator of the food blog *The Amateur Gourmet* (www.amateurgourmet.com), which was named one of the World's 50 Best Food Blogs by *The Times* (UK) in 2009. Roberts is also the author of the book *The Amateur Gourmet* (Bantam/Dell) and is currently writing a cookbook for Artisan Books, which will arrive in Spring 2012. He lives with his boyfriend, filmmaker Craig Johnson, in the West Village, New York.

WHAT I WISH I KNEW

by Ivan Coyote

VANCOUVER, BC

I grew up in a small town called Whitehorse, Yukon, way up in northern Canada, and went to a high school with about 350 kids in it. I come from a gigantic Irish Catholic family, and my parents and most of my aunts and uncles had gone to the same school before me, and my little sister and most of my thirty-six cousins attended the very same school after I did. I graduated in 1987, and could not get out of that school and that town fast enough.

I didn't come out in high school, even to myself. I kissed my first girl about one month after my nineteenth birthday, and then burst out of the closet. One of the things I was always conscious of was that not only did I have to deal with the consequences of being queer in a small town, so did my family. My little sister and my cousins had to deal with the homophobia that splashed off of me and hit them, too. It made me realize that I was not the only one in my family who suffered because of the bigotry of others. Some of my family did, too, even though they were straight.

Now I am forty-two years old, somehow. I am a writer and musician and performer, with seven books and three CDs out. I am a full-time working artist; I spend most of my time on the road, touring North America and Europe. I love my job.

I still go back to high schools, this time as a writer, to do readings. Even though every time I walk back through those big glass doors and into a high school, my mouth goes dry and my heart starts to pound. Even though every time I see gangs of teenage girls gathered in knots around lockers in the hallway, I still feel that old familiar ball of fear start to curdle in my guts. I visit high schools because they are still scary places for me, because they remind me of my own sixteen-year-old self—the misfit, the girl who walked and threw and danced and played hockey like a boy. The girl who none of the boys wanted. I go back into high schools to meet all those kids like me, to shake their hand and look them in the eye and let them know that they are not alone, even if they don't even know who they are yet or haven't accepted it or learned to love that part of themselves that I do. I see them and know them and love them because of who they are, not in spite of it.

I wish I had met someone queer when I was sixteen. Someone who was not ashamed of who they were, someone who I could talk to. It probably would have made my life a lot easier. I would have figured myself out earlier, and loved myself better sooner. It is too late for me to speak to my own sixteen-year-old self, so instead I want all of the misfits and weirdos and artists and queer kids to know a couple of things I wish someone had told me back then.

It does get better. It does. But it is up to all of us to make it better, for ourselves, and for others, too. Always remember that working to make your school safer for queer students, or bisexual students, or gender nonconforming students, is not a selfish act. Creating a safe school for yourself will only lead to a safer school for everyone, and everyone deserves a safe place to learn in. Not feeling safe at school can seriously affect your ability to access your own education, which can impact you for the rest of your life. When you work to make your school better for you, you are doing your school, and everyone in it, and everyone who will ever be in it in the future, a gigantic favor. Never forget that.

You deserve so much more than to just be tolerated. You deserve to be loved for exactly who and what you are right now. This is, of course, a double-edged sword. This also means you must return the favor. Learn more about racism and sexism and ableism, too. You, unfortunately, are probably already well aware of how much homophobia can hurt, inside and out. Learning more about how different kinds of oppression work and where they intersect will help you build better bridges with others and create a safe and respectful school culture for everyone. Bullies are almost always outnumbered by the bullied. We just need to organize.

Remember that not everyone is able to come out to everyone all of the time. Some of us cannot come out to our parents yet, or our colleagues at work, or our teammates, or even our friends. It is okay to know who you are, and keep it private, if your own safety requires it. This does not mean you are any less queer or radical or cool than the guy with the purple hair and the rainbow stockings. It just means that he has different circumstances than you do.

It is getting better. There are lots of us out there who care a whole lot about you, whether it feels like it sometimes or not. I am one of them, and I will never stop coming to high schools to meet kids just like you. Until I stop feeling scared every freaking time I walk through those front doors, I will keep working to make all schools safer for all of us. I promise you that.

I know that school is still a fucked-up place to be queer. Parents and teachers and counselors can do all kinds of things to try to stop bullying, but ultimately, no one can protect you from all the little cruel ways that other people and society and the media try to force you to conform and to fit into their little cookie-cutter ideas of who you should be.

But I want you to know that as I look around myself right now and see the amazing people and artists and parents and activists around me, I see people who took chances, who are brave and honest and unashamed to be themselves. All the best people I know right now were once misfits and weirdos and homos and artists, just like you and me. That is exactly what I love about them.

Ivan Coyote is the award-winning author of seven books, four films, and three CDs that combine storytelling with music from some of Canada's finest independent musicians. She has written a column for *Xtra!* magazine for ten years, and also performs a one-hour anti-bullying show in high schools across the continent.

FREEDOM FROM FEAR

● ●

by Michael Feinstein

LOS ANGELES, CA

Each of us is born into this world with unique gifts, talents, personalities, and preferences. There will always be those who do not understand or accept those who are different from what society perceives as the norm. Yet, fundamentally, we are all the same. While we dream of a time and place where we will be accepted for who we are, we must also learn to cope with the pain and problems that our uniqueness presents here and now. It's important to remember that there are others everywhere who are like us and will love us for who we are.

When I was growing up, I often felt lonely and isolated because I knew that I was different from everyone around me. At the time I could not imagine that there was a single soul who would understand. The fear of revealing my feelings was great, and while I knew that my parents loved me, I also felt that even they would not understand. The erroneous messages I had absorbed made it clear that I was not "normal," and thus, I knew I had to hide my dark secret. Little did I know then that there were people just like me all around, many dealing with their own issues and hiding in their own ways because society made it difficult to do anything else without fear of consequences. It is fear that keeps us from being who we are. When we go through the step-by-step process of dealing with our fear and finding a support system, things can start to change. It is amazing how even the small step of reaching out to another person for help can begin a process of unlocking what is inside us. Finding the right way to do so is not always clear or easy but it is possible. Through the help of friends who saw things in me that I could not see in myself, the tide started to turn and I slowly began to gain more self-confidence. As my confidence grew, I developed clear inner intentions and the ability to ask for guidance to help me reach those goals, something that helped me tremendously along the way.

Today we live in an extraordinary time. Society is changing, but with change comes resistance. Those against change and acceptance know in their souls, underneath their prejudice, that there is nothing that they can do to stop the inevitable. This realization frightens them and makes them fight harder to try and suppress us. It comes down to their fear against ours.

The sooner we get past our fear and look at who we are in our souls, the sooner we'll be able to realize a future where we can all live in harmony. Deep in your soul is a voice that is clear and sure. This inner voice transcends what our thinking mind dictates—a mind not born of our own wisdom but filled with the opinions and judgments of others. Take time to contemplate your inner self, to discover your soul; this inner voice can be heard through self-contemplation and meditation. And know that you are truly beautiful from the depths of your being, because loving yourself is the greatest gift you can experience! What others perceive and say is illusion as far as your true self is concerned.

Do words hurt? Deeply.

Are aggression and violence going to disappear? Someday.

In the meantime, learn to distinguish between the falsity of fear and ignorance, and your life purpose to evolve in love and peace. And remember, you are never alone.

Michael Feinstein is singer, pianist, and historian who has been nominated for five Grammy Awards. His PBS series *Michael Feinstein's American Songbook* was recently released on DVD, and his latest CD is titled *Fly Me to the Moon*. Feinstein serves as artistic director for the Palladium at the Center for Performing Arts in Carmel, Indiana.

A MESSAGE FROM PRIME MINISTER
DAVID CAMERON

• •

LONDON, ENGLAND

We all know that growing up can be difficult. But for young people who are being bullied life can feel incredibly hard and lonely. So there are two things I want to say to anyone out there who is being given a hard time because of their sexuality.

The first thing is to talk to someone about it. You don't have to struggle on, dealing with this on your own. There are so many people out there, whether it's your mum and dad, your teachers, family, friends, people who care about you and who want to help you. Speak to them and you will feel so much better.

The second thing I want to say is that Britain is a diverse, open, tolerant place. This is not the sort of country where we label people for being different. Just look at the massive progress that has been made on making this country more fair. Today, same-sex couples can have their relationships legally recognized. People in our armed forces can be open about who they are. Equality laws are fighting discrimination at work and in society.

Now, of course, there is more that needs to be done, which is why this government is working hard to tackle homophobic bullying and drive it out of our schools. But overall, Britain is a place where you can be who you want to be and we should celebrate that.

So take heart from the kind of country we live in, our values of fairness, responsibility, and decency, and what that means for your future. And now, talk to someone, because if you do, things really will get better today.

Author's Note: If you're in the United Kingdom and need some support, Stonewall can point you in the right direction. Free info line: 08000 50 20 20.

....

David Cameron became Prime Minister in May 2010. He leads a Conservative/Liberal Democrat coalition government inspired by the values of freedom, fairness, and responsibility. Prior to becoming Prime Minister, David Cameron was elected leader of the Conservative Party in December 2005 on a mandate to change and modernize his party. Before he became an MP, David Cameron worked in business and government. He was educated at Eton College and Oxford University, studying Philosophy, Politics, and Economics. David, his wife, Samantha, and their three young children live in London and West Oxfordshire.

YOU WILL MEET PEOPLE WHO CELEBRATE YOU

by Jenn and Erika Wagner-Martin

WAUKESHA, WI

Erika: I grew up in a small Wisconsin town—largely conservative. And, while my immediate family wasn't particularly anti-gay or homophobic in any way, certain members of my extended family were. Many times at Thanksgiving or Christmas or Easter I would have to endure anti-gay comments, and I just knew that it wasn't going to be okay with some of my family to be who I was. And that was really hard.

Jenn: I grew up in a different small town, also in Wisconsin. Some of my high school classmates had decided—even though I didn't know yet, had no idea—that I was gay. So they'd leave notes on my locker or shout out "lezzy" and "dyke" when I was just walking down the hall. This would happen every day. It was tough. It was especially hard to endure because you have to go to school every day. But then high school thankfully ended and I went to college, where nobody knew me. And I don't think I realized until I got there I could be whoever I wanted at college. Whoever I wanted to be. College is different from high school. It's more diverse. It's more open-minded. So, it got better right away.

Erika: When you go to college, or when you go to work, or whatever you do after high school, you have more opportunities to be yourself.

You're not in this little box where everyone's trying to label you and define you. When I started college, I didn't even really understand that I was gay. I knew that I had these intense female friendships but I didn't really know what that was. And then I met my very good friend, Rachel, who became an ally by just letting me be who I was. She was super-supportive of me and just let me figure it out. Soon, I met more people like her, and the more people I met, the more I could become who I was meant to be, the better it got.

Jenn: Our paths crossed for the first time about six years ago.

Erika: We've been together ever since. And in 2007, we had our big fat gay wedding in Wisconsin.

Jenn: We wore beautiful white gowns. And had bridesmaids, we called them bride guys, since we didn't have any grooms. A lot of people told us it was one of the best weddings they'd ever been to. I don't mean to brag, but it was.

Erika: It totally was.

Jenn: Early in our relationship, we talked about wanting to build our family through adoption. In early 2010, we got the call. Two girls—sisters—one tiny, tiny baby and the other about a year and a half old arrived on our doorstep. We've had them now for eight months now.

Erika: They changed our lives forever. I've never been as stressed as I have the last eight months but I have never been happier either because I have everything that I've always wanted.

Jenn: We have a house, two children, and even a minivan. Now we just need the white picket fence. The funny thing, the ironic thing, is that we're not so different from those kids from high school who used to harass us and pick on us for being different. I'm not so different from them anymore. I have my family. I have my life. I get up and go to work every morning. And so, even though you feel so different, you feel like a freak, you feel like there's something wrong with you, there's nothing wrong with you, you're fine. You're fine. You're probably more like everybody else than you realize.

Erika: Be yourself. Be true to who you are and tune out the noise as much as you can. You're going to meet people who support you. You're going to meet people who love you. You're going to meet people who celebrate you. And someday, if this is your choice, you'll get to marry your best friend.

....

Erika and **Jenn**, both counselors in Wisconsin, met in 2004 over a Crockpot of meats. That's really all you need to know.

AN IDENTITY UNFOLDED

by Mark Ramirez

ANCHORAGE, AK

Translated from American Sign Language

Growing up I used to think that everyone was like me, that everyone was interested in and attracted to people of the same sex. But over time I saw that wasn't true; it wasn't like that. I was different. It was then I felt like I had a secret to keep. I felt trapped inside myself; unsure of who I was.

I lost my hearing when I was nine years old. We don't know exactly how it happened, maybe nerve damage, but it did, like it was meant to be. It turned out to be more of a gain than a loss because it introduced me to the extraordinary life I live today.

Soon after, I moved to a deaf school that was located an hour away from my hometown. It was a very difficult transition, especially at a young age. I was mad at the world and didn't want to exist anymore. I felt like I was the only deaf person in the world and that there was no point in continuing my life.

The school was small, but it was like any other place with cliques, peer pressure, labeling, and all the other obstacles kids experience.

In middle school, and the first few years of high school, I went out with many different girls. It was fun but I only dated them to hide who

I really was, to be someone else. I never felt happy or complete because I was not being true to myself. I didn't think I could share my secret with anyone then. There was simply no one I felt I could to talk to.

My family was conservative and religious. Going against the Bible would only mean I was a sinner. My parents were divorced and my two older brothers treated me like an insignificant part of the family—the life of the youngest, I guess. Still, I felt close to everyone in my family; they were loving, caring, supportive, and gave me everything I needed. I just didn't feel courageous enough to tell them the truth.

During my junior year I met someone, and that experience gave me the strength to be more honest because I was so happy, everything felt so right. I felt complete and whole for the first time in a long time. I knew I wanted to feel that way forever so I came out to my friends and the people in my community. Fortunately, everyone was positive and very supportive. I felt great, great enough to tell my mom.

To be honest, I was pretty much forced to tell her. I got suspended from school for participating in sexual activities with another male. She questioned me about it and I told her it was with one of my girl-friends. Mothers seem to know when you are not telling the truth so I ended up confessing to her. She said it was fine and that she loved me but I could tell she was not happy.

About a year later, she asked, "Are you sure you are gay?"

"Yes, I am very sure," I said, and from that day on, it got better. She's been there for me.

I decided to tell my brothers, too. They were both okay with it. Unfortunately, I have not found the strength to tell my dad or my grandparents yet, but I think I'm ready. The next time I see them I will go ahead and come out—because I know it will only get better if I do.

So for those of you who feel confused, or lost, or alone, know that you're not alone. I was there. I was picked on; people called me names and put me down. I experienced this all before I even came out. I was a target just because I did things differently from everyone else, even though what I was doing was good—good for me and good for those around me. But at that age, doing good was not cool, and they made sure I knew it. I know what it's like to feel hopeless and to think there is no future for you. I also know from experience that the future is a great place but you have to want to be there to see it. If you stand strong, be who you are, and know that even though people might not support you now, the days only get brighter if you believe in yourself. It gets better, it really does.

Mark Ramirez was born in Albuquerque, New Mexico, and attended the New Mexico School for the Deaf after he lost his hearing. He graduated and enrolled in Gallaudet University in Washington, DC, the only university in the world that serves deaf and hard-of-hearing students. He currently works at the university and will continue his graduate studies there with the School Counseling and Guidance Department. After obtaining his master's degree, it is his goal is to return to the high school setting to provide guidance and support to the deaf youth and do advocacy for human rights. He enjoys traveling, the outdoors, working with people, and being in touch with nature and the world.

A MESSAGE FROM
SUZE ORMAN

• •

NEW YORK, NY

've spent my entire life—and I'm sixty years of age right now—I've spent my entire life being gay, being a lesbian woman. And back then—back in the '50s—when I was born (I knew I was gay from day one) there wasn't anybody to talk about it with. Still, it did get better.

In the '60s, when the movement first started to happen, and one by one we started to talk to one another, I had a conversation about my life with somebody who understood my life. And it got better. And as every day passed, with everything that I did, I knew that if I was just willing to be who I am, that the world would eventually change and accept people like me. And look at me now.

So my message to you is this, just stick with us. People are listening to you, people are supporting you. People want you to be who you are. And if you could just have faith that things will change, and stick in there, I promise you it will get better.

Is it going to be easy? No. Nothing in life is. Is it worth the struggle? It is. There is nothing greater in life than to be able to be who you are. Tell the world who you are, to not be ashamed of who you are. I am proud that I am a lesbian. I am proud that I'm the personal-finance expert of the world. I am proud of my accomplishments. I am proud that I can stand in my truth, unafraid to tell anybody who I am.

Because, it does get better. But it only gets better when you're willing to be honest—when you're willing to fight to be able to be who you are. Fight for your own right to stand up and say, "I'm proud. I'm gay. Maybe I'm different, but I am still *who I am*." It gets better. I ask you to hang in there. I ask you to accept our support. And I ask you to just give it time. Because, in the end, it really does get better.

Suze Orman has been called "a force in the world of personal finance" and a "one-woman financial advice powerhouse" by *USA Today*. A two-time Emmy Award–winning television host, *New York Times* mega-bestselling author, magazine and online columnist, writer/producer, and one of the top motivational speakers in the world today, Orman is undeniably America's most recognized expert on personal finance.

BROTHERS:
IT GETS BETTER

· ·

by Lenox Magee, Rannon Harris, David Dodd, and Kean Ray

CHICAGO, IL

Lenox: Yo, I'm Lenox.

Rannon: I'm Rannon.

David: I'm David.

Rannon: And we want you to know that it does get better.

Kean: It gets way better. Extremely better. All-the-time better. Especially with your friends.

Lenox: Yes. It does.

Kean: First of all, let me tell you about my story and how it got better for me. I'm thirty years old. But at the time, I was around seventeen or eighteen, I had just started discovering myself, who I was, and I wanted to come out of the closet. It was very traumatic time for me because my family is very anti-gay. Very homophobic. I come from a family of women who believe the main thing homosexuals want to do is molest children. The ironic thing is that my father was bisexual. So clearly my mom's a bit fucked up.

David: Can you say that?

Kean: Of course I can say that. I love my mom but she got fucked up from that experience. Whatever the case, during that time I was really worried about what my mother would think about me and what my grandmother would think about me because I was living with her at the time. And what my brothers would think about me because I am the oldest of six boys. And then what my friends would think about me. I was in high school and I had a lot going on. I was popular. It was that "TV" scenario where I thought at the time I had a lot to lose. So I tried to commit suicide. I took three hundred aspirin, maybe it was six hundred. It was one of those big, bulky bottles you get at Sam's Club. I swallowed all of them and went to sleep, figuring I'm going to have a peaceful death. Grandmother walked in, saw me passed out, saw the aspirin bottle—very dramatic scene—called the ambulance. Having my stomach pumped was worse than trying to commit suicide. I had to drink liquid charcoal and they forced this big, long tube down my throat and forced me to throw up. It was the worst thing I had experienced in my life. I had to stay in the ER for a week on different IVs. They said that had my grandmother not come—fifteen or twenty minutes later—I probably would have been on dialysis for the rest of my life.

After that I had to seek counseling. That's when it hit me. During the transition from eighteen to nineteen, I said to myself, "Forget everybody. I should live for myself." I was going away to college and made a big 180 on worrying about what other people thought or felt about me. I knew I needed to be there for my brothers, because like I said, I'm the oldest of six.

So I went away to college and started living my life for myself. Then my brothers came to live with me. I became their caretaker. And I really couldn't think about what anybody thought about me because, at that time, I had to raise my two brothers. I had to make sure that they finished school; one was still in grammar school and one was in high school, and I was still trying to finish my studies at Northern Illinois University. It was a very hard time but it made me a strong person because I know that no one can tell me what to do. All of my friends can tell you that I don't take any crap from anybody, not even my mom.

Everybody knows who I am. I say what's on my mind and if you ask me my opinion, I'll tell you how it is, and I leave it like that.

Taking care of my brothers helped me to become a strong person. No one can dictate to me what's going on in my life except Kean. I feel that speaking out to young brothers or young sisters—white, black, Asian, whatever you are—saying that you need to live your life for yourself is important. Because nobody can take care of you like you'll take care of you.

Lenox: And the world is changing, too. I came out when I was fourteen, when nobody I knew was out at all. Now we have shows that are gay. When Ellen came out on television it was not the cool thing to do. I did it in high school and I was accepted and I had a great experience. I was around really positive people. So there are people out there that can help you and can be there for you and can support you, and will love you for who you are. So it does get better. It really does.

David: I didn't have a traumatic experience like Kean. But, growing up, I was always teased by kids for being "different." But you know, when you're a kid, you don't really understand what different is. Until you get older and you realize that's what they were talking about when they said you were a faggot or you were gay. I went from being teased in school to being hit to being beat up, and always being scrutinized by kids on the block.

The silver lining to all of that was I realized that I create my future; I create my destiny. Just because these things happened to me doesn't necessarily mean that they should continue to happen to me. So I became stronger, and I built a support system with family and some friends. I think that no matter what you're going through, as long as you have someone to support you—100 percent, totally—it gets better.

Rannon: I can definitely say it gets better. Growing up I remember feeling like I was different. I was always the smart kid or the proper kid. And because I was a late bloomer, I didn't realize I was gay and start messing with guys until the end of college. It was very, very difficult for me to tell my parents because I had always heard gay slurs growing up. So for them to hear me say, "You know what, I like men," I thought it was the end of the world. My mother locked herself in the bathroom and cried for two days straight, I believe. Yes, she did. She cried herself to sleep. It was a traumatic experience for me.

I love my parents very dearly. I'm their Golden Child. I'm the only one that's gone to school. I'm the one that has tried to live my life the way my parents wanted me to live it. So to do something outside of the norm and come to them and say, "Hey, I'm doing something different. Something that you didn't put in this plan for me," was very hard for me. I had a lot of sleepless nights, a lot of nights where I cried myself to sleep, but you know what? It got better.

Now I've graduated from school. I've got a great job. I have this great group of friends. I have a great support system. And my family came around. They love me for who I am. They don't care what my sexual preference is and they don't care who I'm with. They still love me for the person that I am.

And after that, I started mentoring students, I started talking to people, talking to students and telling them that it gets better. And, although it may look hard, just remember that you are the master of your fate. You are the captain of your soul. You are the one that determines what happens to you. Don't let those people out there tell you that because you're gay, you're wrong. That's not true. You can be gay. You can be successful. All of us are successful. All of us have a great future. All of us have great lives. And you know what, it does not matter what our sexual orientation is, it just matters that you have the will to succeed. That's all that you need.

Kean: Let the choir say:

All: It gets better. Amen.

Kean: It gets better, and gaymen!

Kean: We are successful. I'm a director of finance. David does PR. Lenox is a journalist. And Rannon is an analyst/HR/business man.

So we're all very successful in that aspect but that's not what *makes* us successful. What makes us successful is the fact that we didn't let our gayness define who we are. It's a part of us, but it doesn't define who we are. And I think that's what makes us a unique group of guys and a unique group of people. Because "we is who we is," but we're not letting anybody tell us that just because you're gay you can't do things. You were meant to be great. Everybody's meant to be great. It's the question of what are you going to do to make yourself great. That's the question you have to ask yourself.

Lenox: And you will find the answer to that question. It's really hard but you just have to keep the faith and keep believing in yourself and loving yourself and it will come. It all comes to you. It really will.

David: What I do now, and what I did back then, are affirmations. I know it sounds crazy talking to yourself in the mirror. But, honestly, I kind of have a theme song I carry with me throughout the day. I think it was Ellen who talked about that, about having a theme song every day or having some type of mantra to get through my day. It's really been a positive thing for me. It's given me a shield of armor, if you will, against all those elements that were negative affecting me. I started seeing things in a different perspective. Think about doing something like that, saying something that's great about yourself every day and wearing that on your sleeve. Letting that guide you through your day and for the rest of your days, even as an adult.

All: It gets better!

· ·

Lenox Magee has had more than ten years of national and international experience in journalism as an on-air personality, journalist, blogger, and writer. The Chicago native was the former editor-in-chief of *Bleu Magazine*, a national LGBT publication; a radio cohost/producer for Windy City Radio, Chicago's only LGBT radio station; a reporter/producer for Vatican Radio, in Rome, Italy; and online content manager for the GLO TV Network, a new urban gay network.

Outside of his full-time responsibilities as an associate director for AT&T, **Rannon "Ray" Harris** still finds time to work as an entertainment editor for two major publications (*360 Magazine* and *Bleu Magazine*), write his book, and further develop his locution by working on press releases, interviews, stories, and reviews.

David Dodd currently serves as communications manager for Windy City Black Pride (WCBP), a volunteer-based 501(c)(3), not-for-profit organization that provides resources, conducts outreach, and hosts the largest event in the Midwest for the African American LGBT community. He is responsible for developing and implementing the organization's local and national advertising, marketing, and public-relations strategies while writing for his popular blog, *The Real BGC (Black Gay Chicago)*.

Kean Ray has such a passion for educating that he has served in the higher education sector for the past six years, working for Northwestern College as the director of finance; the University of Phoenix; and Ellis University as an adjunct professor facilitating business communications and interpersonal communications. He is currently working on his PsyD in business psychology at the Chicago School of Professional Psychology and has just started his first business venture, K Dock Media, an event-planning marketing firm.

DROP DEAD, WARLOCK

· ·

by David Sedaris

LONDON, ENGLAND

'm so old that when I was in junior high school calling someone a queer was like calling him a warlock. This is not to say that the word was never used, just that no one had actual faith in it. A kid might be girlish. He might tape pictures of other guys to the inside of his locker or pack for Scout camp in a patent leather purse but no one believed he could truly be a homosexual, as such creatures didn't really exist—did they?

We certainly didn't see them on TV. My school had no information on gay people, and neither did the public library, not even in novels. Perhaps it was different for kids in big cities but in Raleigh, North Carolina, in the late '60s and early '70s, I honestly believed I was the only homosexual on earth. It's the way that a zoo creature might feel—these seals, for example, I saw on a recent trip to New York. Born in captivity, what do they know of the oceans, and of all the other seals living contented lives out there?

A gay fourteen-year-old in the year 2010, even one living in the smallest of towns, must surely know that he's not the only homosexual on earth. He might need reminding, though, that all the best people are tormented in junior high school. If they're not getting harassed for being gay, they're bound to get it for being too smart, too loud, or too independent. It's always something, and then you get older, and things change for the better.

If you had told me when I was young that by the turn of the century, I'd be a published author, I would not have believed you. If you told me that I would have a long-term boyfriend, and that the two of us would live in New York, and then Europe, I'd have accused you of reading my mind—the innermost section where I hide my wildest fantasies. With the exception of owning a proboscis monkey, everything I wanted when I was a teenager has come to pass.

This is not to say that every homosexual automatically gets what he or she dreams of. A miserable youth doesn't guarantee you a happy adulthood—that would be too fair. It helps to be flexible, especially in regards to what you might think of as your "type." Decide you will settle for nothing less than Thor, the Nordic God of thunder, and you've essentially drained your dating pool. Loosen up. Be kind. Allow yourself to be surprised.

It helps, too, to keep a diary, to record the many injustices you've suffered, and later turn them into stories. You can't do anything with people being nice to you. People being awful, though; that's gold, so mine it while you can.

David Sedaris is the author of seven books, the most recent of which is *Squirrel Seeks Chipmunk*. He is a regular contributor to *The New Yorker* and Public Radio International's *This American Life*. He and his boyfriend, the painter Hugh Hamrick, currently live in London.

GWENDOLYN GONE

•••••••••••••••••••••••••••••••••••••••

by Meshell Ndegeocello

HUDSON, NY

To be honest, bullying was such a regular part of growing up for me that it doesn't seem like days, moments, or events to remember, but just a chunk, an era, and one of the hardest parts of my life.

I do remember the first time like it was yesterday, though. In the fifth grade, I had a friend named Gwendolyn. We stuck together at school and hung out in the afternoons. Gwendolyn was tall, athletic, kind of a big girl. We were alike in a lot of ways; butchy, indifferent to what the other girls seemed to care about, and, the big one, uninterested in boys. But when one boy teased us, saying we were "tomboys together," Gwendolyn turned to me and said, "No way!" and pushed me. She chased me home until she caught me. She told me she wasn't my friend anymore and hit me in the face. I didn't understand what I had done, but I felt terrible about myself. It felt like something must be really wrong with me if Gwendolyn, who I thought I shared a lot in common with, didn't want to be my friend any more than the other kids who seemed so different from me.

I was afraid to make friends after Gwendolyn. And I was teased for years after that. I was pretty isolated and often lonely in middle school and high school. I went to the prom with my own brother. I wasn't sure why I wasn't like more of the girls in my grade, but at some point, I realized that what set me apart was not what I was wearing or eating for lunch or listening to on my headphones, but that I was gay. Once I knew that, which wasn't easy to realize, I looked outside my class and outside my school for a few people who I thought might recognize me. And there were lots of them once I looked. With a little time and a few people on my side, I became brave enough not to care about the people who didn't like me. I even became brave enough not to hate them for being mean to me. My world did get better, but I got better, too.

I don't know what happened to Gwendolyn, but I do know this: When I look back, it is still a little painful. When I think about being a teenager, I don't usually feel nostalgic. But I don't have to feel bad about how I made someone else feel ashamed or unwanted. Despite how painful it was to earn it, I cherish the wisdom I have about accepting myself and other people, all kinds of people, for who they are. When I make a friend now, I make sure they know that I don't care if they are weird, or popular, or straight, or pretty, or black, or like me, or different. I just want them to know that I like them, that I am their friend, and I mean it.

Meshell Ndegeocello was born Michelle Johnson in Berlin, Germany, and raised in Washington DC. Her records, eight to date, have offered lyrical ruminations on race, love, sex, betrayal, God, and power, and she has simultaneously embraced and challenged listeners with her refusal to be pigeonholed musically or personally. Along the way, she has earned diehard fans, critical acclaim, the unfailing respect of fellow players, songwriters, and composers, and ten Grammy Award nominations. Meshell was the first woman to be featured on the cover of *Bass Player* magazine and remains one of few women who lead the band and write the music.

GROWING UP GAY . . . AND *KINKY*

by Dart

MARCY, NY

When I was a teenager, back in the '80s, I went to a boarding school. I was ostracized and hazed and mocked for being different. Not only was I dealing with a very, very tough puberty but I was confused by the gay feelings I was starting to have. Add to that confusion my realization that I was also kinky and into leather.

In this close-knit, little boarding school community, I was treated really, really badly. The boys used to write really cruel things on my dorm room door, like "fag" and "homo." And to this day, I can still remember going to use the bathroom one day and finding all this graffiti written about me on one of the stall walls. The worst of it showed an arrow pointing to my name and, scrawled beneath it, was, "It's because of him we have AIDS." This was in 1983, when so little was known about AIDS and there was so much fear and panic around the epidemic, so you can imagine just how painful that was.

I felt suicidal at the time. I thought there was no hope for me. I knew I couldn't help these feelings that I was having, and I was stuck in this environment that didn't like or accept me for who I am. I just didn't know if I could go on.

I'm here to let you know that you can go on. There is a whole wonderful world outside this teenage high school environment that you may be feeling oppressed in. And it's a world where you can celebrate who you are, you can embrace who you are, and you can actually have fun being you.

After I left boarding school, I went to UCLA, right in Los Angeles, right near West Hollywood. I discovered a whole new environment that nurtured, supported, and celebrated diversity. It was fun being a gay man there; I actually felt encouraged to go out and experience new things. I met some of the most wonderful people during that time of my life, who liked me because I was different.

I also realized then that the rest of the world is not necessarily as the media portrays it. You have to watch the news and watch political commentary with a grain of salt. You're seeing some extremes on FOX News. It doesn't speak for the rest of the world, and it doesn't speak for the rest of America, either. There is a lot of support out there and a lot of celebration for being a gay person.

I love the life that I'm living right now. If I was given the choice to have any other kind of life, I wouldn't choose another one. I like to say, "When I die, I want to come back as me." And recently, I went back to my twenty-year high school reunion and brought the man I was seeing. All the guys that I hung out with at the party were the same guys who used to haze me in high school. But they were awesome; they had all grown up, just as I had. In fact, one of them gave me a big hug and said, "You know what? You turned out really, really good despite all the challenges we gave you. And you know what, if I was gay, I'd do ya."

It does get better. Hang on. I think you are really, really going to enjoy who you are.

. . . .

Dart is an active educator, performer, and player in the leather and BDSM world. He has traveled extensively, teaching various topics in kink and sexuality. He has a monthly podcast available on iTunes called *Dart's Domain*. He also blogs regularly on his website, www .dartsdomain.com.

THE BIGGEST GIFT

• •

by Stewart Taylor

NEW CANAAN, CT

G rowing up in a small, conservative town in Connecticut, I found that being different was not something other kids took well to. I was always the awkward, skinny kid that liked to sing in school talent shows, and most people usually assumed that I was gay. After a while, I felt trapped in the stereotype that all male singers were gay, and grew tired of being treated a certain way for just being myself and pursuing my music.

Middle school became a giant charade for me, as I tried desperately to act cool and prove to everyone that I wasn't gay. I grew my hair out; I tried to act more manly; I only listened to certain singers on my iPod; and I bragged about all the girls I was hooking up with after I got leads in the school musicals. I was suppressing who I really was to please my peers, and I acted like a complete asshole as a result.

But changing myself in order to gain popularity and acceptance wasn't making me any happier. Instead, I discovered that being afraid of my true self was incredibly debilitating, and by high school, I had had enough of the charade. In truth, I not only liked girls but boys, as well. Yet I had become so set on the idea that any form of gayness was a bad thing that I suppressed that side of myself.

In high school, I had to completely relearn how to just be me. Little by little, I clawed out of the hole I had dug for myself and learned to distance myself from the people who didn't accept me. I stopped caring about the way I acted or about what kids I was seen with. I befriended people based on who they really were. I got involved with the school theater program, where I continued to hone my talents. I was around other kids who loved music and performing as much as I did.

The final key to fully accepting myself was coming to terms with my sexuality, something I'd struggled long and hard with. Yet, it is this struggle that's made me who I am today.

Bisexuality is probably one of the more difficult orientations to understand because it's neither black nor white. For years I went back and forth in my mind trying to figure out if it was even possible to like both sexes. But now at eighteen, I can confidently say that I am bi.

Needless to say, the path to acceptance has not been free of obstacles. Much of our society is still extremely homophobic. And many kids get the message that being gay is the worst thing you can be. Getting over that initial belief and reversing the damage it had done to me psychologically was the first step to accepting my orientation. I was also fortunate enough to seek solace in another bisexual schoolmate who came out before I did. She was further proof to me that I was not alone and that other kids struggled with the same issues. With her, I was finally able to experience what it was like to be my true self. I could spend time with her and openly comment on girls and guys without feeling the need to censor myself. Slowly but surely, I came out to my two best friends, both of whom were incredibly accepting.

It wasn't until my junior year in high school that I completely cast aside the apprehension I felt about other people knowing my secret. One evening, at my best friend's Christmas party, I had a conversation with an older musician about orientation that literally changed my life. I'll call him Frank. After talking with him for a while about music, he asked me if I was gay. I was taken aback by his question and told him that I wasn't. Frank then proceeded to ask me if I was bi, to which I fearfully gave the same response. He apologized for being so blunt, but I could tell he knew I was lying. So, eventually, I opened up and told him I was bisexual. He then proceeded to tell me that the moment someone asks you if you're gay and you freeze up and deny it, you're giving that person the power to walk all over you. You're giving them the power to judge you. However, if someone asks you the same question and you immediately, and proudly, respond, "Yeah, got a problem with that?" suddenly you have the power. You're showing that person that you know who you are and you're fine with it.

Frank will probably never know what a profound impact his words had on my life that night. From that moment on, I didn't care what other people thought. I went straight home, logged on to my Facebook page, and proudly wrote that I was attracted to women AND men. I was done hiding. People would just have to take me as I was, otherwise they didn't deserve me at all.

As the week went on, friends confronted me and told me how proud they were that I had made such a brave move. I had my doubts about the way my guy friends would respond to the news, but thankfully, they were all supportive. The news snowballed around school and became a much bigger deal than I ever thought it would be. Unfortunately, the news reached my younger brother before I could tell him myself. He came home from school that afternoon and asked me if the talk around school was true. I simply told him that, while he probably wouldn't understand, I was in fact bisexual. What I didn't know was that he'd go straight to my dad and tell him.

My father did not take the news well. He tried to convince me that my decision to come out was not okay. The next morning he told me he was kicking me out of the house.

Thousands of teens are homeless because their parents don't accept or understand their sexuality, and I could've been one of those kids, had my mom not stepped in that day. Although there was a lot of arguing, my mom assured me that I wasn't going anywhere, and got my dad to back off. With time, the tension in the household eased, but the pain I felt in that situation remains.

It's moments like these that remind me every day that the biggest gift you can give yourself and to others is acceptance. If you can just learn to love yourself for who you are and be the person you were meant to be, it won't matter how many people are against you. Yes, there are probably always going to be closed-minded people who don't condone the LGBT community, and sometimes those people may even be your own parents, but at the same token, there are many more people in today's world who accept people like me with open arms. When I hang out with my straight guy friends and hear them talking about how much they support my different sexuality, I know that times are changing for the better.

I used to suppress who I was, but nowadays, nearly everyone around me accepts and loves me because I have learned to accept and love myself. I'm popular in school because I'm everyone's friend, and I treat others the way that I want to be treated—a far cry from my middle school days. I'm the happiest I have ever been, and I only wish that more teens who are struggling with their sexuality could come to the same realization that I have; that we are all beautiful individuals just the way we are.

Stewart Taylor is a singer/songwriter who lives in Connecticut. He plans to attend Berklee College of Music in the fall. Stewart's video was part of *We Want It to Get Better*, a video created by teachers Jeremy Leiner, Ethan Matthews, and Chris York with the students of the Studio New Canaan (New Canaan, Connecticut) as a way to give teens an open platform to share their generation's perspective and send support to their peers.

A MESSAGE FROM
SENATOR AL FRANKEN

• •

WASHINGTON, DC

I'm Senator Al Franken, and I wanted to take a moment to talk about the recent string of suicides by LGBT youth across the country. It's beyond heartbreaking that so many students have taken their own lives for being bullied for being gay or perceived as gay.

To any young people out there who are reading this, you may feel alone and that there's nothing you can do, but you're not alone. There are people who want to help, so please reach out to someone. If you don't feel like you can talk to somebody in your family or community, you can call the Trevor Project—a totally anonymous hotline that you can call twenty-four hours a day to talk to someone. The number is 866-4-U-TREVOR.

Just know that there are people and communities all across this country who care about you and are working to make your lives better. I, and more than twenty-five of my colleagues in the Senate, am taking part in this effort. We're working hard to pass a law that would provide you with the same legal protection against discrimination and bullying as other students have now.

And it will get better. When you're in school I know many of you feel pressured to fit in and be like everyone else. And that means, some-times, hiding who you really are. But you can believe me when I tell you that once you leave school, once you start making more choices for yourself, you'll find that the same things that made you feel different in high school are what make you interesting and unique.

Bullying is a deadly serious and an all-too-frequent part of school life. And, tragically, it's often ignored by teachers or administrators. This needs to change. It does get better, and we are going to make it better. Visit my website at Franken.Senate.Gov to learn how you can help.

Senator Al Franken was born on May 21, 1951, and grew up in St. Louis Park, Minnesota. He graduated from Harvard in 1973, where he met his wife, Franni. They've been married for thirty-four years, and have two children: daughter Thomasin, twenty-nine, and son Joe, twenty-five. In 2008, Al was elected to the Senate as a member of the DFL (Democratic-Farmer-Labor) Party from Minnesota, and was sworn in July of 2009 following a statewide hand recount. He currently sits on the Health, Education, Labor, and Pensions Committee; the Judiciary Committee; the Committee on Indian Affairs; and the Special Committee on Aging.

TRANSSEXUAL PRAIRIE GIRL

. . . .

by Tamsyn Waterhouse

SAN FRANCISCO, CA

I'm a transsexual woman. I grew up in rural Canada in really conservative surroundings, and in a rather conservative family. I went to a pretty conservative school as well, and when I was growing up, it was all about conforming, fitting in, and doing what was expected of me. I was never even able to think about issues like my gender identity or sexual orientation until I had grown up. In my high school, you just had to fit in. It wasn't a particularly bad time for me; there was just no opportunity for expressing or discovering myself then.

I always felt awkward and different, but that was all I knew, so I came to assume that that was just what being alive feels like. This is high school we're talking about, after all. So I learned how to fit in, and I think I did pretty well at it. I'm mostly gay, so living as a boy and being attracted to girls didn't create any problems. I love hockey and pizza, too, so there you go.

It got better when I came out, when I was able to tell my friends and family that I'm still me but I'm not quite who you thought. When I was able to say, "I'm transgender," it got a lot better. My friends were there for me. My family was there for me. My colleagues were there for me.

When I came out to my mom, who is a retired bassoonist, I had been dreading that conversation for a long time, not knowing how she would react. Finally, I just said, "Mom, I'm transgender." She replied, "That's all right, dear; we had a lot of that in the orchestra."

Overall, my family and friends have been great: supportive, kind, and curious. Sometimes I think they treat my transsexuality as a sacred cow, though, and I find myself wishing they'd just lay in and razz me about it for once.

Right after I transitioned, I was really self-conscious. Any time I was in public and I made eye contact with someone, I got really nervous and thought, "Oh, this person is staring at me because I'm transsexual." And then straight guys started asking me out, and I realized that there's more than one kind of staring.

It's always okay to ask questions, especially when it's questions about yourself. It's okay to ask, "Who am I?" It's okay to ask, "What gender am I?" You should never be afraid of those questions.

If I could tell my teenage self one thing, it would be: "Hurry up and get your wisdom teeth out, please. Do me a favor." And if I could tell my teenage self two things, it would be: "Dude, you're a girl. It's okay. Get used to it and enjoy it. Be yourself and don't be afraid of anything."

I love who I am. I'm very proud to be transsexual, and I wouldn't have had it any other way.

• •

Tamsyn Waterhouse grew up just outside Winnipeg, spent a decade in university studying mathematical physics, and dropped out when she finally achieved her life goal of owning her weight in LEGO. She now lives in San Francisco and works in renewable energy R&D. She loves film, food, games, airplanes, and communal living, but she does not love writing autobiographical paragraphs.

ART FROM RAGE

• •

by Jake Shears

NEW YORK, NY

I was fifteen years old when I came out. I went to a big high school, and since there were so many kids there, I thought it would be as good a time and place for me to come out as any. So I started telling other kids that I was gay, launching what was probably the worst year of my life. I was harassed; I was followed; I was threatened; kids wanted to kill me. I couldn't go from class to class without being accosted. Kids would throw desks and chairs at me in class and the teachers would just pretend that they didn't see what was going on.

I would get sent to the principal's office with these kids that were obviously *torturing* me, or I would go on my own accord, and be told that this was happening because I wasn't keeping my private life private. Any school administrators with that attitude today should be put in prison in my opinion.

I'm here to tell you that even though it's horrible and these terrible things happen, and you may have this idea to kill yourself, to hurt yourself, don't. I thought about it. I thought about killing myself quite a few times during this period of my life but I'm so glad I didn't, because I'm living the dreams now that I created when I was fifteen years old. I'm living out those fantasies that I had. It's such a rewarding, amazing life that I've gotten to lead.

I'm having so much more fun than I did when I was fifteen, that's for damn sure. The experiences that you have when you're a queer teenager—and I'm using the word *queer* in a very broad sense, covering everyone who feels different—are going to give you a whole new perspective on the rest of your life. And they can instill in you a sense of joy, a sense of inspiration, and an amazing sense of humor.

I get to run around onstage in front of a ton of people and rip at my clothes and shake my ass and act as gay as I want to be. I get paid to express myself however I want to in an explosive way. That's a direct response to the fact that I didn't feel like I could do any of that when I was fifteen. I've made a career out of my rage. I've turned it into a job. I still have a lot of rage in me and I still have a lot of anger about that time of my life, and I probably always will. But you can take that anger and use it for your own good. They say blondes have more fun. Well, I say queers have more fun, and blonde queers have the most fun.

However hard it may seem, however bad it gets, whether it's from your parents, or from fellow students, or your brothers and sisters, or your crazy religious next-door neighbors, or whomever, breathing down your neck, telling you that you are a bad person, or that you're full of sin, or that you don't deserve to have as good of a life as anybody else, just realize they're crazy. Those people are *crazy*. If you remember that, that they're just crazy people who have nothing better to do than insinuate themselves into to other people's lives and try to control them, if you just remember that, then you'll be okay. Then you can go on to make lots of friends and create a family full of people that don't behave that way.

You are a special person and you've got so much to offer the world, and even though you may feel sad right now, you can turn your sadness into joy and you can turn your rage into art.

....

Jake Shears lives in New York City and is the lead singer of the band Scissor Sisters. He's also cowritten the musical version of *Tales of the City*, which will open at ACT in San Francisco in June 2011.

IT GETS BETTER /
بتكون أحسن
(BTKOUN AHSAN)

. . . .

by Bashar Makhay / بشار مخأي

NEW YORK, NY

Original transcript:

من أول طلعتي في نفسي فهمت ليش ماكنت فرحان بحياتي، كنت في دولاب
وما كنت عايش حياتي في الحقيقة. من أول طلعتي كنت كثير خايف علشان
اصدقائي وعشيرتي، ايش يفكرون ويسوون. خفت يعذبوني، خفت يعوفوني.
قلت بلكي يحبوني على ما أنا. بالأخير مع كثير من الحكي، وكثير من الوقت، أكثر
الناس حبوني على ما أنا. بس أقرب الناس صعب يفتهمون ليش أنا أحب نفس
الجنس؟ أفكر المشكلة بجماعتنا أننا مانحكي عن الجنس. قبل ما أن اطلع أنا من
الدولاب - خزانة - ما أحد في حياتي حكى عن الجنس. جماعتنا مايريدون أي
واحد يسأل عن الجنس أو يقول عن هويته الجنسية، وهاي مشكلة. بالأخير أنا
طلعت من الدولاب، وقلت لكل العالم. قلت لكل اللي أعرفهم، قلت للمجلات، قلت
للإنترنت . كثير ناس حكيو عليها، وكانت أول مرة أشوف ناس يحكون عن
الهوية الجنسية. اليوم أنا فرحان كثير بحياتي، عندي كثير أصدقاء، كثير ناس من
عشيرتي، فرحانين بي. بصدق بتاخد كثير وقت، وكثير حكي، بس الحياة حتكون
أحسن، راح تكون أحسن بكثير.

Original translated transcript:

When I first came out to myself, I realized why I wasn't happy with my life; I was in the closet and I wasn't living my life truly. When I first came out, I was really scared of what my friends and family would think and do. I was scared they would hurt me, abandon me, or just maybe love me for who I am. In the end, after a lot of time and a lot of discussion, more people in my life came to love me for who I am, but there are still many people in my life that have a difficult time understanding why I love someone of the same gender.

I think the issue of our people is that we do not talk about sexuality. Before I came out of the closet, nobody I knew spoke about sexuality. I think that when our people think about sexuality, they don't want anyone to ask about sexuality or tell anyone their sexuality. This is an issue.

In the end, when I came out, I told the whole world, I told everyone I know, the news, Internet, newspapers. For the first time in my life I started to see people talking about sexuality, a lot of people. Today I am very happy with my life; I have a lot of friends and people in my family who are proud of me. All I can say is that it takes a lot of time and discussion but life gets better, life gets a lot better.

· ·

Bashar Makhay proudly identifies himself as a Progressive Gay Chaldean Iraqi-American Christian man. He began his organizing work with ACCESS (Arab Community Center for Economic and Social Services), providing HIV/STD counseling, testing, and referral services to Arab and Chaldean gay men. Working at ACCESS, after struggling with his own coming-out process, Bashar realized that the Middle Eastern gay community needed and wanted to be organized. Bashar left ACCESS and then cofounded Al-GAMEA (The LGBT Association of Middle Eastern Americans), a first-of-its-kind organization, created to provide a forum for support, socialization, education, and awareness inside and outside of the Middle Eastern community in metropolitan Detroit. Bashar currently works as a program associate for the Arcus Foundation, a private foundation that works to achieve social justice based on sexual orientation, gender identity, and race.

TOO GOOD TO BE TRUE

•••

by Cameron Tuttle

SAN FRANCISCO, CA

N o one bullied me in high school because absolutely no one knew I was gay. Definitely not me. It took me years to figure that out.

I was one of those squeaky clean, annoyingly mainstream, over-achiever types. I got good grades, did student government, sang in musicals, played team sports, and joined lots of clubs to fatten up my college applications. But even though I was popular and friends with lots of different people, I felt alone, really alone, like no one knew the real me.

How could they? I was trying so hard to be perfect.

On the outside, I was a thriving, active, make-my-family-proud, successful teenager. But on the inside, I was emotionally numb, coma-tose, flat-lining. My mom had died of breast cancer two weeks before the beginning of ninth grade. She was an amazing mom, loving and supportive, and she gave me enough freedom to explore who I was so I could succeed or fail with my own personal style. After she died, I was devastated. But I was determined to prove to the world and to myself that I was okay.

I found myself working really, really hard to be the best because I was scared. Scared of being different. Scared of being defective. Scared of feeling my feelings. So for years, I didn't let myself feel.

I got a lot done in high school but I didn't have a lot of fun. And even though I wasn't ever bullied by other people, I was relentlessly bullied by my own thoughts and fears about who I was, how I was supposed to behave, and what would happen if I didn't.

I actually had this pathetic idea that I would somehow let down my community—people I barely knew in the conservative, snooty neighborhood where I grew up—if I ended up being a lesbian. How ridiculous is that?

Bullying isn't just what real people in real time say to you or try to do to you. Bullying is everywhere—it's in the words of fearful, judgmental parents who are trying to control you. (BTW: it's also in the words of well-meaning but misguided parents who are trying to "protect you from being hurt.") Bullying is in the news and in government policy. It's in the imagery of pop culture. It's in religion. And as a result, it gets into your head.

How did it get better for me? Slowly. It helped that I went to college across the country, as far away as I possibly could go from my hometown without needing a passport.

I eventually found the guts to stand up to my inner bully, the judgmental, fearful, bossy voice in my head that kept telling me, *You can't . . . You shouldn't . . . Don't you dare!* And then I finally found the confidence to listen to my body and to my heart and to be honest with myself.

And then I moved to New York.

When I was living there, I met tons of people who were a lot like me—squeaky-clean, annoyingly mainstream overachievers who just happened to be gay: former high-school cheerleaders, homecoming kings, class officers, student leaders, star athletes. And I realized . . . yeah, I can do this. Yeah, I can be this. And now, I love being different—in my squeaky-clean, annoyingly mainstream way.

If your school is like the rest of the world (and it is—no matter how weirdly "normal" it seems or tries to be), 5 to 10 percent of the other students around you are gay. Whether you're trying to fit in and hide in plain sight like I was, or you're determined to stand out and never fit in, you are not alone. Others are there, wondering, doubting, fearing, experimenting, exploring, and struggling just like you, struggling to find their place in the world. Not just a place—the place, the right place, the honest place, that feel-good happy place. They may not look gay, they may not act gay, they may not even know they're gay—yet. But they are there. Trust me.

In my twenties, in New York, was the first time I really relaxed and let myself fall madly in love. And you'll never guess who I fell in love with: a girl from my hometown, from my own high school, a girl from right up the street. And it was amazing.

· ·

Cameron Tuttle is the author of the bestselling series The Bad Girl's Guides, *The Paranoid's Pocket Guide*, and the new Paisley Hanover series for teens, which in no way resembles her own high school years. She lives and writes in San Francisco.

JOURNEY TO A BETTER LIFE

by Juan Carlos Galan, MS

MIAMI, FL

I grew up in the small conservative town of David, Panama, in Latin America. Ever since I was a little kid, I felt different from all the other boys in the neighborhood. I was not good at sports. I did not like aggressive games. I hated having to hit the piñata at birthday parties. And I always preferred reading books and playing with the girls. I was raised by my very traditional and religious grandparents in a culture of homophobia and machismo. In my hometown, it was culturally acceptable for gay and lesbian people to be publicly subjected to humiliation, disrespect, and discrimination. I remember hearing stories of gay men being verbally and physically attacked.

Because I was not masculine, the kids in school made fun of me constantly. They would write profanities about me in the bathrooms, taunt me during PE class, and call my house and say nasty things to me on the phone. I remember walking into a classroom and having all the students yell offensive and derogatory things at me while the teacher did nothing about it. The school staff just let the bullying happen. They believed that I was asking to be bullied by being different from everyone else. At school, I only felt safe around my friend Angie, whom I had known since I was a little kid. She stood up for me when I was threatened by my classmates. At home, I was bullied by my own family, which was even more painful than the harassment I received at school. My family was constantly telling me that I needed to change my mannerisms; they would criticize the way I spoke and walked.

One day, my mother took me to a psychiatrist who was supposed to help me change. I felt so guilty and humiliated for having a doctor tell me how to sit properly. He tried to change my tone of voice, and even prescribed the antidepressant Prozac for me, which I thought then was a magic pill that would make me manlier. I lied in every session in hopes that I could stop going. I told the psychiatrist that I was acting tougher in school, and the kids were not making fun of me anymore. The reality was that the bullying was getting worse, and I did not having anyone I could trust to talk to about it.

I ended up believing the false, negative stereotypes that I heard growing up because I lacked any evidence of the contrary. I did not know anyone else who was gay. I felt lonely and isolated, and I was barely speaking to my family. One night, while I was riding in the car with my grandfather, he demanded I tell him why I always seemed so sad. I did not want to talk about it with him because I knew that he was extremely homophobic. I was definitely not ready to come out but he pressured me so hard that I ended up telling him that I was gay. He told me that gay people could never have happy lives because no one loves them. He asked me to think about the rest of the family and how much I was going to shame and hurt them. He said that all gay people are promiscuous, and not worthy of respect or success. He told me that I was abnormal. He said that everyone hates gay people, even in bigger cities and more progressive countries. And then, he cried.

I had never seen him cry so hard. It was so traumatic to see him so upset and hear him say these terrible things that I ended up blocking my own emotions. I decided that it would be easier to lie to him. So a couple of days later, I told him that I was no longer gay, and I had just been confused. I knew this was not true, and I was lonelier than ever because now I felt like my family would never love me for who I was. I got so depressed that I started thinking about ending my life. The future scared me. I contemplated a life of suffering and loneliness and figured that I would never be able to be happy. Killing myself would be the only way to truly end all of the pain.

I was very close to committing suicide before I decided I should at least tell someone else my secret. I was not sure if I could tell Angie. Even though I knew that I could trust her, I was afraid that she would react negatively and that I would lose my only ally in the school. I decided to tell her anyway because I knew that if I did not share my secret with anyone, it was going to end up killing me. I came out to her. I told her everything that had happened with my grandfather and how bad the bullying at school was making me feel. Telling her was the best decision I have ever made. I was able to release so much anxiety and repressed feelings. She was happy that I trusted her, and made me feel like I was special for being different. It was so refreshing to suddenly have someone to count on. I had been keeping this secret my whole life, and I was finally able to experience what it was like to be completely honest with another person. I realized then that I was capable of developing true friendships; having someone that loved me unconditionally made it clear to me that life was still worth living.

When I moved to the United States for college, I met new people and started building deep connections and friendships with other gay people and straight allies. I got the chance to finally experience what it was like to belong to a community. I helped set up an agency that provides a safe space for LGBT teenagers so that they are supported through their coming-out process and won't have to go through what I did. I came to appreciate the beauty and magic of the LGBT culture. Most importantly, my LGBT peers inspired me to truly embrace myself and understand that there was nothing wrong with me. I didn't need to change for anyone.

I have come to realize that every single negative stereotype that my grandfather recited that dreadful night has turned out to be completely false. Not everyone hates gay people. In fact, there are many LGBT people who are loved and respected by their community and have built successful careers. I know openly gay people who are politicians, artists, lawyers, writers, doctors, and activists. Gay people are not perverts. LGBT individuals create healthy, fulfilling, and happy lives. I'm a happy person today, surrounded by loving friends and a partner whom I am planning to marry. The reality is that, little by little, even my family has come to accept and love me for who I truly am. But none of this would have happened if I were not here. If I had ended my life, I would not have been able to meet so many wonderful people. I would not have experienced the togetherness and belonging that comes from truly deep friendships. I would not have been able to fall in love. I would not have known what it feels like to be embraced by a community. I would not have been able to see that life does get better.

I promise that your life will get better, too. I fact, you can start creating a better life right now. Even when you think there is no one to talk to, you can reach out to the Trevor Project or the Alliance for GLBTQ Youth and ask for help when you are feeling depressed. If you are being bullied, say something. Supportive adults can be your allies; they can help you file a complaint to stop the bullying in your school. If it is safe for you, you can make your school a more inclusive place by starting a Gay-Straight Alliance with the help of understanding adults. You can also contact your state equality agency and get involved in developing a safe schools policy and training for your district. Most importantly, always be on the lookout for warning signs of depression and suicide so that you can help yourself and your friends stay safe.

No matter how hard it may get, or how isolated and sad you may feel, remember that you are loved despite what your grandfather, relatives, neighbors, or anyone might say. The LGBT community needs you and all your unique gifts and talents to help us build a better future. Above everything else, deep within your heart, you must know that IT GETS BETTER.

Juan Carlos Galan, MS, is a writer, activist, and social researcher. He has worked with the Alliance for GLBTQ Youth (www.glbtqalliance .org), an agency that provides a full range of social services for LGBT youth in Miami-Dade county. Galan developed and coordinated the agency's information systems and research efforts. He's also heavily involved with immigration equality, lobbying Congress for comprehensive immigration reform that is inclusive of LGBT families and raising media awareness about the legal struggles that bi-national same-sex couples have to face.

THE GAY GUY IN THE BAND

. . . .

Kevin Samual Yee

BROOKLYN, NY

When I was eleven, I saw an episode of *Sally Jesse Raphael* where she was interviewing a young gay teen and his religious family. I watched his family bickering and crying, trying to convince him that it was just a phase. I remember thinking to myself, "Gee . . . what a hard life. I hope that I don't grow up to be gay."

I was an awkward teen and never quite fit in with any crowd. I'm pretty sure that every teenager feels this way no matter who they are or how comfortable they seem on the outside. I liked musical theater and dancing and spent my free time participating in the local theater scene. I was basically a male version of Lea Michele in *Glee*.

At the age of fifteen I was hired to be part of a boy band. The Backstreet Boys and 'N Sync were at the top of the charts so being in a boy band was a pretty big deal. I figured I was on the road to superstardom.

It was another story all together.

From the moment I was hired, the executives at the record label took issue with me. They thought I came off "gay." And that was a problem if I was ever going to appeal to the throngs of teenage girls who would buy our album. It began with several closed-door media sessions where we discussed how to talk "straight." *Don't articulate as*

*much . . . Mumble more; use more current slang; if asked who your
favorite singer is, Celine Dion is not the right answer, etc. . . .*

They tried to change my appearance by bleaching my hair, piercing my ears, and dressing me in an array of oversized baggy clothing mostly worn backward. Why they thought these changes would make me look less gay I will never know. Their interpretation of straight was actually more offensive then they're negative view of gay. At one point, the group's manager even marched me up and down the aisles of a grocery store so I could practice my "straight" walk (which essentially looked like I had sprained my ankle and was trying not to put pressure on it).

It was humiliating.

I spent three years in that group learning to act "straight" before our album bombed and we were all sent home.

The first thing I did when I left the group was come out of the closet. I was gay. And after years of being someone else, I wanted to finally be myself.

I've been lucky enough to find my place on the stage working in musical theater for the past ten years. You can be whoever you want to be here. When I think back on my time in the boy band, I laugh at how silly it all was. Of course, then I was devastated, feeling judged for who I was. Now I see how big this world really is—there is a place for everyone. And to truly enjoy it, you have to be able to celebrate yourself.

• •

Kevin Yee is a Broadway actor who has been seen in companies of *Mary Poppins*, *Wicked*, and *Mamma Mia*. He is also a singer/songwriter with two albums, and creator of the YouTube webseries *The Kevin Yee Show*. His video contribution to the It Gets Better Project featured actors from the *Wicked* 2nd National Tour.

WILL I GROW UP TO BE PAUL LYNDE?

by Andy Cohen

NEW YORK, NY

Back when I was a kid in the suburbs of St. Louis in the '70s and early '80s, there were no gay people on TV with the exception of Paul Lynde and Charles Nelson Reilly, who were basically these two huge queens. They were very funny but everybody kind of laughed at them. So in my mind, gay people were laughed at and didn't really have any impact or any value as members of society.

I realized that I was gay somewhere around eleven, twelve, or thirteen years of age. And the only time I would allow myself to face that fact would be late at night. I'd be alone in my room, just lying there in the dark of night thinking, *This isn't going to happen for me; this life is going to turn really bad. No one is going to accept me, and no one is going to love me, and my family will not have this, and all my friends who I love will be no more, and I will never be able to be the person that I know I am.*

It was heartbreaking.

And it was something that I didn't allow myself to face that often. But, every once in a while, I would have a very long, sleepless night—those were some of the longest nights of my life. And they did not stop until I went to college in Boston. There, I slowly found my way. One semester I went abroad and was able to find out who I really was.

I could express myself to the new friends I was making and create my own identity. And was able to figure out on my own how all of that was going to play out for me in my life.

After that trip I was nothing other than who I am today. It didn't change me; it didn't define me; it was just that part of who I am was finally able to emerge. I found acceptance and I found love. So for anybody who's having a sleepless night or a sad day, or has some asshole picking on them, just know that you're going to wind up way better off than that asshole. They'll probably get really fat and lose their hair; it'll be a nightmare for that person. But you're going to be okay, because it gets better. I promise.

Born in St. Louis, **Andy Cohen** is Bravo's executive vice president of original programming and development, responsible for overseeing the network's current development and production slate of such hit shows as *Top Chef, Top Chef Masters,* The Real Housewives series, *Kathy Griffin: My Life on the D-List, The Millionaire Matchmaker, Flipping Out,* and many others. In addition, Cohen is the host and executive producer of *Watch What Happens: Live.* Cohen received an Emmy Award for *Top Chef* and has been nominated for nine additional Emmy Awards. In June 2010, he was listed as one of *TV Guide*'s "25 Most Influential People in Television."

FINDING WHO I AM

•••

by Hunter Adeline Brady

STAMFORD, CT

I am a happy sixteen-year-old girl with a great group of friends, but when I was younger I always seemed to be the odd one out among the kids in my neighborhood. I was rarely invited over to play, until one of the kids' parents would demand that I be included. I assumed it was just because they could only have a few people over at a time, or it was a family thing, until I got older and realized I wasn't being included because I wasn't like them. Eventually, they just cut me out of their lives all together.

I was told middle school was going to provide a fresh start. That everything was going to be great because I would be able to change everything and magically make it all better. That wasn't the case. I felt like a newborn infant being thrown into a tidal wave. It all started off crazy and scary: getting my first locker, moving from classroom to classroom, making new friends, or at least trying to. And then I met my future worst enemy, my first bully. His name was Alex and he was about my height and weight and was actually nice to me after school that first day. But as the days went by, he started calling me names like "Big Red," "Ginger," "Freak," and anything else he could think of.

Alex bullied me by calling me names, commenting on my clothing and the way I looked in general. He made me want to stay in bed all day and hide from the world. I was scared to walk into school and hear what he would say next. I did not know who to turn to, so I ventured off into the world of theater. And that is where I found my true home—a place I felt safe and where I could be myself. I got a lead role after my first audition, and felt that I could really show people that I was actually someone who was passionate about something. I wanted to prove to Alex that I wasn't a "nothing" like he always told me I was. I continued to shine on the stage, unafraid to go all out.

I still wanted to fit in, which meant having a boyfriend like all the other eighth-grade girls. I'd had crushes but it didn't seem like any of the boys liked me back. I thought there was something wrong with me. And then I began to wonder, "Do I even like boys?" I was scared of what the real answer might be. I didn't say anything to anyone about these thoughts and feelings that I was suddenly having. Then, during the summer after eighth grade, I was sleeping over at a friend's house. It was all fine until she kissed me. I instantly called my mom to pick me up. I did not understand what had just happened. I knew what it was like to kiss someone because people had dared me to before. But I didn't know what it was like to kiss a girl. I didn't think it was wrong but I was afraid that maybe she would think that it was a mistake. I couldn't help but smile as I got into the car to go home. I couldn't deny it, it felt right.

That summer came to an end and it was time for me to go to high school. I was entering a massive school that both my sister and mom had attended and loved. It started off amazing and I was enjoying it until I started struggling with grades and all of the normal things that happen in your first year of high school.

I wasn't happy. Something was missing and I didn't know what, until I met the girl that would be my best friend. She was awesome. I could be myself around her and we shared the same curiosity. Actually, she wasn't curious. She knew she was bisexual. We never had anything beyond friendship, but after meeting her, I was able to proudly say that I was bisexual. She helped me realize that it was normal to feel what I was feeling. I was afraid to tell my parents about my sexuality until halfway through my sophomore year. When I finally did tell my mom, she was completely fine with it. I think she thought it was just a phase. I think she still does. I didn't tell my dad, though. I was afraid to for some reason, and still kind of am.

I began hating that school. The teachers did not seem to care too much if you were doing your best, and the students did not care at all. They were also extremely rude. When I walked down the halls, it turned into middle school all over again, with people calling me names and even occasionally shoving me into lockers. I knew that I deserved better. I wanted to be in a better environment so I could go to a good college. I transferred to a new school—an all-girls, private school. Girls at my school know that I am bisexual and are completely okay with it. I know who I am and am truly happy with the person I have become. Finding my true sexuality has changed my life and I wouldn't change anything that I went through for the world. I have found who I really am and I am happy now. And that is all that matters.

Hunter Brady is currently a sophomore, getting good grades and loving life. She is studying voice and acting at the Studio in New Canaan, Connecticut. She loves photography and performing onstage. As long as she can bring a smile to another's face, she can smile. Hunter's video was part of *We Want It to Get Better*, a video created by teachers Jeremy Leiner, Ethan Matthews, and Chris York with the students of the Studio in New Canaan as a way to give teens an open platform to share their generation's perspective and send support to their peers.

COMMUNITY

●●●●●●●●●●●●●●●●●●●●●●●●●

by Chaz Bono

LOS ANGELES, CA

G rowing up is really hard, and when you're an LGBT youth, it's even more difficult. You can feel like you're the only person like you in the world. Maybe you're dealing with bullying in school or judgment from your family, and it's really easy to get into the mindframe that life is never going to get better—that this is what it's going to be like and I'm always going to feel like an outsider. I'm always going to feel bad about myself.

I just want to let you know that it gets better. When you grow up, you realize that you're not alone and that there are lots and lots of people—communities of people just like you—who are willing to embrace you and support you and love you. You just need to hang around and wait for that magic to happen, because life is really great. Even when you're different, life is really a wonderful thing.

I've gone through a lot of that stuff, of really feeling different. I only came out as a transgender man about a year and half ago. So, even as an adult, I was living with this secret and feeling weird. And I got it out and now I feel great. I've been embraced by a new community. That's what happens when you're finally honest about who you are; you find others like you.

I have a wonderful life. I have a wonderful partner who I've been with for over five years now. Yet if I had let any of the fear that I had at different points throughout my life—in high school, feeling different (even feeling different as another person)—if I had done something drastic then, I would have missed out on the best times of my life. Don't let anybody tell you that there's something wrong with you if you're different. There's not. So hang in there and just remember it does get better.

The only child of famed entertainers Sonny and Cher, **Chaz Bono** is an LGBT rights advocate, author, and speaker. Chaz recently underwent gender transition in the public eye, where he continues to impact change and create awareness and visibility for this cause. He has written two books: *Family Outing: A Guide to the Coming Out Process for Gays, Lesbians, and Their Families* and *The End of Innocence: A Memoir*. He is at work on a third book, *Transition: The Story of How I Became a Man*, to be released by Dutton in May 2011. Chaz is also currently filming a documentary, *Becoming Chaz*, which will debut at the Sundance Film Festival in January 2011. He resides in Los Angeles with his partner, Jennifer Elia.

A MESSAGE FROM
NANCY PELOSI

••••••••••••••••••••••••••••

WASHINGTON, DC

Hello. I'm Speaker Nancy Pelosi. Today, to anyone who feels different, to those of you who feel lost or think you don't fit in, to those who feel singled out because of who you are, I add my voice to the chorus of parents, friends, teachers, mentors, and leaders in your neighborhoods and across the country, to say: It gets better. You are not alone.

As a mother and a grandmother, I want to tell you that a better tomorrow awaits, filled with opportunity, with hope, with the promise of success, with respect, and progress for all. There are resources and people ready to help.

In America's rich history, we've overcome barriers and obstacles before: for women, and for religious, racial, and ethnic minorities. And we are doing it again for gay, lesbian, bisexual, and transgender Americans.

During this challenging time for so many, you should know that I am on your side. In the Congress, we are striving to advance our nation's pledge of equality, our heritage and our hope. That is why we passed a fully inclusive hate-crimes bill, ensuring protections for the LGBT community alongside all Americans. And now it is the law of the land.

In our communities, homes, and schools, and as a country, we must state clearly that bigotry and bullying have no place in our society. Bullying contradicts our American values and our aspirations. Diversity is an American strength.

We will overcome the forces of prejudice and hatred among us. We will build a future that welcomes every family and every child, regardless of background or sexual orientation. We will foster the talents, hopes, and dreams of all of our young people. Together, united, we will remind our LGBT youth and all Americans: It gets better.

• •

Nancy Pelosi is the House Democratic leader of the U.S. House of Representatives. She served as Speaker of the House of Representatives for two consecutive terms, having been elected in 2007 as the first woman in American history to serve as Speaker. Serving in the Congress for more than two decades, Pelosi has proudly represented the city of San Francisco since 1987. A native of Baltimore, Pelosi is married to Paul Pelosi and is a mother of five and a grandmother of eight.

GUNN'S GOLDEN RULES

● ●

by Tim Gunn

NEW YORK, NY

As a seventeen-year-old youth who was in quite a bit of despair, I attempted to kill myself.

I'm very happy today that that attempt was unsuccessful. But, at the time, it was all that I could contemplate. I thought I needed to end things right then. And I have to tell you that when I woke up the next morning, after taking more than a hundred pills, I was in a whole other level of despair. I thought, "I shouldn't be here. This isn't what was meant to be." I, frankly, just wanted to start life all over again.

There are people who can help you. You cannot do this alone; that's another very profound message that I want to give to *all* of you. It really requires collaboration between you and the people who love you, the people who you can depend upon—no matter who they are—as mentors. In my case, it took a very serious intervention to help me. And it was the result of the botched suicide attempt—to be blunt.

I am a huge advocate for the Trevor Project. The Trevor Project is a suicide-prevention hotline for LGBT and questioning youth. Please visit their website (thetrevorproject.org) and seek them out. Your identity will be protected; you don't have to worry about getting parents involved. I understand the desperation. I understand the despair. And I understand how isolated you can feel. People really care about you, and I'm included in that group. So reach out, get help. You're not alone. It will get better!

I promise.

....

Tim Gunn is chief creative officer of Liz Claiborne Inc. Gunn has also served as a member of the administration and faculty at Parsons School of Design for twenty-four years and has a rich and deep history with the institution. In August 2000, Gunn was appointed chair of the department of Fashion Design at Parsons. Gunn serves as cohost of the six-time Emmy-nominated *Project Runway* and is the author of two books, *A Guide to Quality, Taste and Style* and *Gunn's Golden Rules.*

PERFECT, JUST THE WAY YOU ARE

•••••••••••••••••••••••••••••••••••••

by Darren Hayes

LONDON, ENGLAND

I am a gay man who loves his life. I have a career that I love. I've got a partner that I adore beyond all comprehension. And I am surrounded by friends and family and a community who accept me and support me for who I am.

But it wasn't always so. Growing up I had a real tough time. By the age of thirteen, I was bullied so much so that I didn't want to go to school anymore. It seemed that everyone else in the world knew that I was gay before I did. There was something about me that some of the kids didn't like, and, boy, did they let me know about it. I was picked on; I was tormented; I was called names; I was beaten up because I was gay.

I was also artistic, a born entertainer. I could sing. I could dance. You could see from space that I was meant to be doing what I do for a living today. Yet, back then, the thing that made me extraordinary made me a target.

It took me a long time to realize that I was gay. You don't need to know my long, boring coming-out story. Suffice to say that parts of it were quite dramatic and fun, but it was also quite tragic at times. I eventually accepted who I was and was lucky enough to have pursued a career in music and the arts that I could throw myself into. Though, when I think back on it now, I realize I spent a lot of the early part of my career disguising a deep sadness. Those early experiences of being picked on in high school had an impact. They made me believe that who I was, was wrong, that the happily-ever-after they sell you in the movies wasn't for me, wasn't for gay people. That scenario only applied to straight people. Even then, in my early twenties, I didn't have a role model that I could look up to. I didn't know a single gay person. Yet, in my heart, I knew that I wanted to get married one day, maybe even be a dad, but certainly meet someone that I could live the rest of my life with. And I was led to believe from the people who picked on me, and the society that I lived in, that this wasn't an option for me.

And yet, even though I struggled with sadness and depression, I was lucky enough to have people in my life who loved me for who I was and made me feel confident and secure that being gay wasn't a choice, it was simply the way I was born. It was just who I was. It was really no more significant than the color of my eyes or the color of my hair.

I eventually found love. Richard and I just celebrated our fifth anniversary of our civil partnership here in England. We got married in a circle with all our friends and family and I was lucky enough to hold Richard's hand and my mother's hand, and look across the circle at my sister and my nieces and nephews and all the people who loved me for me—who loved me for who I was born to be. It was the happiest day of my life.

It wasn't always that easy, though, and for anybody who is struggling, anybody who is being made to feel guilty about who they are, I just want to remind you that it gets better. It gets so much better. It gets amazing. I know things might be tough right now but you must never give up. You must never forget that there's a light at the end of the tunnel and, more importantly, that you are beautiful. You are perfect, just the way you are.

....

Darren Hayes is an Australian-born recording artist who first found fame as the lead singer and one-half of pop group Savage Garden. He lives in London with his civil partner, Richard Cullen, and their cocker spaniel, Wally.

WHERE HAPPINESS IS

• •

by Natalie Sperry Mandelin

PLEASANTON, CA

was born and raised a good little Mormon girl in Sandy, Utah, a city about thirty miles south of Salt Lake. I went to church every Sunday and was baptized at eight. I went through the church's entire young women's program. By the time I was in high school, I felt that I had a testimony of the Gospel.

I also developed a crush on the girl who sat in front of me in my sophomore history class. She was super-cute and had been out for two years; and we were only fifteen. I was ill-equipped to deal with my feelings. All I had in the form of education about homosexuality were admonitions from my family and the church that it was wrong and that if you were a homosexual, you were going to hell unless you repented. I remember writing diary entries when I first met my girlfriend about how I feared for her immortal soul and how I needed to try and save her. Well, I told my mom about this girl that I had met and my mission to save her from hell, and her response was that we were not allowed to be friends anymore. I couldn't even talk to her on the phone. My mother said that what she was doing was evil and I was incapable of helping her. What I needed to do was protect myself against the devil.

I was kind of a strong-willed child and didn't really believe that my friend was evil or that she was going to hell. Plus, as I already mentioned, she was pretty cute, and we had a really great time when we hung out together, so we started hanging out more and more, and I started hiding it from my parents. I also started experiencing a lot of anxiety. I was afraid my parents would find out that I was still spending time with this lesbian, and more than that, I was afraid of the feelings that I had toward my friend. I was afraid that this meant either she had succeeded in dragging me down to hell or that there was something wrong with me that needed help—that *I* needed to be saved.

The more time I spent with her, the closer we got, and the more I fell in love with her. We became clandestine girlfriends. We would sneak out of school because we weren't allowed to see each other in the off hours. No one knew about us, aside from a couple of her friends. Certainly no one in my circle of friends was aware. They were all Mormons. I knew I had no support there. They all knew she was a lesbian and they were really curious about why I was hanging out with her. I loved her so we started having sex, and I detailed it in my diary. I remember experiencing brutal anxiety attacks, and feeling totally alone, feeling like I was hiding myself from everyone that I knew and loved. But I didn't know what else to do; I had no other choice. So I wrote it all down.

I'd hidden my diary, of course, but my mother found it anyway. She confronted me and gave me an ultimatum: I was to either renounce my relationship with my girlfriend and any homosexual feelings I might have, repent all of it, go to church weekly, and continue to be a good Mormon girl, or I could leave home and move in with my dad, who was living in Seattle.

I was devastated. I felt as though I had betrayed everyone in my family. I had betrayed God. I had betrayed all my friends. And as a result of my inability to deny who I was, I was now being forced to sacrifice everything. I was still just a kid. I wanted to continue going to my school. I was in the honors society. I was on the debate team. I had plenty of friends. I was a happy, good kid. I wanted to keep all of that, but I had to make a choice and I knew I could not continue living a lie.

So I simply vanished from school the next day. I moved to Seattle and fell into a deep depression for several months. I missed my girl-friend, but more than anything, I felt my family and my friends had abandoned me. I believed that my faith had abandoned me. And I thought that I was being punished for being honest, for being true to the deepest feelings in my heart.

My dad finally agreed to let me go to a youth group in Bellevue, Washington, called BGLAD. He dropped me off in the parking lot and later told me that he came back five minutes later to see if I had chick-ened out. But I hadn't. I walked into the building and right up to the door. They had this little window where you could look in to see what was going on. I was really nervous, but I saw this semicircle of chairs, and in the chairs were all these kids. Everyone was laughing and joking and so I thought, "What do I have to lose at this point?"

In the one hour that I was in that meeting, I experienced more com-passion from these total strangers than I had felt from my entire family, from all my friends, from everyone who had found out about me prior to walking in that door. I was blown away by the love these strangers extended to me, by how understanding they were of everything I was going through, and how much their stories looked like mine. Some of the kids I met in that group are still my best friends today.

From that moment forward it got better. I realized that I wasn't alone. I realized that there was an entirely different narrative about the feelings I had had than the one I had learned as a Mormon. That, in fact, nothing horrible was going to happen if I continued to love women. I wasn't going to be miserable and unhappy, as was predicted by all of the adults in my life at that time.

I really learned to start trusting myself that day. I learned to stand up for myself, even if my opinions were unpopular, even if what you stand to lose is greater than you can even imagine. Because you just cannot go on without voicing the truth that's in your heart. That's where happiness is. Ironically, this was something we had always been told in church but it wasn't until that day that I really learned how to do it. It was difficult; I'm not going to lie. I'm not going to say that I am totally over it. I'm still very hurt and very angry for that little kid who had so much placed on her, so much judgment and so many expectations that she couldn't fulfill. I'm angry that people in my community didn't reach their arms out to me and show me the compassion that Christianity is so famous for.

If you're in the LDS Church and you're gay or bisexual or transgendered, or just curious, and confused, I want you to know there's a whole other world out there of people who support you, of people who love you. Even your family and friends, who reject you today or you fear would judge you if they knew, even they change with time. My relationship with my mom has improved dramatically over the years. I refused to give in and I refused to give up. I shared my feelings with her and we agreed to disagree over many things. I love her to death and I *know* she loves me. There were times when I was young that I feared our relationship would never recover. But it has. And that's the beauty of it. I can live my own life now, free of ultimatums. I am able to be true to myself and still love, and be loved by, everyone in my family.

It might feel like you have no choices, like you'll be left alone. Maybe you're not as lucky as me; maybe you don't have a place to go; maybe your alternative is to be on the street. If that's your choice, than you might have to wait and make a different choice than I did. That's absolutely okay. Just know that you are not alone. If someone tells you that the feelings that you have, and that you might express through a sexual encounter with someone you love, if someone tells you that's wrong, that's their thing. That's not your thing. You get to decide. You don't get to "choose" in the way that you have to choose your eternal salvation or love. You get to decide what it means. Just hang in there. Please.

• •

Natalie was born in 1976 and lived in Sandy, Utah, until 1993. She attended the University of Washington in Seattle, where she received a bachelor of arts degree with distinction in 1998. In 2004, Natalie graduated from the University of California, Hastings College of the Law. In September 2010, Natalie married David Mandelin in a ceremony officiated by her friend Mark, one of Natalie's best friends and one of the first gay people she met after coming out in 1993. Natalie hopes with all her heart that marriage equality will come to the United States soon, and that Mark will finally be able to marry his partner of seventeen years, Todd.

NOT-NORMAL

. . . .

by Michael K. Wells

SEATTLE, WA

I grew up in a town called Normal, Illinois. Go ahead, laugh. Everybody does. Here's the thing about being from Normal: You don't realize there's anything funny about being from Normal until you leave.

A typical midsized midwestern town, Normal is home to a state university, the headquarters of a few major corporations, lots of churches, and some folks (some, mind you) who don't much care for gays and lesbians. I wasn't bullied in Normal, but I was deeply in the closet. I was always aware that the wrong gesture, look, or tone of voice could grab the attention of someone who might want to hurt me. And I didn't want to get hurt. So I monitored my actions and behaviors very closely.

Growing up there meant being wary of how my churchgoing family might react if they discovered that I liked boys. We attended a Southern Baptist church that wasn't all fire and brimstone, but it wasn't exactly forward thinking either. I heard rumors of a gay bar in town called My Place, and rumors that guys found going in and out of there were beaten up. Keep in mind that this was the pre-PFLAG, pre-*Will & Grace* 1970s—not all that long after Stonewall. Jimmy Carter was in the White House, followed by Ronald Reagan; *The Bionic Woman* was on TV; and the Eagles were on the radio. Change was around the corner but it hadn't arrived for this sixteen-year-old Normal boy. Not yet.

Being out in those days was unthinkable for me. I had a friend in high school who was more effeminate than I was and I remember how we would throw ourselves into school activities in an effort to shield ourselves from being perceived as different. We joined student council, wrote for the student paper, participated in the speech and debate club. And we excelled. I became editor of the paper; he was elected president of the student council. That's how we protected ourselves, and that was the crux of our existence in Normal—being different could get you hurt, could get you fired, could get you in trouble. Neither one of us wanted trouble.

What I wanted was escape.

The closet was all I knew and being in it was killing me. My closet was small and dark and filled with frightening things; but the scary things in the closet were not nearly as frightening as what lay outside it. My crushes on boys left me sick with fear—both because I imagined I'd get beaten up if anyone knew and also because I had come to believe that I couldn't possibly be happy and gay. I was terrified of my adult life and what I would become. I had no images or role models around me to prove that LGBT people could be happy and healthy. I was gasping for air and no one around me had any idea.

As I got older, I began to question the shame that came from feeling different. I had always been a big reader, and as I started reading more sophisticated books, I encountered people whose lives were startlingly different from my own. Happy people. Smart people. Funny people. People who lived in other places and led other lives. People, like me, who wouldn't have felt at home in Normal. I started to imagine a different world, a different place. A Not-Normal. I began dreaming of the day I would leave. I spent countless hours fantasizing about what my life in Not-Normal would look like: where I would live, who my friends would be, what love would feel like. I imagined a safe place, a place where I could stop holding my breath, a place where people around me would love and support me. I had read about these places, so such a place must exist! It must!

Here's what I really want to tell you: I found it.

I left Normal for college in Iowa. Overhearing my high school journalism teacher say that Iowa City was probably the most liberal town in
the Midwest sealed the deal. My parents (whom I love dearly) couldn't
quite understand why I wanted to go all the way to Iowa when there
was a perfectly fine college in Normal. But I knew that this was my
chance. It was a baby step, from Illinois to Iowa, but it was a baby step
that saved my life. I became human in Iowa City. I didn't come out of
the closet for a couple of years, but I could see the light shining at the
end of the tunnel. I met all kinds of people and put to rest forever any
notion that being different was a bad thing. I learned to celebrate difference; I learned that the world was full of people who thought, ate,
dressed, spoke, and acted differently than the folks in Normal; and I
learned to love.

One day I ended up in Seattle, Washington, specifically, in Capitol
Hill, the city's densest, gayest, greatest neighborhood. A place filled
with art and music. Filled with other people who came looking for
their own Not-Normal. There are some oddballs who grew up here,
but they are well aware of how lucky they are. My first boss in Seattle
was an out, proud, successful lesbian named Barbara Bailey. She owned
Bailey/Coy Books, a magnificent bookstore where I went to work. Barbara was politically active and well respected in the Seattle community, gay and straight. I curated the reading series at Bailey/Coy for
twenty years, hosting events for Armistead Maupin, Lily Tomlin, Tony
Kushner, Dorothy Allison, Gloria Steinem, Quentin Crisp, and lots of
other people who have made such a difference in the lives of others.
I marched, I chanted, I worked, I played. I had come home.

After twenty years of running a bookstore that proudly welcomed
everybody, I now run the Capitol Hill Chamber of Commerce. My
job is to tell people about how great, how loving, how welcoming this
neighborhood is. Every day I celebrate the place that I found, the place
that my escape from Normal led me to. Make no mistake, the desire to
find a new home is not the challenge of LGBT folks alone. Capitol Hill
attracts people who come for its celebration of urban life, its embrace

of culture and community, its texture, its energy . . . its funk. Some of those folks are LGBT, some aren't. Doesn't matter. They're all welcome.

For me, it got better because I found the right place. The place I would have been born if I'd been given a choice. Capitol Hill is home, has always been home. It took some time to get here, but sometimes the trip home is a long one.

You can find your Not-Normal, too. Enjoy the ride.

. . . .

Michael K. Wells was the manager and owner of Bailey/Coy Books, a beloved institution in Seattle's LGBT and literary communities, for more than twenty years. Michael has worked as a neighborhood advocate, serving with the mayor's task force on Broadway and working to bring economic vitality and a touch of the fabulous to the Broadway corridor of Seattle's densest neighborhood, Capitol Hill. He is currently the executive director of the Capitol Hill Chamber of Commerce.

BORN THIS WAY

• •

by Perez Hilton

LOS ANGELES, CA

I f you're in high school, or if you're in middle school, and you're finding it difficult to go to school or to be accepted by your family, I'm
here to tell you: It gets better. Not everything gets better. You'll still
get pimples, but most everything in life will get better because you'll
be older. You'll be wiser. You'll have experience. And if you're in a really
unpleasant situation, in a year, in two years, in three years . . . you'll be
out of there. I know it may seem like a lot of time now but, when you're
thirty-two like me, a year, two years, three years is not that long.

When I was fifteen, I was *so* closeted. I went to an all-boy Jesuit
school in Miami, and I remember once, vividly, in theology class (aka
religion) the teacher said, "You know, there are studies that say that
ten percent of everybody is gay." And I was like, "Wow! That's a really
revolutionary thought for a Christian school, for a Catholic teacher."
And then, of course, she had to add, "But you boys are not like everybody else. So I don't think that ten percent of you are gay. Your percentage is much less."

Actually, the percentage was way more than ten.

High school wasn't the easiest of times for me. I didn't have that
many people to look up to. I didn't have role models—good, bad, or
any kind of models—on television. I remember the only gay person I

saw on TV when I was young was Pedro Zamora on *The Real World*. Now we have a whole gamut of people, from Neil Patrick Harris, who is amazing, to myself, whom a lot of people find annoying. But I would have loved to have had me around when I was a teenager. I might have looked at Perez Hilton and found him extremely annoying or thought he was really cool, but I would have loved the fact that Perez Hilton was able to create something from nothing and become successful, and not have to be something he's not.

So you should be proud of who you are, too, because it's not a choice to be who you are. You were made this way. As Lady Gaga says, you were born this way. So if you're having a hard time, talk to someone. Talk to a friend. Talk to your parents if you can. Talk to a stranger. Call a hotline. Talk to somebody online. Talk about your feelings, because suicide is never the solution. I have been there. I went through a point in my life where I was suicidal daily. I was so depressed and miserable— hating life. I felt like I was in a black tunnel, and I saw no light at the end of it. I was thinking about how I could kill myself daily: Today I'm going to slit my wrist. Today I'm going to hang myself. Today I'm going to jump off my building. But you know what got me through that? Time. Over the course of time, my problems got better. Things changed. I got fired from that job that I hated. So things you think are bad now, in hindsight, in the future, may turn out to be some of the best things to have happened to you.

If you need somebody to talk to, if you need advice, if you're having a hard time, I am here for you. Okay? So know that you are special and you are loved. Your life and your spirit are of great value.

Cubano and Miami native **Perez Hilton** is the Internet's most notorious gossip columnist. Perezhilton.com averages more than 280 million page views and 13.5 million unique visitors per month. Since launching in 2004, perezhilton.com has become one of the leading go-to sites for celebrity news. He has been featured in or on the *Los Angeles Times, The View, The Wall Street Journal,* MTV's *TRL,*

Larry King, CNN, E!, *Time, Paper* magazine, *Life, Spin,* CBS News, *BusinessWeek, MuchMusic, Los Angeles* magazine, *The Advocate, Dateline, Howard Stern, Us Weekly, InTouch Weekly, The New York Times, Billboard,* and many more. He is the author of two bestsellers, *Red Carpet Suicide* and *True Bloggywood Stories.* Visit www.perezhilton.com.

DARN IT

. . . .

by Kate Clinton

NEW YORK, NY

t did not look good. I was a secret, serially and seriously, crushed-out, wildly girl-loving-girl, living in the proto-don't-ask-don't-tell world of my middle class, Irish Catholic family, in upstate New York, 1950s. Though the bully pulpit of the Catholic Church had not yet come out so stridently against gay rights, I got the message that the flames of hell surely awaited me. As a baby butch, I knew I did not want to marry or have children. I pictured myself as a sere spinster darning socks before my oldest brother's cold, cold hearth. I had read *Silas Marner*.

My teens and twenties were a low-grade depression of overachieving, overeating, and being overserved. I did all the high school, college-y things—proms, homecomings, student government, pep club, protests—but since all my energy went into not coming out, I was in an emotional blackout. I have few memories of that time. When I became a teacher, I Peggy Lee'd, "Is this all there is?" And began to wonder idly about suicide.

But then, by something like gay grace in the form of one of my oldest high school drools who had come out as a lesbian, I met some defiantly gay and lesbian sexual liberationists. They threw great parties. I slept with a Quaker who had no concept of guilt. The next day, when she joyfully shared that she had told her sister the good news, I choked out,

"You what?!" She said, "Why not?" I thought, "Really. Why not?" I came out. I was twenty-eight.

For almost thirty years I had been kept in the closet by the systemic bullying of the hetero-family, the church, and the state. Coming out was the most natural antidepressant ever, better than cold whole milk sucked through two rows of mint Oreos. I was no longer alone. I came into a community of courageous, out gay men and lesbians. We made love, trouble, culture, and changed politics so that LGBT people could come out younger and younger.

Now I have vivid memories. Of wild partying in spontaneous speak-easies. Of deep listening to friends. Of being heard. Of marching for AIDS treatments, the freedom to marry, against war. Of shared meals, created rituals, kiss-ins at the WNBA. Of supporting friends during family shunnings, breakups, child-rearing. Of arguing fully. Of beginning my career as a lesbian humorist. Of being with my gal-pal of many years. The more out and active I become, the better it gets.

Of course, I hope I can remember some of those stories when I am finally sitting with old friends in my lesbian retirement RV park and some young queers come by to sing old festival chanteys. I hope to be able to tell them how in the early decades of the century we blew the whistle on bullying and made the world safer for all difference. Then I'll show them how to darn.

....

Kate Clinton is a humorist, stand-up comic, blogger, vlogger, and activist. She has written three books and recorded nine comedy collections. She lives with her partner, Urvashi Vaid, in Manhattan. For more information visit kateclinton.com

LOOK AT THE MOON

by Agustín Cepeda

COLLEGE STATION, TX

Imagine what your high school looks like from the moon: its shape from above, how big it is in comparison to your city, the country you live in, the world. How important it is compared to all the places and experiences and people you have yet to meet. Try to envision your incarceration as a good time to plan your escape. It can be a very elegant and stylish and fabulous escape—you can plan your outfit and pick out the song you want playing on your iPod, because when you walk out the door, you begin the adventure that is the rest of your life. And it's going to be an amazing life.

Right now I'm studying in Italy so my life seems *unusually* better. But it wasn't always this way. I grew up in College Station, Texas, home of Texas A&M University, one of the most conservative campuses in the U.S. This conservative spirit was alive and well in my high school, which was not a place I felt comfortable being myself. I was lucky enough to pass, so I evaded taunting and humiliation. I didn't come out until my second year of college.

The struggle I faced was internal. Even though I knew my family would be very supportive, I couldn't imagine a future in which I would be gay and also successful. It just wasn't part of my plan and I didn't even want to try to imagine it.

When I finally decided to come out, I told a friend who was very supportive and not at all surprised, which kind of surprised me. Then I came out to another friend who encouraged me to tell my family, so I came out to my sister, who was over it in a matter of seconds. My sister and my friends took it better than I had ever hoped for and it was their collective indifference and their capacity to love me unconditionally that laid the foundation for me to accept and love myself. When I told my parents, it wasn't news, just an acknowledgment that I was able to finally say it. As expected, it was a nonissue for them as well. I had their full, unconditional support. I'm aware of how lucky I am.

When people ask if it got better, I always feel strange saying yes, because it's such an understatement. It does get better but it's much more than that. Once I came out, my life was split in two and I was able to take everything that was great about my life at the time and integrate it with a new, confident, proactive, assertive me.

I suggest getting your hands on some gay literature or gay media. It helped me a lot to see other people being gay and confident and loving themselves. You'll find out soon, I hope, that gay people are some of the most talented, hilarious, capable people you'll ever meet. And the world really needs those kinds of people, so stick around. There are amazing adventures to be had with really funny, attractive, open friends and lovers. You just need to get through high school so that you can have all those adventures.

· ·

You will most likely find **Agustín Cepeda** agonizing over some detail or other, whether it's figuring out a design problem at architecture school, smoothing out a wrinkle on his bed, thinking of the perfect gift for each of his three younger siblings, or committing to memory the feel of a down-the-line, heavy-topspin, one-handed Ping Pong backhand, and always trying to go with the flow.

CRITICAL SHIFTS

••••••••••••••••••••••••••••••••••••

by Jesse Barnes

BARCELONA, SPAIN

'll never forget driving down the freeway every day to school and looking at the light poles on the side of the road thinking, "Which one has my name on it? Which one is gonna end my life?" I felt like I had lost the battle. I felt like I was a huge disappointment and that there was nothing left for me. I was sixteen years old, and I had already been sexually active with men for a few years. Coming from a religious family, I felt like it was already over, that my life was over.

Fortunately, I didn't give up. Seeking help, I started seeing a "gay reform" counselor who was supposed to make me straight. He was the saddest person I had ever met. He was "gay reformed" himself, married with children. Seeing the sadness behind his eyes and in his life, I just realized that's not what I wanted and that there still was hope inside of me.

So I moved. I moved far away. I left it all. I said good-bye to my family and I said good-bye to my friends and I started over. This is the power behind being gay. At some point, you have to make a decision in your life about who you are and what you're gonna do. A lot of people don't have to do that. They just go through life one step at a time. But when you're gay, you have to make a big choice in your life to be who you were meant to be and to follow your heart. It makes you strong.

Make this decision. Be a part of a beautiful culture and a beautiful people—gay males and females who have all had to make difficult decisions and leave people behind in the wake who couldn't accept them for who they are. But you will be accepted and loved by many other people as long as you're true to yourself. So don't give up. Don't give up. It's gonna get better. It gets a hell of a lot better.

••

Jesse Barnes survived high school in Anchorage, Alaska, and currently lives in Barcelona, Spain, and Paris, France. He's an entrepreneur.

FOR AIDEYBEAR

by Ava Dodge

CHEVY CHASE, MD

In memory of Aiden Rivera-Schaeff

I met Aiden Rivera-Schaeff my first year of high school. He was soon my best friend. Aiden was transgender, female to male. He transitioned in his first year of high school, so, as you can imagine, the bullying was pretty intense. He was almost constantly harassed at school and online. About two months into his senior year, he dropped out. Some students in one of his classes started calling him his old name, Caitlin, and most of the class got into it. Some of them referred to him as "she" or "it." He refused to come back after that. On April 22, 2010, he committed suicide. He was one month away from his eighteenth birthday.

The thing is, Aiden wasn't unpopular by any means. He was basically friends with everyone who accepted him as Aiden. The entire time I knew him, he'd always had a girlfriend or a girl chasing after him. He had a group of younger kids he was friends with that he looked out for and who treated him as a big brother. At his memorial service, they ran out of room on the benches and there were rows of people standing in the back of the room. Almost everyone who spoke at Aiden's memorial said that he was the one person that had always listened and never judged.

My favorite photo of him hangs on my wall, as well as a drawing he gave me a year ago. Our friend, Maddie Hook, took the picture of him a few days before his death. He looks so happy in it. He'd started to grow a little facial hair because of the testosterone treatment and I remember he was so proud of that. I wish Aiden was here to see all the videos and read all these stories so he might see it would get better. I know that there are a lot of people out there like Aiden who are amazing and beautiful and loved; and many like him, who can't see any of this about themselves because they have to deal with so much hate every day.

One of the most frustrating things for me after his death was that, outside of his friends and family, no one knew what had happened to Aiden. There was no media coverage; no one was outraged that this boy, who I had loved, had been harassed until he couldn't take it anymore. That was the worst part. It felt like no one really cared. And then I saw this project and the thousands of videos people were making. So I guess I just want to say thank you to everyone who made a video, shared one, watched one. Thank you for caring.

Ava is a junior in high school in Maryland. She's an active member in her school's Gay-Straight Alliance.

A MESSAGE FROM
JOHN BERRY

● ●

WASHINGTON, DC

H ello. I am John Berry, director of the United States Office of Personnel Management. To all youth out there who are in a tough place right now—know this—it gets better.

I was lucky—I was never bullied. But I was afraid of who I was. I was afraid God wouldn't love me. I was afraid my parents wouldn't love me. I was afraid I couldn't be successful in politics. Now I know God does love me, more than I could ever have imagined. And God made me just the way I am—and God doesn't make junk.

My parents, whom I was walling out from my own fear, loved me all the more. But it wasn't easy. My dad, a Marine sergeant who went to Mass every day, asked me when I came out to him not to bring my partner over to the house. Ten years later, when my partner was dying from AIDS, my dad held him in his arms and told him, "I love you like my own son."

Things do get better.

And as to my career fears? I am the highest-ranking openly gay man in United States history. I have stood on the North Pole and the South Pole. I have managed 40 percent of United States law enforcement, including the Secret Service, and the Park Service, and I've even been director of the National Zoo.

You can be whatever you want. You can *love* whomever you want. But only if you first love yourself. Trust me—it's worth it. It gets better. Live. Love. Live.

. . . .

John Berry serves as director of the United States Office of Personnel Management, where President Obama appointed him to modernize the federal government into a twenty-first-century workforce. John has a passion for service, and his federal career has taken him to both the North and South Poles, seen him manage more than 40 percent of federal law enforcement—including the Secret Service—and to the Obama administration, where he is responsible for setting employment policies for 1.9 million federal civilian employees. At this time, he currently serves as the highest-ranking openly gay federal official in history.

THE SHOW MUST GO ON

●●●

by Kyle Dean Massey

NEW YORK, NY

grew up in Arkansas in the '80s and '90s and took dance lessons so, as you can imagine, I was endlessly made fun of. But I loved dancing. I loved it so much.

And I eventually quit.

By the time I was eleven or twelve, right around puberty, the teasing and bullying just got so bad that I actually gave up dancing. In retrospect I wish that I had had the courage to keep doing it. Don't ever let anybody talk you out of doing something that you love because it makes you feel different.

I didn't start dancing again until I was eighteen years old and on my way to college. It took time for me to realize that being "different" is actually a good thing.

There were no gay people in my town at all, at least none that I knew about. And I was led to believe that it was subversive or wrong or evil to be gay. There was no outlet. I was made to believe that I was odd and weird and different to the point where it was just debilitating. I was so consumed with being gay then. It was on my mind constantly. I was always thinking, "If I walk this way, or talk this way, or dress this way . . . will people think I'm gay?"

Today it's such a nonissue. I never think about it. It hardly ever crosses my mind. Except for when things come up in the news about a gay kid killing himself. And then I can't help but identify with those people and remember what it was like at that age and how I went through the same things.

By the time my senior year of high school started, I was *done*. I asked my parents if I could skip it and go to college instead. I was desperate to get out of there. People always say, "Your high school years are the best years of your life." *Uh-uh. I mean, how depressing is that? Like, it's all downhill from eighteen?* I'm telling you: The best years are yet to come. And while all that bullying takes a toll, and it's so hard when it's happening, if you give it time, it will get better. It will. Everything you have endured makes you a much stronger person in the end. And although I ended up not skipping my last year of high school, once I got to college, things quickly changed for the better

I know there are a lot of people out there who are in their high school drama productions or take dance classes or do other things that boys aren't supposed to do. And I know there are girls out there who do things that girls aren't supposed to do. And, let me tell you, keep doing them. Because one day you could end up on Broadway like me; you could be dancing on Broadway.

Kyle Dean Massey is a Broadway actor best known for his starring roles in *Wicked*, *Next to Normal*, *Xanadu*, and *Altar Boyz*. He is originally from Arkansas and currently lives with his boyfriend in New York City.

DEAR UNCLE RONNIE

by randy roberts potts

DALLAS, TX

My uncle, Ronald David Roberts, was born in 1945, the oldest son of the late televangelist, Oral Roberts, my grandfather. My uncle Ronnie, like me, was gay. He wrote in letters, published after his death, that he came out in high school, but only to close friends and family, including his father. His father, Oral Roberts, was the first televangelist, and likely the most famous faith healer since Jesus Christ, with a worldwide audience in the hundreds of millions. He did not want a gay son. Oral's anti-homosexual rants were so vehement that they can still be found on YouTube, forty years later. In his thirties, six months after getting divorced and coming out, my uncle Ronnie died, on June 10, 1982, by a self-inflicted gunshot wound to the heart.

I'm gay, too. And my mother, like her father, does not want a gay son. My mother made a point to tell me, only a year ago, at my grandfather's funeral, in front of four thousand people, that hell does exist and I'm going there. My uncle and I were raised in a world dominated by Evangelicals who taught, and still teach, that the fires of hell await all gay men and women. This is the Evangelical "Christian" legacy for gays like my uncle and me: Threats. Bullying. Damnation. Death.

But for me, and many others, the story doesn't end here. Five years ago, when I was divorced and came out, I found myself, like my uncle Ronnie, in Oklahoma, in my thirties, and terrified of losing my children because I was gay. I was regularly called a faggot, both by strangers and by my ex-wife, and, like my uncle before me, reached a point of despair. Suicide among gay men and women in Evangelical communities is still prevalent. Evangelicals may not be killing gays outright—the police report suggests my uncle killed himself. However, while the Evangelical community might not pull the trigger when one of their gay members commits suicide, they provide the ammunition.

When I came out, I started writing a letter to my uncle Ronnie, a letter meant for me, for my uncle, and for friends I have who are still closeted—terrified their family will reject them. Five years later, I'm still writing this letter—it's become a way for me to record this experience.

It all started for me one summer afternoon when I was twenty-seven years old and I stood in my kitchen and said to myself, out loud, that I was gay. It was the most liberating feeling I've ever had, and for the next three days I was on top of the world. But then reality came crashing down on me—I was married, with children, and I didn't know what being gay would mean in terms of my family, my wife, my children. It was a horrible place to be. It took a few more years of being scared to death, and going to two different therapists, before I finally decided that the best thing for everyone involved was for me to get divorced and come out. I had been suicidal for years, and I eventually realized that my children needed a father who wanted to live, who looked forward to tomorrow, and the only way I could be that man was to get divorced and come out.

That's when I started writing my letter to my uncle because I felt like he was the only one who would understand. My parents didn't understand, most of my friends didn't understand—it was something I didn't know how to explain, so I started writing.

Coming out was TERRIFYING. I remember going to gay bars and standing against the wall like a thirteen-year-old kid at a middle school dance. I was awkward and shy and didn't have a clue how to talk to people. I drank a lot; it would take two or three drinks just to get the courage to step away from the wall and actually talk to people. And the feeling of talking to a guy who seemed to like me was great, and scary, and nerve-wracking, and amazing, all at the same time. I'd spent my whole life aching to find a nice guy who wanted to hold my hand so the first time I went on a date and held a guy's hand was AMAZING. I'd never felt happier.

But I was living in Oklahoma at the time, and someone driving by yelled "faggots!" at us. A couple weeks later I was in line at a bar with my boyfriend and two tough guys in front of us said they hoped "no fucking fags" came into their bar tonight. My boyfriend and I were both over six feet tall, so I tapped one of the guys on the shoulder and said, "Hey, you're looking at two fags right now. What do you want to do about it?"

I had never been in a fight in my whole life, but I was ready. I wanted a black eye. I wanted everybody to know I was out, that I was a fag, that I was ready to fight for the right to be who I was. The owner, Edna, leaned over the bar and said, "Nobody's gonna fight about something that stupid in my bar! Free round for the four of you as soon as you hug each other. Do it! Now!" And so we all awkwardly hugged each other and drank tequila together.

Even a year after coming out, I can't say things had really gotten better. My ex-wife was still calling me a fag in front of my children, and screaming all the time. So I eventually took her to court for that and other custody violations, spending $50,000 I didn't have. But it was worth it—she hasn't called me a faggot since, and my children haven't heard their mother or new stepfather talk disparagingly of gays in their presence either. My ex-wife and I share our children equally, and the kids are doing great. We get along just fine now.

And me, I'm doing great. Finally. I've had a lot of different boyfriends. I've fallen in love a couple times. I've felt that wonderful, giddy feeling you get when someone you like likes you back, and the gut-crushing feeling you get when that same someone lets you go. I'm finally not desperate anymore. I'm just me, happy and gay, but not defined by my sexuality. The best thing about coming out has been to watch myself go from someone terrified of being gay, to someone willing to fight for my right to be openly gay, to, finally, just another guy living his life who happens to be gay. That's the best thing of all. I had to fight hard for it, but it finally happened—the freedom to just be myself, no apologies, no fighting, no drama. The day I thought would never come finally snuck up on me and surprised me. My grandfather was famous for telling people, "Something good is going to happen to you!" And, it's strange to admit it, but he was right.

That's what I'd like to tell my uncle Ronnie today: It really does get better.

randy roberts potts is the gay grandson of televangelist Oral Roberts. He has worked with juvenile delinquents on the East Coast, was a social worker in Oklahoma City, and spent five years as a middle school English teacher.

MY OFFICE WALL

● ●

by Trevor Corneil, MD

VANCOUVER, BC

Not only does it get better, it can get pretty fabulous. I have a husband named Leyton and a dog named Blakelee. My life is happy and full. I get to play the piano and build *Star Wars* LEGO with my nephew Cameron. I have another nephew, baby Benjamin. He's not big enough to build *Star Wars* LEGO yet. But he will be soon enough. There's our best friend, Shelley, a teacher and a lesbian (now you know, kids!), and the rest of our urban family. We all go for sushi every Friday night after school or work. So have I always been this happy?

Absolutely not. Let's go back to grade seven, junior high, in a place called Calgary, Alberta—redneck central. There were these people—kind of like boogeymen—they were called homosexuals, gays, fags . . . and they did nasty things to nice people. The problem was that deep down inside I had this feeling that I might be one of them. But I was a nice person. None of this made any sense. Jump forward to high school: 2,499 straight people, apparently, and me. Alone. Isolated. Obsessed with the captain of the volleyball team. But to hit on him, that was a death sentence. Slice and dice.

My solution was to study, study, study, so that I could be a medical doctor. I just wanted to be able to say, when someone called me a fag, "F-you, I'm a doctor."

Jump forward to 2010. I am a medical doctor. For many more reasons than—well—that! I went to university for thirteen years learning biology, medical sciences, epidemiology, primary care, and finally, public health. Sure I wobbled in and out of the closet along the way. But I didn't fall down. I now have five degrees hanging on my office wall. Every once in a while, a colleague or patient will ask why I bother showing them off. If only my "F-you" wall could speak!

Now I spend my time finding, supporting, and creating access to health care for marginalized populations, including lesbian, gay, and transgender persons. I'm proud of who I am. I'm proud of what I do. Sometimes I look back and I'm shocked that I got here. But I did. I worked hard. I built self-esteem. I built an identity. How? A huge desire to survive, and the right people around to support me. Leyton is one of the people I was lucky to find along the way.

But most important, I just hung in there. If there's one thing I ask you to do, it's to hang in there. It will get better.

Dr. Trevor Corneil is a comfortably out clinical professor at the University of British Columbia, and a medical director for the Vancouver Coastal Health Authority. He sees patients at Three Bridges Community Health Centre, a free public clinic in downtown Vancouver. Dr. Corneil runs a mentor group for queer medical students, where members support each other as they negotiate the "medical closet."

KEEP ON LIVIN'

by JD Samson

Look up to the sky sky sky
Take back your own tonight.
You'll find more than you see
It's time now now get ready.
So you can taste that sweet sweet cake and
Feel the warm water in a lake (y'know)
What about that nice cool breeze and
Hear the buzzing of the bumble bees
Just live beyond those neighborhood lives and
Go past that yard outside,
Push through their greatest fears and
live past your memories tears
You don't need to scratch inside just please
Hold onto your pride.
So don't let them bring you down and
Don't let them push you around cuz
Those are your arms, that is your heart and
No no they can't tear you apart
They can't take it away now. Cuz

This is your time this is your life and
This is your time this is your life and
This is your time this is your life and
This is your time this is your life
Keep on livin'!

These are the lyrics to the Le Tigre song *Keep on Livin'*, written by
JD Samson in 2001. Used by permission of the author.

• •

JD Samson is one-third of the electronic feminist punk band and
performance project, Le Tigre. In 2007, MEN begun as the DJ/
Remix team of JD Samson and Johanna Fateman of the band Le
Tigre. Eventually, MEN became a live band focusing on the energy
of live performance and the radical potential of dance music, with
lyrics speaking to issues such as wartime economies, sexual com-
promise, and demanding liberties. MEN's debut full-length record
will be out February 2011 through IAMSOUND Records. JD Samson has DJ'ed internationally since 2001 throughout many different
party scenes and music genres and is currently touring as a solo DJ
and live with MEN.

IT GETS BETTER *BECAUSE* YOU'RE A LITTLE DIFFERENT

by Dave Holmes

LOS ANGELES, CA

I grew up Catholic in the Midwest, in St. Louis. And when I was a boy, I did not like to do things that boys did. I didn't like to play sports; I didn't care about sports. I didn't like to play with guns. I didn't like to wrestle. I didn't like to get dirty. And I felt strange about it. I felt like I had somehow chosen to be different. I had somehow chosen my self, and I had chosen wrong. Because even the people who loved me said, "Do this, because this is what boys do. Here's a football. Go play with it, because that's what boys do. Here, let me take the *People* magazine, here's a football. Go outside and play with it, because that's what boys do."

I felt defective growing up. In my teenage years, when puberty happened and sexual feelings started to pop up, I had them. I just had them about men. I had them about Huey Lewis. The first few seconds of that "I Want a New Drug" video still get me to this day.

I got picked on a lot growing up because I was different. Kids are terrible. Kids are cruel. I was at my cruelest when I was a kid. And kids are cruel because they're terrified. Everybody feels a little bit different, and because of that, they lash out at people with more obvious differences. I had them, so I got picked on. You might have them, so you might get picked on.

To me, much worse than getting picked on was when people I looked up to—my brothers, the cool kids at school, or whoever—would talk about someone who they perceived as gay, that's all that person was to them. If there was a boy who was a little girly and their name came up, they would do the limp wrist or call them a fag or whatever, and then that person was just dismissed. There was nothing else important about that person. Why even bother talking that person anymore? They're a fag. That's that. Those who conformed to gender norms got to be multidimensional people with traits and flaws and the whole bit, but gay people were just gay, end of story. No need for further discussion.

That scared me to death. Because I felt like a real person and I wanted to be perceived as a real person. I wanted to grow up to be someone who was proud and who made the people he loved proud. Yet I didn't think that I could because inside I felt different, and that is a terrible burden for a kid to carry. I should not have had to carry it, and you shouldn't have to carry it either. But you don't have to carry it forever, because I am here to tell you that it gets better.

Once you get out into the real world, you will notice that there are not only a lot of people, there're a lot of different ways to live. I moved to New York, which is a huge, dense city, with an enormous breadth of people. There are so many different kinds of people and so many different ways to live and so many different interests, and so much going on, that the fact that I was gay was like, "Who cares? You're gay and what else?" The fact that I was interested in things that weren't stereotypically male was not even a consideration anymore. In fact, it wasn't until I embraced those things; it wasn't until I started to look at the things I was passionate about as assets—rather than liabilities—that my life really changed. And the life that I wanted when I was a thirteen-year-old with a crush on Huey Lewis became my life because I got truer to myself.

Now, growing up, I never dreamed that I would be gay and proud. And I am. It never occurred to me that I would have a family who knew the real me and loved the real me. And I do. It never, *never* occurred to me that I would be able to bring a boyfriend home and have my parents like him. And I have. In fact, they love him. I never dreamed that I would have the kind of friends that I have, friends who are so smart and so confident and so funny. And some are gay, some are straight, and nobody cares. And if there's a football game on, some people want to watch it and some people don't. And nobody cares which of those groups you fall into. It just doesn't matter.

So if things are bad right now, here's my advice to you: Use this time in isolation to figure out what it is that you love to do. And then do that thing as often as you can. Learn as much as you can about it. Read everything you can get your hands on about it. And be the best that you can be at the thing you love to do. And that way, when this time ends—and it will—and you get out into the world, you will have a talent. You will have a passion. You will have attracted some good people to you. And you won't let this time make you an angry person, or bitter person. Do what you love to do, and I guarantee you there is a place in this world where someone will pay you to do it. So find it.

Now, I am not telling you that you are never going to come across someone who judges you for your sexuality. We see this every day. On the news, each day, there is a new jackass. You are going to come across some people who think differently of you because you're gay. I can tell pretty easily when someone is judging me for being gay. And that is a quick and easy way for me to know that I am talking to an idiot, someone who is not worthy of my time or attention, somebody who can't come to my party. And, it's a good party, my party; and your party is going to be a really good one, too.

Just keep in mind there is a big, beautiful world out there waiting for *you*. It gets better. Trust me.

Dave Holmes is a comic/actor/writer who lives in Los Angeles with his boyfriend, musician Huey Lewis. He is kidding about that last part.

UNAPOLOGETICALLY, ME

by Demetrius Gittens

BREMERTON, WA

'm a gay, twenty-two-year-old, African American man, and I can honestly say it does get better. It gets great. And I wouldn't have my life any other way.

It wasn't this easy all the time, though. When I was younger, I felt like I needed to hide behind sports, music, and baggy clothes. Being the middle son of three boys made me question my differences rather than embrace them. As a young kid I never really got into sports, though both of my brothers excelled in basketball. My mom always introduced me as the "thinker" of the three. She always assumed I'd be the doctor or lawyer of the family.

After a very short stint in peewee football, I thought I'd never play sports again. But in high school, like my older brother, I tried out for the basketball team and realized it was something I really enjoyed! To fit in with my peers and avoid any question of my sexual preferences, I wore the latest styles—baggy denim shorts with boots, sweat suits, and huge T-shirts. I had two playlists on my iPod, one for when I was alone (Destiny's Child, Alternative, and R&B), and one for hanging with friends (2Pac, Biggie, and other rap artists).

But as I got older and with help from an openly gay friend, Keala, I realized that this wasn't me. There's no way I could be happy if I continued to fake this lifestyle and personae. Keala and I were in the same circle of friends, and everywhere we went he was the same person. He never attempted to deepen his high-pitched voice; he wore whatever he felt like wearing with no fear of scrutiny; and he was genuinely the nicest person I have ever encountered. I really looked up to him, and he was a big factor in my decision to come out.

Before moving away for college, I decided I was going to begin the coming-out process. I started with a couple friends who received it well. Then I told my mother. Growing up with Christian values, I knew she wouldn't take it as well as my friends had. She quoted the Bible and there were tears on both sides. That would be the first and last time we discussed the issue for almost two years. While I was away at school, I made up girlfriends to satisfy my family's (mostly my older brother's) inquiries. I knew he would be the least understanding of all.

On New Year's Eve 2009, with twenty friends waiting downstairs, he finally asked the question: "Do you like dudes?"

I was shocked, and although this was not how I envisioned telling him, I could not pass up the opportunity so I replied truthfully. He took the news better than I expected. And, although he still thinks my orientation is a choice (and a sin); he says he loves me regardless. On the upside, my mom tells me she has always known and is sorry for how she originally reacted. She now asks questions and wants to know about my life away from home. We're even to the point where I would be fairly comfortable bringing home a serious boyfriend.

Unfortunately, none of my close friends are gay (Keala passed away last year in a car accident), so I spend most of my nights with guys and girls at straight bars and clubs. Recently, I was dancing with a girlfriend at a bar when a guy next to us called me a faggot. I was so angry I pushed him and started cussing at him, as did my friend Charlene. We were quickly separated, and my friends got me out of the bar. I'd never experienced this before (I was lucky to have not been bullied in high school). Once outside, I broke down and began to cry.

I am glad I stuck up for myself. Hopefully, he took something away from the experience as well, and no one else will ever have to be the target of his ignorance again.

Thank God we now have people like Tyler Oakley and B. Scott. We have books. We have the Stonewall Movement. We have *The Matthew Shepard Story*. We have Ellen, and Kathy Griffin, and now we have Gaga, as advocates for gay and lesbian people, and for the LGBT community as a whole.

You can be yourself. It's no longer the road not taken. In fact, we can choose to go whichever direction we feel is the one meant for us. No one can tell you who you are, but you have to pick the right time to tell people, to show people, who you are. Don't just spring it on them, don't feel forced into it. No one can make you come out, not a boyfriend, a girlfriend, a family member, or a friend. Do it on your own time. Just do it, though. Because, once you do, you'll feel so liberated, so much happier with yourself, with your life.

It gets better. It honestly, truly does get better.

Demetrius Gittens is a hospitality student from Bremerton, Washington, a small town right outside Seattle. With big-city aspirations, he hopes to move to Los Angeles or New York and become a successful hotelier after graduating from college this year.

A COLLECTIVE VOICE

by Gabe Milligan-Green,
Addy Cahill, and Russell Peck

NEW YORK, NY

Addy: So we've known each other for fourteen years.

Russell: Fourteen years

Addy: We met at church.

Russell: In the children's choir.

Addy: We sang together and we were altar servers.

Russell: My mother taught our Bible study class.

Addy: We were really, really lucky because we were in a loving and open community.

Russell: Our priest was really supportive and open. Very liberal. It was nice to have that kind of community and that kind of support from a very young age.

Addy: We were all there for each other.

Russell: Especially in a church setting, you know?

Addy: Yeah, because we were coming together for a love of one God and one spirit.

Russell: And each other.

Addy: And each other. So, after growing up in such an amazing community, I guess my first real reality check was when we finally got confirmed.

Russell: We had taken CCD for years together, since I was in first grade. So we finally get to this time, during middle school, and I had kind of been figuring out that the Catholic Church was this place that said that they supported loving your neighbor as yourself, but in actual practice the institution itself didn't actually accept everyone for who they were. I wasn't sure if I wanted to stay with the church. My mom said, "Well, just get confirmed and then you can make your own decision and figure it out."

Addy: So we go and we get confirmed by this substitute bishop.

Russell: He was this very old man who had been in retirement for five or ten years.

Addy: This guy is coming out of retirement to come and talk to us, as a new crop of Catholic youth, going out into the world to be good people, to be loving people—the way we were taught in this church.

Russell: And he gave this homily all about loving your neighbors.

Addy: How, as young people you have to kind of band together and support each other because it's a really rocky time, and we're coming into our own.

Russell: And at one point, I was sitting next to Addy and he [the bishop] started talking about gay people. He said something along the lines of, "If you have gay friends you should support them and love them, but try to get them help and let them know it's not okay to be gay."

Addy: He basically said, "Don't let your friends be gay. It will be harder for them; it's against God's rules. You should support them and help them get help. But don't let your friends be gay."

Russell: And I remember sitting there, feeling stunned. Here I was surrounded by this community of people that I had been with for years, that I loved and had done choir with, and been altar servers with. I was surrounded by all these parents and children, and sitting next to Addy, and it was just this weird moment where even though I knew all of these people loved me and accepted me for who I was, here I was being told that what I was, was wrong. My uncle, who was sitting across the way, almost walked out when the bishop said this, and Addy grabbed my knee so hard and wouldn't let go.

Addy: It blew my mind. I remember just sitting there with Russell in the pew and feeling astonished.

Russell: It was just crazy that there are people in this world who feel like they can tell you who you are and who you should be, but can still preach the importance of loving everyone equally.

Addy: It doesn't make sense to me. It never made sense to me. It frustrated me.

Russell: And at the end of the service, my mom tried to make me go over and thank the bishop for speaking, but I refused.

Addy: How could you be teaching someone to not let their friends accept themselves? How could you be teaching someone to tell their friends, "I love you, but I don't love this part of you"? If you love someone, you should love *all* of them, you should support all of them. You should be able to be there for all of them because that's what friendship's about.

Russell: Even though I don't go to church anymore, I always appreciate what I learned at church and the community that I found there.

Gabe: It gets better. But it won't j ust happen. You have to go out and search for it. There are people out there that will love you, that will accept you, that will stand up for you, and support you, and love you for just who you are. But you have to find them. Even if you live in a small town out in the middle of nowhere, find your closest Gay-Straight Alliance chapter. Hop on the Internet. There are millions of people out there who are just waiting for you. Find the right people and make it happen. Build a better community for yourself. Believe me, it gets better.

Terence: There are people in the world who aren't tolerant.

Gabe: There are people in the world who are tolerant, but judge . . .

Addy: who are filled with discomfort and feelings of separateness.

Jason: There are people who will view you as the other . . .

Zach: who will be bystanders to all sorts of horrible behavior . . .

Austin: because of fear . . .

Terence: or refusal to sympathize.

Maria: But there are also people who love without judgment.

Gabe: There are people who love other people in their entirety . . .

Michael: for their entire selves.

Arianna: There are people who love like you . . .

Austin: no matter what gender you are . . .

Maria: no matter what gender you love.

Jason: You don't have to settle for tolerance.

Gabe: You don't need to settle . . .

Zach: for people who don't help you in your times of need . . .

Maria: or stand up for you when you need it.

Peter: You deserve better.

Addy: There are so many people in this country . . .

Max: in this world . . .

Gabe: and you can find your community.

Addy: It will get better . . .

Gabe: if you make the effort to find your family.

Addy: Build a family . . .

Michael: a support system of people who love the whole you.

Gabe: Friends who love with all the trimmings: support, care, and understanding.

Addy: It gets better.

Terence: If you trust your ability to get through.

Addy: If you trust that, yes, we are out here.

Arianna: We are out here.

Michael: We are out here.

Arianna: People who love.

Zach: Love

Maria: Love.

Gabe: Love.

Ray: Love.

Addy: Love.

Peter: Love.

Max: Love

Arianna: Love in full.

Addy: Love wholly.

Arianna: And people who are waiting to be loved, just like you. Just like all of us.

Russell: It gets better.

· ·

The contributors to this essay are students who hail from all areas of the country, with different cultural and religious traditions, who have come together as a community of artists, dreamers, and friends living in New York City. **Gabe Milligan-Green** and **Addy Cahill** called together this group of beautiful people from school, theater, and Greenwich Village rooftops to share our secret of survival: Finding the right people and support systems to help you survive climates of intolerance and create a life worth living.

I DIDN'T ALWAYS WEAR A TUXEDO

●●●●●●●●●●●●●●●●●●●●●●●●●●●●●●●●●●●●

by Murray Hill

BROOKLYN, NY

didn't always wear a tuxedo. Or use Layrite (the waxlike pomade responsible for my pompadour). I didn't always have a mustache or dress like a man. Or sing, dance, and tell jokes. I didn't always have a smile on my face. I wasn't always Mr. Showbiz. There was a time when I had only one double chin. I wasn't quite "Murray" then. I was a confused, lonely, androgynous tomboy.

I rarely talk about my childhood, and when I do, I pay someone an hourly rate to listen to me for forty-five minutes. I'm an old-school entertainer who doesn't share my past in public or as part of my act.

What was it like for me as a kid? It wasn't easy. I come from a conservative New England town, an Irish and Italian Catholic family, and a generation where being gay wasn't discussed. There were no resources that I knew about for kids who were different. No Internet. There were no "out" celebrities, gays on television or magazine covers, and certainly no visible gay people in town. Lesbian and transgendered people were invisible. I didn't even know what those words meant.

As far back as I can remember, I've been judged, teased, picked on, and embarrassed in public for my ambiguous gender. I didn't look or act like the other girls. Growing up, I could never just "be." I was always questioned: Are you a boy or a girl? What's with your voice? Why do you wear boy's clothes? Why don't you have a boyfriend? Why do you have a boy's haircut?

I was taken out of my first-grade class and put in special program to make my voice more feminine. When I'm singing on stage now and accidentally hit a high note, I blame that experience. I'll save the other details—like being forced to wear dresses—for the memoirs.

My body was under constant surveillance. I've been kicked out of bathrooms and locker rooms for being the wrong gender. I still sometimes feel guilty and keep my head down every time I go to a public bathroom.

I didn't set out to wear boy's clothes, have no visible hips, prefer short hair, or be good at sports. It was just what came naturally. I didn't think about it. I didn't think anything was wrong with me until people started asking questions. I didn't see myself as a boy or a girl, and had no idea where that left me. Today in my act I always say in the opening monologue to a confused audience member: "I can read your mind. . . . You're thinking . . . man or a woman? The answer is No."

Today, people ask me how I "identify." Do I identify as drag king, queer, lesbian, trans, boi? These days the list of choices is long. But I still don't have an answer for this question. I've never felt my personal identification was contingent on gender. I like to say I'm D. All of the Above. Sammy Davis, Jr. sang it best in his hit song from 1968 "I Gotta Be Me": I gotta be me, I've gotta be me. What else can I be but what I am.

So how did I survive? I survived by making people laugh. It was my personal defense mechanism. Making people laugh—and getting them to like me—saved my life. Who is going to judge or pick on me, if they're laughing? Comedy has the incredible power to disarm, and little did I know that I'd make a career out of it. I'm still getting people not to judge me, by making them laugh first. Now, instead of the kids in the cafeteria, it's audiences all over the world.

I also survived by leaving my hometown and family at eighteen, which led to more than a fifteen-year estrangement. I eventually made it to New York City and made a home for myself in the downtown queer nightlife scene. A decade ago, I started producing and hosting the Miss LEZ pageant in the Lower East Side because there was so little visibility for lesbians. I wanted to create an event that showcased the diversity of the lesbian scene with an accepting atmosphere in a fun, campy, empowering way through political, yet nonthreatening, entertainment.

The It Gets Better Project has made me feel more connected to the queer community than ever before. I decided to shoot my It Gets Better video live at the ten-year anniversary of the Miss LEZ Pageant.

The positive energy that night, seeing all different kinds of queer people having fun, laughing together, dancing, cheering on the performers, getting along—it gave me goose bumps. My heart was filled with pride, acceptance, and love. It's that feeling that I always wanted as a kid, and the feeling that I want for all queer people and all people who feel they don't belong.

It got better for me because I created my own inclusive community. I want to show young people, and everyone, how much love there is out there. We can coexist. There is strength in numbers. We are each other's family. We don't have to be isolated, not anymore. The proof is in that video. I've come a long way from being that confused kid alone in my room to being Mr. Showbiz on stage. I've turned all that hate into love by way of laughter.

I'm living proof that it gets better. And you can make it better for you, and for other people, too. I hope I get a chance to meet you. I'll start off with a few jokes and a megawatt smile. You'll know right away: I'm on your side. We're in this together.

XXOO MURRAY

....

Comedian and renowned entertainer **Murray Hill**, "the hardest-working middle-aged man in show business," is a relentless retro-shtick slinger, buster of audience chops, and freewheeling ad-libber. Murray's razor-sharp wit and frenetic showman antics have been favorably compared to the legends of another era, but he has always kept his patent leather loafers planted firmly in downtown hip while delighting folks worldwide for over a decade. *The New York Times* anointed Murray "Downtown's New 'It' Boy." He's been included in "Best of New York" lists in the *Village Voice, Paper* and *New York* magazine; inducted into *Paper*'s Nightlife Hall of Fame; and selected as *Out* magazine's Top 100 Influential Performers. For a good time, visit mistershowbiz.com

HOW I GOT OVER

by Tuan N'Gai

ATLANTA, GA

I come from a big family who lives in a small town—Wichita Falls, Texas. Everybody knew who my family was and who I was; largely because of my grandfather was such a well-known and respected pastor and preacher. It was kind of hard growing up in his shadow. I think everybody sensed from a very young age that I was different, that I was gay even then. I knew it and I think everybody else did, too. I imagine pretending I was Wonder Woman, spinning around at recess in the playground, kind of gave it away. I was ridiculed throughout my school years. But since I had the shelter of such a large family, people didn't mess with me physically. I was called every name in the book, though. And I was taught by my parents everything they felt the Bible had to say about homosexuality. So I learned all of the anti-gay scriptures at a very young age, which created a lot of spiritual turmoil for me.

I was outted when I was twenty-two years old. The woman who outted me proclaimed to be a prophet at a church I was attending at the time. She did it in front of the entire congregation during Bible study. It was one of the most painful experiences in my life.

I lived in fear that God was going to kill me for three years. Eventually, I got to a point where I told God, "If you don't take this away from me, I want you to kill me. I want you to take me out of here because I don't want to live like this anymore. I don't know how to deal with this feeling of conflict." And God said, "My will for your life is not deliverance but endurance." God let me know that I was loved, and that before I was put in my mother's womb, he knew exactly who I would be. And he's happy with who I am. And he let me know that my life wasn't an accident, that I'm supposed to be here and I'm supposed to be gay. And that's something I should be proud of. That's something I should be happy about. And it's a beautiful thing, the fact that I am one of the people in this world that shows off God's diversity. God loves diversity. So it is an honor for me. From that moment, I started on a journey to fall in love with myself and try to see the person that God sees when I look in the mirror. Life has just gotten better and better the older I get.

One of the best things that God did for me was put a mentor in my life. Kerry James, who I affectionately call "Mother James," was dropped into my life at the most difficult time, when I was suicidal. And Kerry has been a mother and a father to me. The things I can't discuss with my parents, I've been able to discuss with him. Having an older role model, who's been there and done that, has made my life so much better. There are a lot of others out there who are willing to be role models and mentors if you just reach out.

After a string of bad relationships, I'm now madly in love with someone who I feel I am going to be with for the rest of my life. I'm happier now than I have ever been. I have a great career and a great ministry where I am able to not just share by testimony but be an encouragement to people. I want you to know that God loves you. You're a beautiful person. Your existence is a wonderful thing. And there's no one else in this world who can do what you have been sent to this earth to do. Your life is precious. And before you decide to take yourself out of here, please go online, seek some help. There are hundreds, thousands even, of affirming churches that will show you the love of God and show you how beautiful you are. There are people and organizations all over the country, all over the world, that can help you get through this. And the best thing about going through this is that you're going *through* it. It is not your final destination.

What's going to keep you strong, and what's going to help you get through it, is learning how to love yourself. Seeing yourself as good enough. Seeing yourself as beautiful enough. And sharing what makes you, you. Falling in love with what makes you unique is going to help you get through this difficult time. Trust me. I've been there. Thousands of other people have been there. There are more people out there like you than you can imagine, and they share your story.

I wish I knew then what I know now, but I'm happy to be able to share it with you. So please, don't give up. Keep your head up; keep fighting. And if you're dealing with violence, report that to the police, to your parents, to your school. If it doesn't go anywhere, continue to go up the chain. Fight back. You deserve to be respected and honored just because you are here. I love you. God loves you. It does get better.

Peace.

Tuan N'Gai is an activist, author, publisher, ordained minister, and founder of Silence Equals Consent, a nonprofit social justice organization. He also serves as co-founder of the OPERATION: REBIRTH movement, which speaks out against homophobia in the black church. He currently lives in Atlanta, Georgia, with his partner.

A "BETTER" EVOLUTION

by Joseph Odysseus Mastro

BERKELEY, CA

'm straight, twenty-nine, and live in Oakland, California. I was born in Oakland and have lived in the Bay Area my whole life. In high school, I played baseball and a little football. I was relatively popular, and pretty much a jerk. Most of my friends were of that ilk—jockish, dickish. And while it was relatively diverse where I grew up, I had black friends, Asian friends, Latino friends, white friends; I can't say I had a single gay friend. I was raised by fairly liberal, educated parents, but as far as I knew, I didn't know anybody who was gay. Some drunken nights in high school in front of the 7-Eleven, I was belligerent toward kids I recognized as being in the theater group, screaming "Fag! Faggot!" at them. Every time I see anybody from high school these days, I immediately apologize to them because I probably said or did something that was shitty.

After graduation I decided that I'd like to do some volunteer work. I'd done enough shitty things in my life; I wanted to give something back. So at nineteen, I began volunteering at a gay and bisexual men's HIV/STD prevention agency in the Castro in San Francisco. I'd stand outside of bars and clubs handing out condoms and lube. I'd dispense information about STDs, HIV, and the risks of intravenous drug use. Basically, I had a lot of conversations with guys about being safe, and I conducted a lot of sex surveys that would allow the project I was working for to catalog information and communicate with the Department of Health, all with a focus on keeping gay men in San Francisco healthy. Some of my straight friends would ask, "Why are you helping out the gays?" which, I realize, is a reprehensible question in the first place, but I'd respond that in the area I live, there are gay men who have HIV, and they're who I want to help.

I met some wonderful people doing that work. I joke around that sometimes I wish I was gay because most of the gay guys I know are fabulous! What I've found in dealing with the gay community in the Bay Area—and I'm speaking broadly and generally—is as a group they are the warmest, most empathetic people I've ever come in contact with. I love all my gay friends. I've met so many committed people dedicated to bettering the health, the welfare, and the lives of the gay community and the larger community, in general.

If you're in high school and you're gay, bisexual, or transgender, and you're being tormented, find some way to get through school and then get to San Francisco, get to the Bay Area, get to Miami or Chicago or New York City. Not only will you find a burgeoning community of people like you, people who will support you, people who will love you, people who will talk to you about everything you need to talk about, but you'll find people like me who used to be dicks. But I got out of high school and I became nicer, more mature, and more enlightened as I got older. I became a friend to the people I used to mess with. You'll meet people who accept you, want you around, love you, and will be there to place bets on the Academy Awards with you, because, God knows, none of my straight friends do that.

I wish Billy Lucas could have read this. I hope this helps someone, even if it's just one kid out there who reads this and realizes that some of those kids who bullied or taunted you in high school will grow up and get a clue. Whether they do or not, know that it gets better for you. It gets better for your community. Be strong and know that whatever torment you're experiencing, you're not going to find it when you come to the Bay Area. You're not going to find it when you go to New York.

Please let that sustain you, and please reach out to someone. The Internet's a great tool if you're feeling down. You'll get through it. It will get better. It will never be perfect, but it will get better.

....

Joseph Odysseus Mastro is a lawyer who would rather be playing third base for the Cleveland Indians or marauding around the Congo with his bull terrier, Behemoth. Joe knows that whatever else happens, it gets better.

SAVE YOURSELF, SAVE THE WORLD

by Khris Brown

OAKLAND, CA

People said horrible things to me every day, they even made death threats. Kids would throw garbage at me, open my locker and slice open all my pictures, tear apart my books and throw them all over the locker room, pour soda over all my stuff, throw my clothes all over the gym locker room. This kind of stuff happened every day in junior high and high school. And let me tell you it got a little wearing.

You would have expected better from my town of forty thousand people, located near San Francisco. But no, it turns out there is ignorance and prejudice everywhere. I'm forty now, and a voice director. Today I am out to everybody, but I guess I've never really been in. I had a girlfriend in high school, which was pretty shocking for 1985; obviously my schoolmates thought so. People, kids and adults alike, were not big fans of the idea then. It got so bad I was even threatened with rape. There were times in junior high school when I thought that it was never going to change. When I thought it would be better to just not be here.

I was raised Catholic and told that being gay was just wrong, that it was against nature—this, from my mother who now happily tells her coworkers and her friends how proud she is of her bisexual daughter. She even cries when the Gay Pride parade goes by her office, she's so proud.

People will change and people will rise up to meet you. People that I knew in high school—some of the same people who said the very worst things to me then—have contacted me on Facebook and said, "You're so brave."

And "If I didn't know you, I wouldn't have known anyone who was gay."

"You're the first person I knew who was gay and it changed my worldview."

They say that now, these same people who threatened to kill me when I was a teenager. Yet if I had made the choice at the time to end the pain that I was going through, well, one, I wouldn't have had the satisfaction of having them write to me all these years later on Facebook, and two, and more importantly, they wouldn't have had the opportunity, regardless of how scared they were then, to know someone who was different.

I think that being "other"—being bisexual, being gay, being transgendered, questioning your gender, whatever—is so incredibly valuable. It gives you a unique perspective on how to overcome the horrible things that people do to one another in the name of fear, in the name of what they think is religious righteousness. To go through all that and to survive it—without any malice toward those people, with love and forgiveness in your heart, and with acceptance of yourself—is the way to help heal the world. I really believe that you will contribute to that future. I promise you that it gets better. My life is amazing! I travel all over the world; I work with incredible actors. I have a fantastic, fantastic life. So I promise you that it is worth it to stay. Please, please get through this and don't believe what people say to you about it being your fault, or that you're weird, or whatever. Screw those people. You know in your heart that you are good. And I know in my heart that you are good.

Khris Brown is an award-winning director for video games, film, and animation. She grew up in Marin County, California, and has lived in Los Angeles, Paris, and London. She currently resides in Oakland, California, with her fantastic spouse and their cat, Scout.

BECOMING AN AUTHENTIC PERSON

by Nicholas Wheeler

SALT LAKE CITY, UT

There are so many people—gay, lesbian, and transgender—who grow up in religious, conservative environments like I did. Who frankly don't make it out alive.

I was raised in a Mormon home where I learned things about homosexuality that weren't true. In church and at home I was taught that being homosexual was a made-up thing; it wasn't something that was natural. It was something that could only bring sadness. When I was in high school being gay was not something I thought about. I thought I would get older and get married to a woman, just like all other good Mormon boys. It wasn't until later that I realized that this would be impossible. The thought that I wouldn't fit into the religious mold I was raised in was devastating to me; I knew it would also be devastating to my family. Regardless, I began to realize that I needed to come out, that I needed to be open about who I was. It took me a while but, eventually, I discovered the things I had learned were not correct. Instead, I learned to accept who I was—a gay man—and to trust that I was a good person. Because that's what I felt like; I felt like a good person. I decided then I wasn't going to let anybody—anymore—tell me who I was.

It took me a long time; I was twenty-four years old before I decided I was okay, that I could be happy as a gay man, as an openly gay man.

Nearly a year later, I came out and suddenly felt free of the intense feelings of self-hatred that I had carried for so long. Some people rejected the new, more honest me; my family felt betrayed and confused. But being honest with myself enabled me to find people who accepted me for who I was, regardless of religion or sexual orientation.

Ever since I made that decision and ever since I decided to think for myself and to trust myself more than trusting others, it's just gotten better. Every day it gets better. That doesn't mean life's not hard sometimes. Sometimes it's a terrible bitch. But I'm still happy. I listen to myself and I trust myself and I know I'm a good person.

A few months ago, I went to a community festival, and outside the gates of the festival was a street preacher. He was preaching about gays, and he shouted out, "I'm gay. But that doesn't mean that I'm a homosexual. It means that I'm happy. I'm not a homosexual."

I was walking by with all of my friends, right at that moment, and I shouted back, "I'm homosexual!" I actually kind of surprised myself by saying it. There was a line of people waiting to get into the festival and, as soon as I said that, everybody cheered. It was such a great moment for me because I realized that I wasn't afraid to be who I was in front of anybody. And I knew that wherever I was, I would find people who were on my side. It gets better with time. As I became true to myself, my relationships with others became more authentic. That's a wonderful feeling.

• •

Nicholas Wheeler is an ex-Mormon graphic designer living in Salt Lake City, Utah.

ON THE OTHER SIDE

by Jay A. Foxworthy and Bryan Leffew

SANTA ROSA, CA

"No government has the right to tell its citizens when or whom to love. The only queer people are those who don't love anybody."

—RITA MAE BROWN

Jay: When I was a seventeen-year-old kid going to high school in Northern California, I was engaged to my best friend at the time, a woman, and we had a kid on the way. I was a very unhappy young man then. I knew that I was living a lie. I knew that the person I was pretending to be in high school was not the real me.

I could not deal with the fact that I was gay. Raised in a devout Catholic family, I knew that the people I cared most about in my life— my girlfriend, my best friend, my family—would not accept me as a gay man. So I did what I thought was right at the time, and I tried to commit suicide. Luckily, I failed. And before I tell you how my story ends, I want to introduce you to my husband.

Bryan: Like Jay, and a lot of people I know, I grew up in a pretty conservative family where religion was a part of our daily lives. I, too, really fought who I was for a very long time. The hardest coming-out experience for me was first coming out to myself. Even after I acknowledged I was gay, I had to contend with a lot of the fears about what I thought—what I had been taught—being gay meant. I assumed that it meant I was going to be alone, that I was going to be an alcoholic, that I was going to be a pervert who preyed on kids and got AIDS. These were the things I worried about because these were the things that most of the people in my life told me. I had to come out against the backdrop of my family saying, "Oh, if any of my kids were gay, I'd kill them." There's a lot of stuff you have to come to terms with when you decide to come out, and you have to be really strong and really courageous to do that. But now I'm sitting on the other side of that battle and I can honestly say that my life is a million times better.

Jay: Bryan and I are happily married and the parents of two wonderful children. I'm a police officer living in California, and I can tell you that life is a whole lot better than it was in high school. And I am very fortunate that I survived two attempts at suicide to get to this place. I understand that sometimes life is scary and it's hard to really see a future but, if you just give yourself the opportunity, it gets better. Life gets a lot better.

Bryan: You can make it through everything. Not only what your friends throw at you but sometimes even what your family throws at you.

Jay: So hold on and focus on working on yourself. Don't worry about what other people think about you. Once you get through those tough times, I guarantee you, the payoff is worth it. Someday you're going to meet the man, or woman, of your dreams and you're going to create a life for yourself with family and love and security that you can't even believe is possible today.

Born in Santa Rosa, California, **Jay A. Foxworthy** is forty years old. He served four years in the U.S. Army in the Persian Gulf and has an AA in criminal justice. He has been a police officer in San Francisco for fifteen years. He met **Bryan Leffew** sixteen years ago in college. Bryan is thirty-eight years old and was born in Santa Rosa, too. Jay and Bryan have been domestic partners for thirteen years and married for two years in the state of California. Five years ago, they adopted Danile, age ten, and Selena, age five. As a family, they started their YouTube channel, Gay Family Values, right after Proposition 8 passed. They have been trying to change straight people's hearts and minds with their videos.

BULLY ME

· · · · · · · · · · · · · · · · · · · ·

by Rabbi Sharon Kleinbaum

NEW YORK, NY

'm the senior rabbi at Congregation Beit Simchat Torah in New York City, and I am a lesbian.

There are those who say that God hates gays. There are those who say that *HaShem* has given us all challenges, and your challenge is to overcome your feelings: Either be celibate the rest of your life or be with opposite-sex partners. There are those who say we are either criminal or sick or sinful. None of these are true.

We are all created in God's image—all genders, all sexual orientations, all races, all sizes—all of us. All different types of kids are bullied, but the bullying is the same. Cowards who are full of shame and rage take it out on those of us who are different: smaller, smarter, differently abled, immigrants, gay-looking kids, girls who aren't cheerleader types, kids with accents, kids with two moms, two dads, kids with a mentally ill parents, and the list goes on and on and on. But we are all created in God's image, *betzelem Elohim barah otam*. Anyone who says differently is *mechalel HaShem*, blaspheming God's name.

I know this message might not be enough. When I was younger and living in the closet, I thought that I was the only living lesbian on the planet. I even went to a psychiatrist to make me straight. We've come a long way since I was your age, and we still have so far to go.

If you are feeling this kind of hurt, I ask you to hold on. You are not alone. You are sacred, and you are beautiful, and there are people who care about you. I am one of them. So are the over eight hundred members of CBST, the world's largest synagogue for people of every sexual orientation and gender identity. We may not be in the same state right now, or even in the same country, but we care about you and there are communities and people like ours all over the world. E-mail me if you are feeling alone. I will work with you to get you the support you want. Find other kids who are being marginalized for who they are. Pray, knowing that God is on your side, and that God thinks you are fabulous.

And a word to the bullies out there, I know that most people who bully others for being gay or looking gay are often struggling with their own feelings of isolation, loneliness, and often their own sexualities. There's nothing to be ashamed of. Contact me to talk. And if you don't agree, contact me to bully me. I'm a lesbian and I'd rather you bully me than a thirteen-year-old kid.

We are all created in God's image. Now let's live up to it.

Originally created as part of the Strength Through Community Project of Congregation Beit Simchat Torah in New York.

. . . .

Rabbi Sharon Kleinbaum serves as the spiritual leader of Congregation Beit Simchat Torah, one of America's oldest and largest faith-based LGBTQ organizations. She is regarded as one of the most important rabbis in America, and was named one of the top 50 American rabbis by *Newsweek* magazine and *The Jewish Week*. The subject of a profile in *The New York Times*, among many other articles and books, Rabbi Kleinbaum has lectured and published widely. She is a graduate of the Frisch Yeshiva High School and Barnard College, and was ordained by the Reconstructionist Rabbinical College. Rabbi Sharon Kleinbaum can be reached at rabbik@cbst.org.

TO THE BULLIES

●●●●●●●●●●●●●●●●●●●●●●●●●●●●●●●

by Tristan Jackson

SYDNEY, AUSTRALIA

Everyone's talking to young gay people who have been bullied in school, trying to explain to them that things get better,
and to hang in there, but I want to have a little chat with the
bullies.

I'm twenty-five, so let's go back ten years, to when I was a fifteen-
year-old high school kid. I was quite an artistic teenager and I got
picked on for being gay. I'd get pushed and shoved and called "fag." It
seems silly now to think that being called a fag would be that upset-
ting but, you know, when you're fifteen, school is your whole world.
So it really did hurt. I remember one time someone had graffitied a
bench at school, writing vicious things about me on it. And another
time, someone spat at me. There were some pretty awful, pretty hard
times.

But here we are ten years later. Let me just put it this way: I live in
a great city, have a great job, make a good living; life is good. But I'd be
lying if I said I hadn't checked out those same bullies on Facebook to
see what kind of lives they were living today. I'm happy to say they look
like losers. The thing about these people is that no one is born homophobic, no one is born racist. These ideas are given to them by their

parents or religious fanatics, or other negative role models, but when they take on those prejudices and hatreds as their own, it doesn't make for a good, happy person, or a happy life.

Those guys that made fun of me in school? They are pretty much all still living in the same hick town, and they've all got crappy jobs, and they look like awful. They look old. They look like they've had long, miserable lives already. I am sure there are many reasons why people's lives turn out this way. But I can't help but think that harboring hatred, and spending a lot of your time and energy when you're in school making someone else's life hell, can't be good for you.

You know how people always say bullies are really the ones that are insecure? Like they'll find someone weak in a pack to make fun of so they feel better about themselves, and when you're fifteen you think, "Oh, that's just something old people say." But I'm old now, and I'm telling you it's true!

If you were completely content and happy with yourself as a person, then you would have no reason to try to bring other people down. When you're calling someone a fag and giving him hell, what are you trying to achieve exactly? What good is this doing you? What is this giving you? You might think it's funny, but I'm betting it's probably got a lot more to do with your own feelings of inadequacy, something deep down inside you, something that you're probably not even aware of yet.

The point is, bully, you might have a couple of pin-headed minions hanging around you, telling you that you're cool and funny, but you're really not. There's not some glamorous, amazing life ahead for you. There is only one direction for people like you and that is down. You are a loser and you always will be. But the world needs assholes, and bullies, and haters like you to make the rest of us shine. Enjoy the power you think you have now, because I promise you it's not going to last. Soon enough, high school will end, and the people you torment will be free of you. But you're stuck with you forever, and you deserve it. Fuck you. Okay bye.

TJ is an online video blogger from Sydney, Australia, whose videos range from movie reviews, to celebrity gossip, and LGBT activism. He loves music, movies, and photography. His ultimate vacation destination is New York, and his favorite living celebrity is Lady Gaga. To see more of TJ's videos, check out his YouTube channel, http://youtube.com/TabloidJunk.

THE GOOD FIGHT

by Kristel Yoneda

LOS ANGELES, CA

To put it simply, high school really, really sucked. I went to a small school in Honolulu. There were only about fifty some kids in my graduating class. As a junior and a senior, I was trying to figure out who I was, not only in terms of my sexuality but as an individual. I didn't receive the warmest reception. Some people were really awesome, and for that I'm really grateful, because I don't know if I would have survived high school without them. But, in general, it was a hostile environment.

People were always talking behind my back, calling me a dyke, calling me a lesbian. Some people didn't want to interact with me because I was gay. Some people assumed that because I'm gay, I liked all girls. All of this, and other ridiculous stuff, made it really difficult for me to feel comfortable being myself in high school.

One day during my junior year, I got called into the office in the middle of class. I thought that maybe my mom had left me a message, but it turned out the counselor wanted to speak to me. So we sat down and we made small talk for a little while, and then she said, "You know, there are these rumors going around that you're gay. You're not gay, are you?" She didn't say it in an accepting tone, like "If you're gay, it's okay.

This is a safe environment." No, she said it in a way that conveys the message, "You'd better not be gay. Do not tell me that you're gay."

I was shocked. Before I could even process the question properly, before I could even really answer, I just flat-out denied it. But she continued asking me, "Are you gay? Are you gay? Are you gay with your friend, I heard she's gay, too." And I kept denying it. "I'm not gay, my friend's not gay. We're not gay together. None of us are gay." Finally, she just looked and me and said, "Well, I heard she's a slut." I didn't know what to say to that.

Had this conversation happened today, it would have gone so much differently. I would have stood up for myself. I would have stood up for my friend. But then, I was only fifteen years old, and I was talking to someone I was supposed to be able to confide in. After all, she was an authority figure that I was supposed to feel safe with. And, in that one moment, she destroyed all the faith I had in the system. From then on, I knew I really couldn't be myself in high school.

She sent me back to class because I didn't tell her what she needed to hear, I guess. It took every ounce of will in my body to hold it together, and I didn't even succeed at that. I went back to my desk and cried. I didn't tell anybody what happened, not even my friends, until way after graduation. I was really embarrassed and scared. And after that, I was just counting the minutes until the end of high school.

I am really glad that I held on, though, because it gets better. It gets so much better. Those people who treat you like crap now—in a few years, they're not going to matter. You're going to meet people who love and accept you for who you are. If you're feeling alone, I'm going to remind you that you're not. Talk to your friends. Talk to your family about it if you can. Talk to a counselor . . . maybe not so much in my case, because that didn't go very well . . . but talk to somebody. I remember that when I was in high school, I talked to a lot of people online and they were a really great support system for me. In college, I met some amazing individuals and I recently moved to Los Angeles to pursue my dreams as a fiction writer. Life has been a struggle, but it's a good fight. One worth sticking around for. It truly, truly gets better. It really, really does.

....

Kristel Yoneda attended the George Washington University in Washington, DC..She is a currently a freelance writer based in Los Angeles, California, documenting her quarter-life-crisis adventures.

A MESSAGE FROM
KEVIN HAGUE, MP

• •

AOTEAROA, NEW ZEALAND

'm a gay man and I'm a member of Parliament for the Green Party in New Zealand.

I remember being a teenager and starting to realize that I was different from my friends. It took me a long time to acknowledge to myself that I was gay. And it took even longer to tell other people about it. Fitting in and seeming like everyone else can feel really important, especially when you're young. It certainly was for me. I often felt isolated, scared, and depressed by the anti-gay bullying and abuse I was exposed to—but also by the jokes and anti-gay culture that was around me in the boy's school I attended. It all left me feeling pretty bad.

That's a long time ago now, though. And today, I'm happy. I'm a well-adjusted, adult gay man. And I have a great life. I have a relationship with my partner; we've been together for over twenty-five years now, going strong. I've got a great adult son. And I've had a career that's been really interesting and now has me in Parliament.

And so part of my message to you is, even though things might seem bad at that moment, it gets better. It gets better.

Perhaps the most important thing I want to say about my life now is that I don't hide being gay from anyone. It's very, very seldom that I personally encounter any anti-gay discrimination or abuse. So for every one of you out there who's feeling like I did when I was a teenager—scared, isolated—my message to you is this: If I could, I would love to be able to reach out to you, and be able to show you the fantastic future that awaits you. I can't do that. So instead do this one thing, be brave about this one thing: Reach out to someone else. Talk to a friend or a family member or maybe someone at your school, a teacher or a counselor, someone you can trust. Because usually what happens is those people are more supportive than you think they will be. They're better than you think they are. And if there is really no one around that you think you can talk to, check out what's available online. There are lots of queer youth groups around the country, and a fantastic umbrella organization in New Zealand called Rainbow Youth

Remember that no matter how bad things seem right now, it will get better. And we want you in our community. Contact someone, get some support, and be there for us. And we will be there for you, too.

Kevin Hague is a New Zealand member of Parliament for the Green Party. Before this he was a senior figure in the New Zealand Health sector and also had a career in bookselling. He has been strongly involved in the community sector since the 1970s, including the anti-apartheid movement and in groups working for gay, and other, human rights. He led the New Zealand AIDS Foundation for the five years until 2003. He lives on the west coast of New Zealand's South Island with his partner of twenty-six years.

HATERS CAN'T HATE SOMEONE WHO LOVES THEMSELVES, AND IF THEY DO, WHO CARES

by Lynn Breedlove

SAN FRANCISCO, CA

When I heard about this project, I thought, "I never got bullied so I have nothing to offer." But then I remembered they always called me "weird" in grammar school, and I didn't have many pals.

Even the one gay kid in sixth grade wouldn't let me play with him and his girlfriends cuz he said I was a boy. I thought, "Yeah, and you're a girl!" I was jealous cuz his mom dressed him as a flapper, in a dress and makeup, on Halloween because she saw that's what he wanted to be. My mom never let me dress as a cowboy for Halloween. She dressed me as Twiggy. No one in San Leandro knew Twiggy was a Carnaby Street supermodel. And I certainly didn't care.

I spent my thirteenth summer playing softball with other girls, and developed a crush on two older teammates who were already in junior high school. I gave them both sheaves of love poems. They read these to one another, realized I was madly in love with both of them, and in September went back to school, spreading the word I was a dyke.

As soon as I arrived at junior high, their friends greeted me with the nickname "Truck," which I guess was supposed to be an insult meaning "butch." Some Latina gangsta girls threatened me. I charmed my way out of it: Smile, submit, avoid, but don't cower.

My dad taught at an inner-city school. He said, "If anyone tries to beat you up, just ball up your fists and scowl. Do not back down, beg, or cry. This only encourages predators. Act tough and fearless. Chances are they will lose interest. And if not, you will gain a rep as a badass and not a punching bag."

Using what talents I was born with, and learned from my parents, I smiled and said something funny. The mean girls lost interest and eventually in high school—along with most everyone else—ended up my friends.

What I did have going for me was my parents' love. They told me that I could be whatever I wanted in life and that they would be there for me no matter what. Mom said, "You're Lynn Breedlove. Never forget that." I thought that was weird, but later it came in handy.

In my first year of junior high, I busied myself. I was drawn to a boy named Victor and asked him out to the Girl Ask Boy dance. I tried out for the school play, the part with the fewest lines and the most laughs, got the part, and cracked up the whole school. The rejection, ridicule, and threats turned overnight into love. Everyone wanted to be my pal, because I had found what I was good at and was obviously having fun. I skated the hallways, streaked through my gym class, and cut up in French class with jokes in French that were over the teacher's head.

Victor came out to me two years later in high school. I said, "Yeah, me too," and then he said, "We are going to find every gay person in this school and make a gang."

Every day he would come back to me with a report. The guy with the earring. The classical pianist. The bisexual babe. The Queen fan in *Saturday Night Fever* pants who swept up after school cuz he was always in trouble. Pretty soon we had a gang of badass queers hanging out. And no one had the balls to fuck with us, because there were a bunch of us and we were obviously not ashamed. Granted, the only award I won upon graduation was Class Clown, but for someone who was to later become a comic, that was apt.

I got through school by sharing what I loved with others, and the obvious queer that was me got love in return. I served the conservative population of my suburban high school some live queer entertainment, poetry, laughs, and pal-dom. And, I found that if I showed up with my whole self, I would have all kinds of pals, straight, gay, and trans.

When it came time to value myself, to decide whether I would kill myself over my gender issues or not, whether I would clean up my act or shoot drugs until I was dead, the words my mom always said to me kept coming back to me, "You're Lynn Breedlove. Never forget that."

What I learned from my parents was love. I loved myself because they loved me. My mom built up her own tribe because she had left her family behind the Berlin Wall in the '50s, and she had to make a new family. I learned from her how to make one for myself, too.

If I had had a family who said they would love me only if I pretended to be someone I wasn't, things might have turned out differently. But if you have that kind of family, you can make your own family who will love you unconditionally. That's why queers call each other Family. We create one that will love us for who we are. We have drag moms and dads, dyke uncles, and matriarchal mamas.

Thirty-five years later, I have that extended family. (And over three thousand queer friends on Facebook, most of whom think and feel as I do.) I learned in high school, if I hold up an effigy, a mask, or a lie, that mask will get all the love, not me. If I say, this is who I am, I may only get three real pals, but it will be me, not some pretend persona, who will be getting all the real love from those three pals.

If I stand up and say, I am awesome and my life is worthwhile, most others will believe me.

If I encounter assholes who want to hate, I have a joke ready and a posse to stand up for me.

As a kid, I was shy, weird, unpopular, ignored, threatened, and rejected. As a teen, I charmed my way through school, but I thought drugs would make my struggle with being different easier. For fifteen years I tried to off myself slowly with drugs or hang out in dangerous situations hoping someone else would off me. Then one day, at age thirty-one, I was able to draw on some distant past truth, that I am loveable, a truth which inspired me to save my own life, make a bunch of art that makes life worth living, and even pays the rent. Now at the age of fifty-two, I am happy and strong. So let this be your truth too: You are loveable and you have something that no one else has to offer the world, something that connects you to other humans: your heart. And something that sets you apart from other humans: your art.

So don't fuck us over by offing yourself. Bring it. Bring your whole badass queer self. We need you to live. To protect us. To stand up with us. To inspire us.

Create your own scene and find your own tribe. You are not alone. Without us, straight people would be super-bored, and so would we. The more of us find each other, the more exciting the adventure becomes.

We're waiting for you with open arms.

....

Lynn Breedlove is a performer and writer. From 1990 to 2005, he was the lead singer for Tribe 8, the first all-dyke punk band playing music for by and about dykes. In 2005 they won the Cultural Heritage Award for Creativity. Breedlove was nominated for a Lambda Literary Award for Lesbian Fiction, *Godspeed* (St. Martin's Press, 2002), and won the 2010 Lambda Literary Award in the transgender category for *Lynnee Breedlove's One Freak Show* (Manic D Press, 2009). He is currently writing a political memoir with his mother and running a queer car service called Homobiles in San Francisco. He has been clean and sober since January 1, 1990.

NOT PLAYING AT A CINEMA NEAR YOU

by Rebecca Brown

SEATTLE, WA

To look at the popular images of lesbians in mainstream movies, you'd think we were all just failures at being straight. What
a shitty image to have of yourself. Don't buy it. You can be a
lesbian or dyke or queer woman or girl-crazy, or whatever you want to
call yourself, and have a great relationship with another woman who
is smart and funny and cute and sexy and loyal and truly wants to be
with you as opposed to with some guy.

The latter of which is the message you get if you look a little below
the surface of *The Kids Are All Right*. I hate that subtext. In fact, I'm
totally sick of how mainstream movies portray us. Part of the problem
is that movies portray us so rarely that whenever you do see a lesbian
character on screen, that character bears tremendous weight.

When discussing *The Kids Are All Right*, everyone fell all over themselves flashing their "enlightened," and oh-so "tolerant" credentials,
describing it as a story of a "normal family that happens to have two
moms" (played by Annette Bening and Julianne Moore). But of course
one of those play-pretend lesbian moms really wants to sleep with a
guy. In the real world, some lesbians do want to sleep with guys, or
discover they are bi. Nothing wrong with that. And there would be

nothing wrong with portraying this if it was simply one of *many* ways lesbian were portrayed in the movies. But it's not.

At least that so-called lesbian wants to have sex with something. The other movie stereotype of lesbians is that we are cold and bitter, repressed and ancient old bags, i.e., utterly unsexy. Remember *Notes on a Scandal*? It came out the same year as *Brokeback Mountain*. The latter is a beautiful, sensitive love story of two beautiful young men in love, set in a beautiful landscape, and the tragedy of how they could not fulfill their love in the cruel world. (Hey, wait a minute, wasn't the gay rights movement happening at the same time? Whatever.) *Notes on a Scandal*, on the other hand, tells the story of an ugly, old, closeted dyke who preys on a pretty young innocent straight woman. Judy Dench is great as the creepy, manipulative cartoon of Older Lesbian Predator. (Though maybe they should have given her a mustache to twirl to complete the image.)

Older Lesbian Predator is exactly the mythic boogeyman (boogey-woman? boogeydyke?) my mother was afraid would corrupt me when I was young. That didn't happen, though. Far from it. I lost my virginity in my teens with a girl my own age, and have always been treated like a beloved daughter by older lesbians who have mentored me and done whatever they could to help and encourage me in my life and work.

Judy Dench wasn't the only great English actress to play such a part. There's a pair of Heartless Old Dykes in *Never Let Me Go*, a complicated quasi-science fiction story set in the future. When the young and in love straight couple come to ask the two old misses (Charlotte Rampling is one) if they can get them the dispensation they need to marry, the Heartless Old Dykes say no. By the time I saw this yet-another caricature of lesbians I wanted to scream. (This may have been complicated by the fact that Charlotte Rampling appears to me to be profoundly fuckable. Actually, now that you mention it, I wouldn't say no to a go at Annette Bening either.)

The point is, you're a young woman wondering if you are a lesbian. You wonder what a lesbian life might look like when you get older.

Do not—repeat: Do. Not. Believe what mainstream movies tell you about your alleged self. Do not listen to what people who don't actually know any honest-to-God out lesbians tell you. Of course, there are some poor, bitter, fucked-up old dykes out there, but you do not have to become one. And, sure, some women can take a while to figure out their sexuality, playing around with your heart in the process. But you do not have to stay with women like that your whole life. And, yes, some women happily and healthily discover they shift fluidly between being bi and lesbo. Let 'em do so. Wish 'em well. What I want to tell you is that you can have a great girlfriend who will not leave you for a guy. (Or another woman.) And that you can both be out and productive and happy and fulfilled.

I didn't think that was possible for me for a long time. (I dated a lot of people who were not right for me.) Then when I was thirty-five, I met the woman to whom I am now married. (Though not legally. Not yet.) For the past twenty years, I have had a great life with her. Our families adore us (including her six—count 'em, S-I-X!—grandkids) and we adore them. We are not, and do not have to be, closeted anywhere.

I look forward to the day when no one has to be closeted. I also look forward to the day when those pop culture stereotypes of lesbians exist only as a quaint reminder of our culture's unenlightened past. A time when you and your lesbian wife will only dimly remember ever thinking you were anything less than the beautiful, brilliant, funny, loyal, well-adjusted, happy—no, ecstatic—pair of dykes you are.

· ·

Rebecca Brown is the author of twelve books including, most recently, *American Romances*, a collection of essays that won a Publishing Triangle Award.

FROM "FAGGOT" TO FIELD BIOLOGIST

by Christopher A. Schmitt, PhD

LOS ANGELES, CA

I was once a gay teenager, growing up in Milwaukee, Wisconsin. It wasn't exactly the easiest place to be a gay kid, especially since I went to inner-city public schools. I was bullied, called a "honky faggot," called "gay," all of that. At the time I didn't necessarily know what to make of it. I knew that I had been more interested in guys than girls for as long as I could remember, but I didn't really know what it meant to be gay and didn't really think of myself in those terms. There weren't any gay role models at the time so it hurt when people teased me in those terms. All I knew about then were stereotypes of gay people, and I wasn't really interested in being like that.

When I was thirteen, I bought in to the colored jeans and silk shirt look that was so popular in the early '90s, the apex of which was my calico silk jacket. Very hot, I know. Needless to say, it did not help with the bullying. One day, riding on the after-school bus (I think I was wearing purple jeans and a teal silk shirt at the time), seven or eight guys came up to me and started calling me a "honky faggot." I got off the bus early to avoid them but they followed me. For the next eight blocks home, they circled me and spat on me and pushed me and continued calling me names. It was horrible. By the time I got home, I was really upset and I told my mom about it. She listened quietly and then asked me if

I *was* gay. Since I didn't really even know what that meant at the time, and I certainly didn't want to prove the bullies right, I said no.

When I finally came out a few years later, my mom told me that she feared I might be limiting my options by deciding to be openly gay. To be honest, I was afraid of that, too. All I knew about being gay were the stereotypes that society had fed me. Yet it never limited my options at all. In high school, I was a well-respected varsity athlete and a lifeguard. I even saved several people from drowning. After I graduated from high school, I went to the University of Wisconsin in Madison and majored in zoology and English. I also met my first boyfriend, fell in love, and, subsequently, had my heart completely broken (it was worth it, despite the broken heart).

After college, I wasn't sure what I wanted to do with my life, so I moved to Costa Rica and studied monkeys for a year on a volunteer basis. I loved it so much that I went to graduate school at NYU to continue studying primate behavior in the wild. I've been living in New York for the past six years, and just this September I received my PhD in physical anthropology, studying the behavior and genetics of woolly and spider monkeys in the Ecuadorian Amazon. All of the things that I've done since I was that thirteen-year-old kid who was followed home and spat on and called a faggot, all of it's been fantastic. And all of it was worth it just to get to where I am now. Right now, I'm in South Africa studying primates, doing what I have wanted to do since I was a teenager. And I've done it all as an out and proud and openly gay man. I've been able to travel everywhere with this job. I've lived in the Ecuadorian Amazon. I've worked in Peru and Colombia and Nicaragua and Costa Rica and Argentina.

So no matter where you are if you're being bullied, if you're being gay bashed, no matter what age you are, it gets better. Once you turn eighteen, you've got control of your life. You can do with it what you want. And it doesn't matter what other people think. If other people are going to try to push their opinions on you, then go somewhere where they won't. Create a safe space for yourself.

You can do that anywhere. Everywhere that I've worked, I've worked with other gay people. We're all over the place; trust me, even here in South Africa. It gets better for all of us. No matter where you are, it's going to get better for you. You can do all of the things that I've done and come to these amazing places and fall in love and have your heart broken and get married (legal in South Africa, Argentina, Canada, Iceland, the Netherlands, Norway, Sweden, Belgium, Portugal, as well as Connecticut, Washington, DC, Iowa, Massachusetts, New Hampshire, and Vermont; and several other countries recognize civil unions). Things are improving. So please just hold on and make it through the next few years, and I promise you that your life is going to be amazing. You're going to be amazing.

Author's Note: As I mentioned in my story, I grew up in Milwaukee and attended public school. I know how bad it can be there. If you're going to Milwaukee public schools now, and if you're being harassed, if you're being gay bashed all the time, if it's becoming unmanageable, if you don't want to go to school anymore—you have other options. A few years ago a charter school opened, called the Alliance School. It's run by Tina Owen and it's a great place made for kids like you, who are bullied and harassed every day at school. If you can't handle it anymore, visit the Alliance School's website (www .allianceschool.net), write to Tina, schedule a visit, or talk to your parents about helping you transfer. It's a safe space for gay students and for other students who are harassed for being different or unique.

Christopher A. Schmitt is currently a postdoctoral scholar with the Center for Neurobehavioral Genetics at the University of California, Los Angeles. If you want to learn more about his work with wild primates or just see some adorable fuzzy monkey pictures, visit his website at www.evopropinquitous.net.

IT GOT BETTER

•••••••••••••••••••••••••••••••

by Stephen D. Lorimor

BERKELEY HEIGHTS, NJ

W hen I was younger, life was a royal bitch.

On the surface I had it easy. I grew up in Warren, New Jersey, an upper-middle-class suburb of New York City. Most people who knew me well were supportive of my decision to come out in 1986 at age fifteen. My parents were initially upset but over the years grew to be supportive as well.

Loneliness was my real issue. While my straight, male friends learned the art of dating and relationships, I had so few gay acquaintances that my dating experiences were often limited to semi-anonymous hookups with what passed for the Internet back then.

College was worse. Shortly after arriving at Iowa State, I was harassed by the people on my dorm floor. My roommate moved out because I was gay. When I complained to my RA, he replied, "Well, I can't blame your roommate for moving out. Why would anyone want to live with a gay person?"

A number of students on the floor put up signs on their door that read, "SAFE—Students Against Faggots Everywhere." I received threatening phone calls, and a few students harassed me in the hallways. I complained to the residence life staff but was told that the signs were free speech and there was little they could do about the phone calls. So I moved out.

For a while I thought about transferring to another school. My parents even encouraged it. They thought I would be happier somewhere else. I stuck it out, in part, because I didn't know where else to go.

In the end, I'm glad that I stayed. I became active with the campus LGBT organization, which helped me gain a lot of self-confidence. I met a young man named Jeff in 1992. We started dating, and nineteen years later, we are still together and very happy. We adopted our son, Devon, in July of 2009. The following April a judge officially made us his parents and I cannot tell you how happy we are. We've got everything that we ever wanted. We've got a home, we've got each other, and we've got our little guy. Life really does get better.

I know that some of you reading this are feeling lonely or depressed. You feel like no one in the world understands you. All I can tell you is that life does get better and there is help out there. If you're feeling lost or suicidal, and there is no one you can turn to, contact the Trevor Project. If you feel like you haven't got a friend in the world, know there are people out there who will listen to you and will understand.

I've gone from being that lonely, depressed gay kid to being a parent who has his life together. I can't tell you how lost I would feel if Devon ever started thinking about killing himself, or if something awful happened to him. He's everything to me. This little guy and my husband are so much of my life. I love them both so much.

You, too, can be happy. You can have the things you dreamed of, whether that's a house and a kid, a successful career, traveling the world, winning an Olympic gold medal, or whatever else you want to do.

Just don't hurt yourself. It does get better.

....

Stephen D. Lorimor is an Internet webmaster and a stay-at-home dad for his son, Devon. He lives in New Jersey with husband, Jeff Cline.

OUR PARENTS AS ALLIES

● ●

by Lawrence Gullo, Fyodor Pavlov, Eileen Charbonneau, and Ed Gullo

NEW YORK, NY

My husband, Fyodor, and I interviewed my parents for this project, and since they proved to be so much more eloquent and better composed than we were, we'd decided to share their incredible wisdom with you. They have been steadfast allies not only for us but for a lot of other people, too. Thanks, Mom and Dad, we love you!

Eileen: You're a part of creation, a beautiful part of creation. If people have a problem with you, then it's their problem, not yours. The wonderful diversity of creation is manifest in each of us, and we can learn so much from those we think of as different.

Part of it getting better is that you realize that you're part of this wider world; you're part of this world that's been with you since your birth. If your family won't accept you for who you are, it's certainly harder but you'll just have to find new family. You'll have to find your advocates no matter where they are. Find people who honor you, look for people who are lifelong learners because those kind of people embrace difference.

When Lawrence told me he was gay, I knew nothing about being gay. My family did not have a tradition of gay, transgender, and lesbian people—at least not that anyone knew of. I'm sure they were there, they just weren't out. Yet watching my son grow and come out and accept himself has really been such a wonderful learning experience, and one that I continue to learn from. If you look for people who are life-long learners, no matter what age they are, they'll become your family. They'll become your strongest allies and advocates because you're teaching *them*. Most of the people who are very down on who you are and what you are, they have a lot of pain inside them. After all, what you're doing is not hurting them, it's got nothing to do with them, it does not threaten their lives at all, and yet they react so strongly against you. The only conclusion I can draw is that they must have some kind of pain inside them that makes you a threat. They have made you a threat. But, again, that's their problem. It's not your problem at all.

Please, keep yourself safe; my biggest worry for these two fine gentlemen, my son and son-in-law, is that they'll get into a dangerous situation. Honestly, that was my biggest concern when I learned that Lawrence was gay. I was so worried that somehow the world was going to be suddenly very unsafe for him. That all the people out there who have all this pain inside them were going to make him the scapegoat of that pain. That still worries me to this day. But I live with it because he is who he is. And don't worry about worrying your parents, because none of that is your responsibility. Your responsibility is to be who you are and make the world more beautiful.

Ed: My wish is that no matter how put upon you might feel, understand that this is just a moment you're having, a bad moment, but a moment nonetheless. It always seems like it's going to last forever, but it doesn't. It passes and time takes it away and something new and usually better takes over. You just have to get through those really difficult spots and then you find that there are wonderful moments to share.

I always felt that whatever Lawrence and Fyodor felt, I was willing to accept it because they were the ones feeling it. It's their lives. And I never felt for a moment that it was strange or different, or I should talk them out of it. It's what they were feeling. It's the people that they are. I only wanted to encourage them to be as much of themselves as they could. And the years passed, and we had this wonderful wedding, and we're all one family now. There was nothing to work out, it just happened.

If you're having problems with your parents—and I know some parents are more accepting than others—or if you're having problems with friends or whomever, know that it will resolve itself somehow. You will find a better place. Or you'll find better people, more accepting people.

But you should never, ever, ever do anything to yourself that would punish yourself for things that other people do.

Lawrence Gullo is an artist and puppeteer whose work centers around gender variance and sexuality in history. He has studied in London and Prague and is currently saving money for gender reassignment surgery.

Fyodor Pavlov was born and raised in Moscow, Russia. He currently resides in New York City with his husband, Lawrence, where they perform and create art together as the Royal Baritarian Players. He is an illustrator, puppeteer, and comic and performance artist.

Eileen Charbonneau is a storyteller in the Native American tradition and the author of nine published historical novels.

Ed Gullo has worked for several radio and TV news organizations as anchor, editor, and writer. Both Ed and Eileen are cancer survivors.

LESBIAN TEACHER BELIEVES IN YOU

by Kristin Rivers

SAN JOSE, CA

'm a lesbian, and a high school teacher. I was called "fucking dyke" by someone who I thought was my friend. In the early '90s, I attended a Gay Pride Event and had a slough of hateful epithets thrown at me by strangers claiming God was on their side and that I should burn in hell. I've experienced prejudice in my career as a teacher from parents, administrators, and even from other teachers. It took me a long time to come out, stand up for myself, and stop allowing others to define me.

I attempted suicide in my teens. I took a lethal dose of prescription medication and meant to remove myself from where I didn't feel I belonged. When I look back now, I see that I was trying so hard to be who I thought everyone else wanted me to be that I forgot who I was. I lost my sense of place and my own worth. I didn't feel I deserved to be loved, at least not in the way I wanted to be. So, I know how horrible it can be. I know how awful it can feel.

Fortunately, a dear friend came to visit me in the hospital, and when I told him what I had done, he threw himself on me and wept. He told me how much my friendship meant to him. Although I had been unable to conjure any circumstance in which I felt needed (before taking the pills), he gave me one. My friend made me feel useful and worthy of being loved. I didn't dare tell him about my feelings about being gay (not then), but I knew that I mattered and that somehow helped me to know that if I could just hold on until college, that I would grow past those empty moments.

Now, at forty-four, I have been with the same woman since 1998 and I know how demeaning it feels to have other people who don't know us decide whose relationship should be legally recognized. I know how all of this hateful and mean-spirited debate can hurt. My wife and I have three children. I see the flawed world they, and you, are coming up in. But please hear me when I say, it really does get better.

As an adult, I have found friends—straight, gay, bi, and poly (*polyamorous*) who love and support me for who I am. I've even found a church where I am not just tolerated but respected, honored, and cherished. My family and I live in a neighborhood where most of our neighbors are accepting. And perhaps, most importantly, I've come to a point in my life where those who don't accept me can't hurt me the way they did in my youth.

I'm absolutely heartbroken by all the amazing people we've lost. But I want you to know that you are not alone. Each person who has contributed to this project loves you, respects you, and can't wait for you to join us out in the world of acceptance that we found and continue to create every day.

Please don't give up. We really are out here.

· ·

Kristin Rivers was born and raised in a conservative small town in Northern California. She teaches English, Spanish, and prenatal health at an urban public continuation high school. She feels unendingly grateful to her authentic family, friends, colleagues, and students who have filled her life with love, purpose, and truth.

STEPPING OFF THE SIDELINES

· ·

by Wayne Knaub

PHILADELPHIA, PA

My little brother came home one day when I was in high school and told my dad that he had heard a rumor that I was gay. Then my sister called to tell me that my father said that if I was a faggot then, when I turned eighteen, my ass was getting kicked out of the house. She said she didn't care if I was or wasn't. It was nice that she was there for me but I lived with the fear of getting kicked out, wondering where I would go, what would I do, for a long time. So I denied who I was, even to my father. Then, one day when I was eighteen, we had a fight about something financial and when the fight was over, he said he loved me. I told him that he didn't. Otherwise he wouldn't have said that to my sister. He asked me if I was gay and I told him that I wasn't. I denied who I was time and time again.

When I was in college, someone outed me to my father during my sophomore year, but we never talked about it. I finally told him the truth my senior year. He said it wasn't what he would have wanted for me, but that he wasn't going to kick me out of his life.

There was never true acceptance on his part; but for twelve years, there was tolerance. And then recently, he posted one of those cut-and-paste "Will you stand up with me against gay teen suicides?" pledges, listing the names of several young people who committed suicide, on his Facebook page. I thought that was a pretty big step for him, but then I read the comment he posted underneath it. "I am so glad that my son was strong enough to withstand the bullying and my ignorance as he was growing up. I am so proud of him and his accomplishments in life, and I love him for all that he is. Being gay is not one of his shortcomings."

It took many years, but I think my father realized that if all these kids were committing suicide, he could have lost his son, too. It's sad that it took so many young people dying for him to realize that he could have been that parent, but he did. I'm very thankful that he's finally come around after all these years and now we're renewing our relationship as father and son.

This past year I was asked by the founder of the Greater Philadelphia Flag Football League (GPFFL) to step in as commissioner when he relocated for a new job. I've been very active in the gay community and gay sports leagues in New York and Philadelphia and welcomed the opportunity to take the GPFFL to the next level.

If you had told me when I was in high school that one day I'd be the commissioner of a gay sports league, I wouldn't have believed you. I wouldn't have believed that such a thing even existed. I would have told you that you're crazy. When you grow up in a rural area not knowing any other gay people, or even that being gay is an option, the idea of meeting another gay person—let alone a whole football team of amazing gay guys and gals—is quite foreign.

So if you're that kid—maybe a nose tackle or the defensive end for your high school or college football team—living in fear, who doesn't think he can have the life he wants and doesn't even realize that something like this might be out there for him one day, I want you to know you can and there is. This is what it's all about. The gay community, the friendships, and the relationships we have built. I know it may not seem like it now, but it really does get better. I hope to see you on the football field with us one day!

Wayne Knaub grew up in York County, Pennsylvania and now lives in Philadelphia. He is the commissioner of the Greater Philadelphia Flag Football League, which is open to all LGBTQ people and our allies regardless of skill level or ability. For more information, please visit www.phillyflagfootball.com. This essay originated as part of a video directed by Damian Tracy, featuring members of the Greater Philadelphia Flag Football League. A special thank-you is due to Damian for his excellent work on the video.

MY OWN WORST ENEMY

by Jessica Leshnoff

BALTIMORE, MD

grew up in a small town in northern New Jersey about twenty-five miles outside New York City. I'm also Jewish, not just culturally so, but I actually care about being Jewish and have a firm belief in G-d.

I've also always been, as my late grandfather used to say about me as a toddler, "an arch individualist." I cut my own bangs when I was three. I asked for an Atari for my birthday when everyone else was getting Nintendo. I wrote elementary school fan letters (in cursive pencil) to Jon Bon Jovi beginning with "Dear Mr. Jovi." I've always done my own thing, and, luckily, was always encouraged to do so by my parents.

"Different" was always okay. But by the time middle school hit, I'd say seventh grade, something started creeping up my spine and settled uncomfortably in my brain. It made me feel different in a new, uneasy way. It was a question without an answer, something so foreign to me as a twelve-year-old in 1990 that I couldn't even think about it.

Am I gay? a voice whispered quietly. I didn't even truly know what "gay" was. There was no *Will & Grace*. There was no out-and-proud Ellen. There was no Adam Lambert. There was nothing, really. But I knew my feelings, I knew who I had crushes on, and I knew it wasn't "normal."

I kept my feelings to myself because they felt wrong. After all, I had crushes on boys. I loved the New Kids on the Block the same way all the other girls did. But things were off.

I pushed my feelings way, way down. Packed them down so deep they turned into concrete in my stomach—and my heart. They plagued me day and night. *What you're feeling isn't normal*, they whispered. *You're not normal. You're weird. You're a freak. You're different. You're wrong.* And the very worst one: *You're a bad person.*

Here's the catch: No one else was bullying me. I was bullying myself.

Year after year the feelings were there, as was the voice in my head. The self-bullying continued. The feelings got stronger. The voice got louder. The bullying got worse. I was my own worst enemy. I didn't know it at the time, but I was destroying myself. By the time I reached tenth and eleventh grade, *You're a bad person* morphed into *You're a bad person and a bad Jew.*

One by one, my dreams started crumbling. Marriage. Children. A happy life. *I might be alone forever*, I told myself. I couldn't see my way out. I felt doomed.

A loop of self-made insults and self-loathing swirled in my head day and night. I joked around in high school, did well in classes, and had plenty of friends, but I felt crushed and breathless all the time. Instead of hanging out with my friends, I cried alone in my room, scared to death of my feelings. Scared to death I'd be shunned by my family, shunned by my friends, shunned not only by an entire religious community but also by G-d. Looking back at it from the safe distance of a happy, open adulthood, I don't know where all the self-loathing came from. After all, no one in my family ever said anything bad about gay people. No one, absolutely no one, told me that if I was gay, or had an attraction to anyone of the same sex, I would be anything less than a good Jew. But you see, all of those feelings—those feelings of being wrong, being a freak, being a bad person—are indoctrinated in us as we grow. I'm a perfect example of that. I've always been a free thinker. I grew up in the New York metro area. My parents are open-minded.

But I got the message from society at large: Gay is different. Different is bad. Gay is bad.

And so I stayed quiet. I stayed quiet until I came out to my high school best friend in a fit of tears and shivers in the middle of the night just a few days before our senior year started. I came out to her because I literally was making myself sick. I had prepped myself for our friendship ending once she heard my secret.

Instead she wrapped her arms around me and told me it was okay.

"Really?" I said through my tears. "You still like me? You still want to be friends?"

"Of course I want to be friends!" she said, smiling. "I don't feel any differently about you. You're still Jessica. You're still my best friend."

A huge weight was temporarily lifted off my shoulders. I had told someone and she didn't care. She loved me unconditionally. But I was sixteen. And even though I wasn't completely sure about my sexuality, I knew, deep inside, that I would have a long way to go because I didn't love myself.

I'd like to say that I replaced fear and shame with pride and happiness, and came out to everyone that was important to me, but that couldn't be further from the truth. I didn't feel any better about myself. And I would continue carrying the weight of the world on my shoulders, and continue bullying myself until I literally made myself sick—sicker this time—finally coming out to my parents when I was eighteen and in college.

And you know what? When I told my parents, they didn't care either.

No one, not one person, who I've come out to in all the years since—and I'm thirty-two now—*has ever cared*. They don't see me as "gay." They see me as Jessica.

If you're struggling with this right now, I want you to go to the mirror, look at yourself and say "I'm (your name)." If the words "gay" or "bi" or "trans" or "queer" are on your lips, replace it with your name. Because that's who you are. That's the core of you. I hope you can understand that. It's something I didn't understand for far too long.

I wasted years—years!—feeling bad about myself when I didn't need to. It's hard enough when you're a teenager. You don't want to be seen as different. Maybe "different" in the sense of you're a cool dresser or exceptionally creative or something like that. For me, being gay was the last straw. I already felt like I didn't fit in. It pushed me over the edge. But it didn't need to.

I felt so alone, so completely alone, when I was closeted in high school. But let me tell you something: When I got to college everything changed. Everything! I started meeting like-minded people. I started meeting people of every sexual orientation and background. My world opened up. Like a screen door in a windstorm—BAM! And suddenly I wasn't alone anymore. I started becoming the Jessica I once was as a kid, before worries about my sexuality came along in middle school and high school. I started coming into my own. And I started to realize, hey, I am normal. I am totally and completely 100 percent normal.

And you don't need to go to college for that to happen. Once you expand your world—meet new people, go new places, graduate from high school—things will start changing. Because if you're living somewhere now where people don't accept you, or are bullying you, there are so many places where things will be different. You just need to hold on. Even if your family doesn't wind up accepting you, families don't always have to be blood relatives. We can make our own families. And if you haven't come out to your friends or family yet for fear of being rejected, give them a chance. They just might surprise you.

I was lucky enough to never have experienced bullying by other people. But I think what I experienced was just as bad. I bullied myself.

If you're bullying yourself, please stop. I promise you things will get better. Go easy on yourself. You are a good person. And you will find your way.

If you're religious, please know that G-d loves you no matter what. Do you hear me? Gay, straight, or anything in between, no matter what. If anyone tells you anything different, ignore them. Shut them out.

Because it's untrue. Do you know how many LGBT-friendly houses of worship there are? Tons! And you'll find yours one day, I promise.

Life as an LGBT person can be happy, extremely, gloriously happy. And normal. When I was twenty-two—just six years after I came out to my best friend in high school—I met holly, who would become my partner of now almost ten years. She is the love of my life! We have so much fun together. I feel like the luckiest person in the world. We got married not just once, but twice. And you know what? We are ridiculously normal. As in: We fall asleep on the couch together and watch movies and go grocery shopping and do laundry and go to Starbucks and make meat loaf. We have a home and it's filled with love. And you'll have that one day, too. You really will. I promise. You just need to have faith. And give yourself time. And talk to someone you can trust if you feel so hopeless that you're considering taking your own life.

Because you need to be here.

You hear me?

You need to be here. You deserve to be here. I want you to be here. Holly and I want you to be here. We all want you to be here. You might not know us but we're out here. And the people closest to you—that you might not think care—they care more than you know. You need to stick around so you can meet all the awesome, fun, impossibly sexy people that are going to help make your life not just bearable but totally and completely awesome.

Don't bully yourself the way I did. Don't worry about things that are going to work out just fine. I bet you're not all that much different than me. And I've managed to figure it out. And you will, too.

I didn't know at your age that it could get better. But it does and it has and the craziest thing? It just keeps getting better. It gets much, much, *much* better.

· ·

Jessica Leshnoff is a freelance journalist and copywriter with over a decade of national and regional writing experience. When she's not writing, Jessica can be found drinking coffee, taking city walks (sometimes while drinking coffee), fawning over other people's puppies (usually while walking), listening to music way too loud in her car, and reapplying frosty lipstick. Incredibly hungry impossibly early, she lives with her partner in Baltimore, Maryland, and chronicles their lives on her blog, *Lunch at 11:30*. Visit jessicaleshnoff.com.

YOU ARE A BELOVED CHILD OF GOD

● ●

by Presiding Bishop Mark Hanson

CHICAGO, IL

As the presiding bishop of the largest Lutheran church in North America—the Evangelical Lutheran Church in America—and a father of six and a grandfather of four, I've listened with pain and shock to reports of young people taking their lives because they've been bullied and tormented for being different—for being gay or being perceived to be gay. For being the people God created them to be.

I can only imagine what it's like to be bullied for being lesbian, gay, bisexual, or transgender. But I do know how bullying can destroy someone. One day I came home and found our daughter curled up in the fetal position on the floor, weeping uncontrollably. She was struggling to know who she was as a biracial young woman. She felt bruised by words people had spoken about her—words that ate away at her sense of identity and self-worth. I sat down by her on the floor, holding her in my arms.

Words have the power to harm and the power to heal. Sometimes the words of my Christian brothers and sisters have hurt you, and I also know that our silence causes you pain. Today I want to speak honestly with you and offer you the hope I have in Christ: You are a beloved child of God. Your life carries the dignity and the beauty of God's creation. God has called you by name and claimed you forever. There's a place for you in this world and in this church.

As a Christian, I trust that God is working in this world for justice and peace through you and through me; it gets better. "For I am convinced that neither death, nor life, nor angels, nor rulers, nor things present, nor things to come, nor powers, nor height, nor depth nor anything else in all creation, will be able to separate us from the love of God in Christ Jesus our Lord" (Romans 8:38–39).

May it be so. Amen.

The Rev. Mark S. Hanson is presiding bishop of the Evangelical Lutheran Church in America (ELCA) and former president of the Lutheran World Federation. The ELCA is one of the largest Christian denominations in the United States, with approximately 4.5 million members in 10,400 congregations across the fifty states and the Caribbean. The Lutheran World Federation is a global communion of Christian churches in the Lutheran tradition, with 145 member churches in seventy-nine countries all over the world representing more than 70 million Lutherans.

TRANSGENDERED AND SELF-EDUCATED IN MAINE

· · · · · · · · · · · · · · · · · · ·

by Jean Vermette

BANGOR, ME

'm a fifty-six-year-old, postoperative transsexual woman who lives in Maine. And I think the best way to explain to you *how* it gets better is to tell you a little about my life.

I knew there was something "different" about me by the time I was three years old. That's when I began to have a concept of myself as a "gendered" person; that's when I knew that I was supposed to be a girl; and that's when I began cross-dressing whenever I could.

But I grew up in a religious household, Roman Catholic, and I knew, even from a young age, that for me, as a male-bodied person, to associate and be so attracted to feminine things and feelings was *not* going to be appreciated. So even my earliest cross-expressing was done in secret.

It stayed that way until I was almost thirty-eight years old. Looking back, I almost think of myself as *lucky* that my trans identity wasn't so overwhelmingly strong that I couldn't hide it with some effort. After all, when I first had these feelings, it was 1957 and Christine Jorgensen (the first publicly recognized transsexual) didn't even flash onto the front pages until 1959.

My parents were very loving but "old-school" Catholics, as well. If I had come out back then, there's no doubt they would have rushed me off to some psychiatrist in an attempt to cure me. It would have been done out of love, and worry, and with good intentions. But it would have been just as utterly disastrous for me then as it is for kids today whose parents march them off to reparative treatments and ex-gay programs.

Then, and throughout all of my school years, it wasn't okay to be gay or lesbian or bisexual, and no one knew what it meant to be transgendered. So, as a result, I stayed in the closet and didn't try to find support, because there really wasn't any to be had.

Following that path pretty much kept me from getting beat up or otherwise harassed, but in order to keep that secret, I had to withdraw into my own little world. I became a loner; I focused on my studies (even though I absolutely hated school); I avoided most social contact; I could count on one hand the number of friends I had. It was a very lonely, confused, and sometimes depressing life, one I wouldn't wish on anyone, especially not you.

By the time I was thirteen, I knew I was transsexual, not gay, and was trying to figure out how I was going to deal with it. And I was realizing that all the hateful and negative things that everyone was saying about people like me was just ignorant bullshit.

When you're young, you don't necessarily know what's true or right, or helpful, or loving. The adults in your life tell you that *they* know what those things are, and they generally seem to know a lot more than you do, so you believe them.

As you grow older and learn more about the world, you realize that those same adults aren't perfect and that they can be mistaken just as easily as you can. At that point you start thinking for yourself, questioning what you've been told. It became undeniably obvious to me that a lot of what people were thinking or saying—about life, about how things were, about people like me—simply couldn't be true.

At the age of seventeen, after discovering that it was possible to do and with my parents' hesitant support, I quit high school and began educating myself. It was fantastic, and even though it took more time for me to negotiate my transsexuality and to come out, these years were mostly free of the mind-numbing negativity about LGBT people that I had experienced previously. That freedom helped me work out who I was, how I could fit in, and what I had to do to get to that point.

Once I was out of high school, I flourished. I became much more outgoing. I got my diploma by taking adult night classes, an agreement I made with my parents, and I began studying things on my own. I studied whatever I wanted, as much as I wanted. I took a series of jobs, mostly manual labor, where I met all kinds of interesting people with incredible knowledge and varying experiences, and I quickly came to understand how limiting much of our educational system is and, as a result, how limited some of the people who go through it can become. Those bullies who are harassing you now . . . they're *definitely* "limited."

At the time I came out, I was working in the construction trade and I figured if anyone was going to give me a hassle about having a sex change, it was going to be a bunch of blue-collar construction guys. But you know what? It didn't happen! Oh, there were a few folks who stopped talking to me or wouldn't work with me, but only a few. And I was floored by the number of folks who came up to me and said things like, "Wow! That was such a brave thing you did. Thank you for sharing that with me. I wish that I could do exactly what I wanted to with my life but I can't. So I really respect you that you did it." Life is not always what you expect. People can be kind. And, ultimately, more people are going to support you than be against you. But to experience that, you've got to stay alive.

And you've got a lot to stay alive for! I've had a wonderful life since high school and done a lot of interesting things: I worked in professional theater for eleven years doing setting and lighting design, and a little acting. I owned a company that made stained-glass lights. I worked for several telephone companies (and I'll tell you, climbing a telephone pole in Maine, when it's ten below zero, is an interesting experience!). I've been a computer programmer; I've been a dishwasher; I got a paralegal degree; I started a small educational company that trains mental health and medical professionals, businesses, and college kids about transgender issues. And now I'm a licensed electrician, one of the few female electricians in the state. I also have a partner! We've been together for nine years now, and we're building a house together in the Maine woods, near a bunch of lakes and the ocean and Acadia National Park.

So you see, it does get better; we're not pulling your leg. We're telling you it gets better because our experience proves that it does. But to have those great life experiences you've got to stay alive, stick in there, and go after what you want. And you can do it! We know you can do it because we did it, and we don't have superhuman abilities or unusual psychological strengths. We did it, and we're just like you.

So whether you're gay or lesbian or bisexual or transgendered, or even if you're a straight kid who's being bullied and called gay, you can do it, too.

> **Author's Note**: In high school, I read a book called *Summerhill,* about a different way of educating kids, by creating an accepting, imaginative, and supportive environment that utilized the students' interests and personal strengths. I wasn't going to a school like that but it made me realize that if we were given love, and the freedom to pursue our goals, then there's no limit to what we can accomplish. A lot of folks tell you that if you can only hang in there through high school things will get better. That's true, but I'd also like to offer you another option. If you really think that school is just too unbearable, and you have the gumption, you can leave the small-mindedness of high school and still get a great education. That's a lot better than taking your own life. To explore that option, check out *Summerhill* by A. S. Neill and *The Teenage Liberation Handbook* by Grace Llewellyn.

Jean Vermette is a Maine native, educated in the Skowhegan school system, Coburn Classical Institute in Waterville, and Beal College in Bangor, where she obtained a paralegal degree. She is self-employed, the author of a book about sexual-reassignment surgery: *Je Me Souviens*, and the founding director of the Maine Gender Resource and Support Service (MeGReSS).

THE POWER OF "YOU"

●●

by Luan Legacy

HOUSTON, TX

I can't sit here and tell you that everything will get better and that nothing will ever go wrong again. Things go wrong, things always go wrong. But you have to make them right.

I've never been a big advocate of hope, and I never will be because, frankly, hope is for losers. Hope is for people who are too lazy to solve their own problems so they rely on hope. You have to solve your own problems. You have to make that decision that you want to be happy. If you fall down and scrape your knee, you put that Band-Aid on yourself. If you're hungry, you find food to eat. If you get bullied at school for being gay, you stand up for yourself. You find a way to end the bullying, whether that be avoiding the bullies, changing schools, telling a teacher, telling a parent, standing up to your bullies and getting totally beaten up; whatever it takes, you have to stand up for yourself.

I don't understand how someone can have the courage to put a gun to their head and pull the trigger. I don't understand how someone can have the courage to tie a knot around their neck and hang themselves with it. But they don't have the courage to stand up to their bullies. It doesn't make sense. How can you have the courage to kill yourself but not have the courage to stand up for yourself?

Well, what I want you to know is that you do have the courage. Everything you need for a happy life is in you; you just have to direct it. Suicide is not going to solve anything. Suicide is you quitting. Suicide is you not having enough respect for your own life that you just give up. You should never give up.

When I was very, very young and I didn't know everything that I know now, I experienced a point in my life where I considered suicide. But I looked at the bathwater that I was going to drown myself in, and I looked at myself in it, and I said, "What the fuck are you doing? What is this going to solve? How is this going to bring you happiness?" And my answers were, "This isn't going to bring me happiness. This isn't going to solve anything." And frankly, I don't know what the fuck I was on to know what the fuck I was doing. So I stopped, went to sleep, and the next day I woke up and sucked in a big breath of air. I took in a big breath of life, and ever since then, life has never been so sweet, because it's scary to know it could have been the end that day.

I never would have gotten a chance to experience love. I never would have gotten the chance to truly come out. I never would have started YouTube-ing. I never would have gotten a chance to dance and to do something I truly love, and neither will you if you commit suicide. Your life is full of opportunities. Make the most of it. Suicide is not the answer. And at the end of the day, so what! So what if they call you a fag. So what if they say you are a flaming homo. So what if they say you like to take big horse dick up your ass. It doesn't matter. It shouldn't faze you. They're just immature, insecure dickheads with nothing better to do. Don't let them get to you.

I love you, guys. Stay strong.

> **Author's Note:** Learning to accept my sexuality was one of the hardest things that I've had to do, but it was necessary in order for me to find happiness. After I came out, I was able to experience life at its fullest because it was then that I was able to live life how I wanted to, instead of how I was expected to. You only get one life, and no one has the right to stop you from enjoying it how you please.

Luan Legacy is a senior in high school and plans to major in interior design and dance in college. He has lived in Texas all his life, but has dreams of moving to California and becoming a professional entertainer. Luan posts videos on YouTube at youtube.com/luanlegacy.

IT GETS BETTER FOR SMALL TOWNERS, TOO

• •

by Dwayne Steward

DELAWARE, OH

I grew up in Delaware, Ohio, a small rural town just outside of Columbus, and I was picked on mercilessly in junior high and high school for acting "feminine." I was called a faggot on a regular basis. I was called a lot of things on a regular basis. Every derogatory name used for gays was at some point directed at me. My parents are also extremely religious; my father's a Pentecostal minister, so I had to deal with bigotry at home, as well.

All of this, of course, made coming out extremely difficult. I was in church every week hearing the pastor preach that gays are going to hell. There was even a rumor started that I was fornicating with another member of the church and we were infecting each other, and those around us, with AIDS. It was pretty bad. I dealt with a lot of inner turmoil and self-hatred for a very long time.

Even though things were pretty bad growing up, the great thing about high school is it doesn't last forever. After I graduated I went to Ohio University, a school that's extremely open and accepting of everybody and anyone. I met a remarkable group of friends who I still keep in touch with. I came out in college and was even a part of starting an amazing support group for LGBT people of color there called SHADES—the first of its kind at OU.

When I told my family I was gay, there was some resistance but they all said the same thing, that they loved me no matter what. My friends were also extremely supportive, and most of them said they had already known. Altogether, coming out wasn't as bad as I was expecting it to be.

When I came out to my extremely religious mother she said that she didn't agree with my lifestyle but that she loved me just the same. My father echoed this sentiment. My parent's initial reaction was one of avoidance. My sexuality was just something we didn't talk about. Biblically, I knew their stance and they knew mine. But they are slowly coming around. When I first came out, my mother didn't want to hear anything about my love life. Now she actually wants to meet my boyfriends. And my father has even started inviting my boyfriends to family functions. So it gets better.

I moved back to Delaware recently and it has dawned on me how important leaving was. I was able to discover people who were just like me, and live a life that was void of any hatred. That experience made me a much stronger person and gave me the ability to confront the stereotypes and bigotry that used to go on here all the time. And Delaware has changed some, too. There are LGBT groups now where that never could have existed when I was growing up here. So, sometimes it just takes time.

If you're a teen in a city like Delaware, Ohio, seek out the gay community where you live. There are groups and organizations that can help you. One great organization in Columbus is the Kaleidoscope Youth Center. It's an organization specifically designed to be a safe space for LGBT youth in junior high and high school. So find a center like that near you. And if there isn't a gay community near you, go to the biggest city around you. Or find an older gay person or an ally that you can trust, that you can talk to.

Suicide is never the only option. Please, please, please do not let the bullies win. High school is only four years of your life. There is so much more out there that you need to experience. There's a whole world out there waiting for you that is much better than the one you're living in. It does get better.

Dwayne Steward is a journalist and human rights activist working and living in Delaware, Ohio. Along with helping pave the way of acceptance and support for gay people of color at his alma mater, Ohio University, he's been involved with the Columbus AIDS Task Force and the Kaleidoscope Youth Center, an organization that focuses on providing a safe space for gay youth in central Ohio.

TO ME: WITH LOVE AND SQUALOR

• •

by Terry Galloway

TALLAHASSEE, FL

I walk into a rehearsal of my theater company, The Mickee Faust Academy for the REALLY Dramatic Arts, and I see about thirty people—all of them the oddest of odd ducks—milling around, laughing, poring over the scripts, swapping jokes. And I think to myself, "I'm actually happy. How in God's name did that happen?"

It almost didn't.

I've been queer since I was born, suspected it by age five, and was happy to discover its sexual component at age seven with a blonde my age named Sunny during a game we called—and to this day I'm embarrassed to remember—"milking the cow." You can well imagine. Around age twelve, I was finally able to put a name to my inner roilings when I looked up the word *homosexuality* in a dictionary. I had heard my older sister use the word with some vehemence when describing to my parents how she'd stumbled upon her female college roommate in bed with a woman, and the fact that I found the context intriguing made me suspect the word had particular relevance to me. The definition in the dictionary, "sexual desire directed at a person of one's own sex," thrilled me to death. But I wanted further clarification. I thought I was being immensely discreet when I off-handedly mentioned at dinner that I'd looked up the word "*homosex—*" I didn't even have time to finish the word. It was like I'd shot off a gun and stampeded cattle. The commotion it caused left me with the strong impression that *homosexual* was the wrong side of the sheets to be on.

Right then and there I went underground. I didn't want to be outed as any more queer than I already was.

When my mother was six months pregnant with me she developed a kidney infection. My family was living on an American military base in Germany at the time. The doctors gave her an antibiotic that they knew could do harm to the fetus, but it was the only drug they had in their arsenal that might save her life so they crossed their fingers and gave it to her anyway.

After I was born everything seemed hunky-dory until my ninth year, when I started having visions. I'd be sitting on the back of our old Chevy looking up at the stars and then all of a sudden I'd be six feet away looking over at myself looking up at the stars. That's when they discovered that a chemical imbalance caused by the introduction of drugs to the fetal nervous system had left me not quite blind as a bat but definitely deaf as a doornail.

So by the time I was twelve I was a freak. I'd already been feeling out of sorts with my body, and the hallucinations had been the least of it. I'd put on weight and turned chubby as a hamster, had a Moe-like bowl haircut, and my two front teeth were fangs because I'd whacked myself in the mouth with the vacuum cleaner handle I'd used as a bazooka during a game of war. Add to that a pair of Coke-bottle glasses and a box-sized hearing aid that fit between my budding breasts like a third one and the picture you get isn't pretty.

I'd look in the mirror and what I saw filled me with self-loathing and anger. It seemed as if all my secret desires had been turned inside out to expose me as the queer little freak that I was.

The bullying I was to undergo for the next long years of my life wasn't so much from other people as from myself. I hated myself. Hated the picture I made, even when that picture changed as I grew older and I became a pretty girl—exchanging the glasses for contacts, the box hearing aid for a clever little one that could be hidden behind my ears.

The image of my body as ridiculous and shameful was permanently burned into my brain.

But what I hated even more was loving girls while pretending to love boys.

I liked the boys, considered them my friends, even liked the sexual games we played together, but I could never really reciprocate their more tender emotions. If they ever got moony, I'd turn brusque or standoffish or just plain curt and cruel. I sometimes deeply hurt the boys I liked the most. As for the girls, I felt as if I was constantly tricking them—trying to trip them up into making admissions of longing for me that I could never dare make to them. All of which added more layers of self-loathing.

I grew up admiring certain principles, "to thine own self be true" primary among them. And there was no way I could honor that principle, lying the way I did. But I was also a child who wanted to be loved. Always the kid in the family who needed to be told, "I love you," over and over again. I was convinced that if I ever admitted any of my queer longing, no one on earth would ever love me again.

So, as I grew older, I started drinking and drugging myself into oblivion and twice ended up in a mental hospital after trying to kill myself. I was being made sick from all the lying; made sick from the fear of losing love.

And then one day, who knows why, I got tired of making myself suffer. I knew in my heart that my self-loathing was misguided—that what I ought to hate wasn't myself but the forces in the world that made me hate myself; the people who were so unimaginative that they couldn't see me for the sweetheart that I was. And I knew, too, that being true to myself, loving myself, would be one of the strongest political statements I could ever make. It was then, in my early twenties, after I'd simply changed my mind, that I came out of the closet, and began to look around for people in the world who would love me for who I was.

I was surprised to find those people everywhere—they were my teachers, my coworkers, my doctors, my childhood friends. And those people included my family.

My parents and older sister, who had once had such vehement reactions to the word *homosexual* had over the years learned new ways of thinking themselves. And when I came out to them they were nothing but loving.

Even to this day my queer friends and I have to face idiots who, with sorrowful fury, warn us of the hellfires that await us for being true to ourselves. When I was younger, those idiots filled me with fear and anger. But as I grew older and happier, that anger and fear evaporated and turned into . . . well, a kind of laughter. The ones who would judge me as harshly as I once judged myself have themselves become the ridiculous ones. Because I have the irrefutable evidence that belies their savage and silly condemnation of queerness: my own happy life.

Terry Galloway is a deaf lesbian writer, director, and performer who writes, directs, and performs. Her memoir, *Mean Little Deaf Queer*, published by Beacon Press, was a finalist for the Lambda Awards and a winner of a Golden Crown for creative nonfiction. She splits her time between Austin, Texas and Tallahassee, Florida, where she lives with Donna Marie Nudd, her longtime love.

HAPPINESS IS INEVITABLE

. . . .

by Henry Winfiele

RICHMOND, VA

When I was in middle school I didn't know about the whole negative stigma about being gay. I certainly didn't know I was any different from any other kid. When I came out to my best friend in middle school, he told everybody. As a result I lost every single friend I'd ever made since childhood, including him. From then on most of the guys at the school started mistreating me. I was called fag, had things thrown at me, was singled out and humiliated daily.

High school was hardly any better. I was a really anxious kid and loathed interacting with other people. I remember having to give a report in front of my whole ninth-grade English class. The entire time I was trying to give this speech, a group of boys in the back were heckling me, trying to make me mess up, which, of course, I did. I was shaking. I was so upset and nervous and couldn't go on. And the teacher just sat at her desk doing nothing about it. But another girl slammed her hands on her desk and shouted, "What's your problem? Why are you doing this to him?"

One of the boys in the group spat back, "Because he's a fag."

Finally I just went back to my seat, crying, and slumped out of sight. The only way I managed to keep my sanity was in art and theater class. None of my bullies took any of those classes and it was full of weirdos so it became my sanctuary. I later attended an art college a comfortable distance away, where I met some of the most amazingly open people you can imagine, the kind of friendships that last a lifetime. But even in college I struggled with crippling anxiety, depression, and internalized homophobia. It took two years of counseling and therapy to overcome those dark years of being harassed and made to feel ashamed for simply being who I am. But I got through to the other side.

I came out to my parents shortly after graduating college. My mom said some of the most beautiful things I've ever heard from anybody, things I wished I'd been told when I was growing up and being bullied. She said, "You are beautiful because of who you are. And there's absolutely nothing wrong with who you are." Those words really stick with me.

Life for gay kids gets infinitely better after high school. You learn who you are and realize that actually *because* you are gay you're going to have a much more exciting and interesting life than the assholes who tried to make you feel bad about it in the first place. If you kill yourself in high school, you can't have the rewarding experience of reclaiming your life. You deny yourself the chance to meet and fall in love with someone. Worst of all, you deny yourself the best revenge possible on your bullies: living your life to the absolute fullest.

Don't deny yourself a future and, at the very least, don't deny *us* the chance to meet and get to know you. Don't kill yourself. Happiness is inevitable if you endure and persist. It'll be glitter and sunshine and sparkles and rainbows all the way.

· ·

Henry Winfiele is a recently graduated, young, rising artist living and working in Richmond, Virginia.

I WISH I'D BEEN SASSIER!

by Brian Gallivan, aka Sassy Gay Friend

LOS ANGELES, CA

hat, what, what are you doing?!

W It gets better. It really does. In middle school, high school, even college—I went to a pretty conservative Catholic college—I was not out at all. I wasn't bullied, because I tried so hard to fit in. I regret that. I regret not being who I was more. But it's hard. It's hard to do that sometimes.

A lot of times in high school I wouldn't do the things that I wanted to, like acting, and writing, and doing improv, all of the things I get to do now and love. I didn't do them in high school because I thought it would make me seem gay and I thought I'd get picked on. I didn't even take an improv class until I turned thirty years old, which is ridiculous. Why did I wait so long to do something I love so much?

I felt the same way about coming out. I didn't even go on a date with a guy until I was twenty-four. When I finally did, it was so great. I really liked him, and it felt so good to just go out with somebody who I really liked. I immediately regretted all that time I wasted trying to fit in and be something I wasn't.

So I'm telling you: I know we wait because we're scared. And if you're scared right now, try and find those couple of people, or more, who are trustworthy, who you feel can help you. Or look on the Internet for resources, or read books. I love books. Most young adult books—I still love young adult literature—are about people who are outsiders, who come to realize that they're okay. So think of your life as a book. If high school's hard, imagine you're just in that part of the book, and you're going to get to the good part soon. And that good part could be meeting new friends, or doing things you never thought you were allowed to do, or meeting someone you could date, or living in an exciting new place. Or, maybe, the good part is just staying where you are and getting more confident about who you are. There are a ton of ways your story could get better, and high school is just a few chapters in a really long, exciting book.

Today I have so many great friends—gay friends, straight friends. And my relationships with everyone I came out to—my family, my friends—are so much better. But that all happens later in the book, so please stick around for the whole story. It will be great. I make these videos poking fun at Juliet for killing herself in *Romeo and Juliet*. And I just wish I could zoom into every scared gay kid's life and say, "*What are you doing*?" I can't. But you can do it for yourself. I believe in you.

It gets better. So stick around.

Brian Gallivan grew up near Boston, Massachusetts, and used to be a middle school teacher before he started improvising. He was part of the mainstage cast at the Second City in Chicago, and he now lives in Los Angeles where he writes, acts, and makes *Sassy Gay Friend* videos for the Second City Network.

PROTECT AND SERVE LOVES SEMPER FIDELIS

by J. D. Davis and Allen D. Stone

BALSAM, NC, AND SAN JOSE, CA

Allen: I was raised in rural southwestern Ohio. The closest town was five miles away. Monday through Friday was for school and work; Friday and Saturday nights were for parties; Sunday was for church. Homosexuality was not discussed and the term *faggot* was the worst name that a person could be called. Faggots were limp-wristed, effeminate guys who walked with a swish and were attracted to other men. . . .

Hence my dilemma. The only part of the definition that applied to me was that I was attracted to other men, but I was worried: If a faggot was a limp-wristed, effeminate guy who walked with a swish and was attracted to other men . . . and I was attracted to other men . . . would I eventually fit the rest of the definition, too? Would I start walking with a swish?

Primarily motivated by this fear, I joined the United States Marine Corps. Known for being the most macho of the armed services, the Marines are also the most respected. Off to boot camp I went.

The first few years of my stint in the Marines were relatively uneventful: I became more mentally fit; I became physically stronger; I became a well-respected leader in my units. However, my attraction to other men never ceased—but somehow I never started walking with a swish.

That made me begin to question the faggot stereotype that had inspired such fear in me. Soon I realized that I was an ignorant and naïve where homosexuality was concerned—but I was learning.

Years later, while still in the Marine Corps, I had my first real relationship with another man.

It was wonderful to see him when I was on leave, but sadness would arise when I returned to my unit. I could not seek comfort or advice from my superiors and friends in the Corps as that would "out me." I loved the Corps and didn't want to leave, but I loved my significant other, too. Sadly, my significant other could never be there to greet me when I came home from deployments. My significant other could not participate in unit functions and was not entitled to the same privileges that the heterosexual spouses of my fellow Marines enjoyed.

Due to the stress of our separation and the discrimination we faced as a couple, my first relationship gradually evolved into a friendship, so I was alone again and had two more years remaining on my second tour.

Eventually I was forced to choose between my military career and being with a man I could love. I chose the latter. And soon after leaving the Marines I would meet and fall in love with an incredible man named J.D.

J.D.: When I was in high school, even when I was in middle school, I was picked on constantly. My biggest bully was a person who had been one of my best friends in early childhood, but he decided to start calling me a faggot in adolescence. We were both in the band, and I can still recall exactly how terrified I was every day walking to band practice: Would today be the day he attacks me? I would think. Would he and the other bullies be lying in wait for me to beat me, call me a queer, throw me down the stairs?

On one of the worst days of my life, this bully nearly killed me by running my car off the road with his pickup truck. Although I was proud of myself for being able to outmaneuver him, the memory of this injustice clung to me through college. Then, when I started graduate school, I briefly dated a gay police officer, and through him, I remembered how much I revered law enforcement officers when I was a child.

After I came out, I decided I could be anything I wanted in spite of all the negative messages I had received about gay men. I was strong, smart, and capable—and I could make a difference. I became a police officer myself and swore to protect the rights of the oppressed, including my lesbian and gay sisters and brothers. I was tough and brave and well trained. I certainly wasn't weak, as I had been led to believe all gay men were by the homophobes who had tormented me in my youth.

Allen: Years after leaving the Marines, with the help of the Internet and social networking, I reconnected with several of my military friends. We shared memories of the Corps and the changes that had taken place in our lives since leaving. I finally came out to these friends and it turned out that many of them had other friends who were gay. They were very accepting.

Today, we are much closer to LGBTQ persons being able to serve openly in the military. (I honestly feel that the superiors in one of my units knew of my sexual orientation—and didn't care—as long as I did my job.) Soon gay soldiers will be able to share their stories with their families and friends and have their same-sex partners and gay friends see them off at deployments, and welcome them when they come home.

The old stereotypes are slowly dying off. We are doctors, homemakers, trash collectors, executives, factory workers—and, yes, some of us are hairdressers. Some gay men are effeminate and some lesbian women are butch. But none of that has any bearing on our potential.

From this Marine's perspective, it's clear that the fight for our rights will soon be won and the perception that we are somehow less than other people will fade to nothingness. We will be accepted—in spite of the actions of an increasingly smaller minority of bigoted persons who hate and bully us—for who we are.

J.D.: We want you to know that no matter what you think about yourself right now and no matter what stupid or hateful names you might be called—whether they say you're too feminine, whether they say you're too masculine—you are perfect and wonderful exactly as you are.

And we're here today to tell you that it does get better.

Allen: And it will keep getting even better.

· ·

J. D. Davis holds a PhD from the University of Georgia and currently teaches Spanish and French at a university in the South. He resigned from his position in law enforcement shortly after the inception of the It Gets Better Project in order to devote more time to writing about his experiences in law enforcement and about his battles with bigotry during his career as a cop. He is the cowinner of the 2005 Fetkann Prize for Literature for his contribution to the anthology *Hurricane: Cris d'Insulaires.*

· ·

Allen D. Stone is currently a doctor of chiropractic in the state of California. He was raised in the farming fields of southwestern Ohio and spent eight years in the United States Marine Corps. Allen left the Marine Corps due to his inability to both serve and be in a loving, intimate relationship with a man.

THE DOORS OF ACCEPTANCE

by Shaun Ridgway

SAVANNAH, GA

When I was twelve years old, I had my first crush on a girl. I had been raised in a Catholic environment and was in seventh grade at a parochial school at the time. I didn't know then what having a crush on a girl meant; I just thought I was crazy. All I wanted to know was why God had made me so terrible. Why God had made me gay; why I'd been cursed with this. So I kept it a secret.

Since I didn't actually know what to do with this information at twelve, I ignored it. When sixteen rolled around, I was the weird kid in high school—the one that's kind of chubby; the one that no one really understood. And then I met the most beautiful, wonderful girl and I fell instantly in love. Though nothing ever came of it, and I continued to date men, somehow people found out that I had a crush on a girl. Word got out, even the administration found out, and instantly, *instantly*, people were saying, "Shaun's a lesbian."

Honestly, I didn't know how to respond, what to tell them. So I told them that I couldn't change who I was. That I had a crush on a girl and someone found out, and that wasn't my fault. From that moment on, I was considered even weirder.

I wanted to die. Everything was so sad and so horrendous. Before this all exploded, I was trying to get into college; now, on top of that, I was supposed to figure out how to be gay, too. I felt overwhelmed and hopeless.

Yet the moment I walked through those high school doors for the last time, diploma in hand, it instantly, *instantly* got better. In fact, it got wonderful. I immediately fit in at college. It was like everything I had ever worked toward meant something all of a sudden. College let me be who I was meant to be. And that crush on that girl when I was sixteen grew to better and better things with someone else.

I remember one day in college I commented to no one in particular, "Oh my goodness. Look at that cute girl." I heard someone else say, "Man, she is really cute." When I looked to see who had responded, I realized it was a girl, and she had agreed with me that another girl was cute. Coming from a family where my sexuality had never been accepted and then going to a high school where we didn't talk about sex of any kind, to realize that someone else agreed with me that a girl was attractive, was beautiful. I knew right then that this was who I was. This was the acceptance I needed. I knew I was going in the right direction, and from there on out, I experienced four years of just 100 percent, pure individuality.

I discovered who I was. It didn't matter to me, or anyone else, if I liked girls, or if I liked boys, or even if I was transgendered. I learned during those four years that my attraction wasn't based on what other people thought.

Killing yourself means you won't get to go to college and say, "Man, that girl's cute." And have another girl say, "You're so right." You won't get to go dancing and enjoy being twenty. You won't get to experience all that life has to offer.

It gets better. It will always get better. And you have no shame, no fear, and no hatred after this. Because what you realize is that other people are hateful because they don't understand. And maybe they're hateful toward themselves, too. Ignore them. Accept yourself. You are so beautiful and you always will be. Love yourself, and it will always, always, always get better.

Shaun Ridgway is a twenty-two-year-old college student studying art history. She is looking forward to teaching abroad and experiencing the art of travel as much as possible.

HOPE OUT OF TRAGEDY

• •

by Matthew Anthony Houck

KALAHEO, HI

n 1998, Matthew Shepard was brutally murdered in Wyoming. His death weighed heavily on my heart. I knew that I had something in common with him.

That same year I started at Columbine High School in Littleton, Colorado. I was fourteen, and freshman year was already difficult. It is for many teenagers, but I also had a secret. My church taught that homosexuality was a sin, so I thought that some demon was growing inside of me tearing me away from God. I struggled with these thoughts, and finally confided in a friend at school about my sexuality.

That same day that I talked with this person about my deep, dark secret, my best friend, Dan Rohrbough, was killed in the shooting at my school.

On April 20, 1999, after making my "confession," another friend invited me off-campus for lunch. I *always* spent the lunch hour in the library doing homework. That way, I could keep my lunch money for a new CD and eat at home later. By the time we'd gotten our food and headed back to school, the campus was in chaos. Police cars were everywhere and we weren't allowed anywhere near the property. After being directed to a nearby neighborhood, a news broadcast interrupted the radio program to announce that there was a shooting in progress at Columbine High School. We had no idea the gravity of the situation until a few minutes later when we turned on the television at a friend's house. What we saw was indescribable.

The fact that I was out of the building during the time of the shooting was a miracle. I missed death by mere minutes. By the time our car was pulling out of the parking lot to lunch, the two killers were already on their way toward the building, guns fully loaded.

Later that day I ended up at a local elementary school where survivors were gathering. I ran into Dan's parents, who asked me if I had seen him. We had second-period science together and were lab partners so, of course, I had seen him, but not since lunch. I figured he was probably fine, that maybe he just couldn't get in touch with anyone. No one, yet, knew anything about anyone for sure. Our suburban community had erupted with kids running everywhere, parents abandoning their cars in the middle of the street in search for their children, and the police trying to get victims to safety.

I eventually made it home that evening with no new information on Dan's whereabouts. My mom, on business in Florida, was on the next plane home. My brother, a senior that year, was lucky to make it out of the school in one piece. Late that night, our family was reunited. My mom walked into the house and hugged me and my brother so tight, afraid if she let us go, her sons would disappear forever. She held us for what seemed like days and just cried.

The next morning my dad arrived with the newspaper in hand. I opened it, and right there on the second page, large and in color, was a photograph of Dan's lifeless body lying on the ground outside the cafeteria. I ran upstairs to my room, crying so hard that it hurt. I immediately opened up my middle school yearbook. I needed to see a picture of his smiling face, instead of what I had just seen in the paper.

Dan was one of twelve students and one teacher who were murdered that day. It was the largest school shooting in history. I went into shock. When the day had started, I was as a frightened teenager in fear of my own sexuality, and hours later I was a survivor of a shocking massacre that took my best friend's life away. Coming out had gone to the back of my mind. I was now in mourning.

Even before Columbine, I remember being scared and in the closet and not knowing if life was worth it. Coming out was the scariest thing that I could have imagined. I remember thinking it was the end of the world. And then, after the shooting, my perspective changed. I suddenly realized how vulnerable we all were. All my fourteen-year-old concerns about adolescence, awkward puberty, and popularity meant little in the scheme of things.

Columbine made me grow up fast. It taught me not to take for granted my relationships, and to forget petty arguments and disagreements and move on. It taught me that if I said good-bye to someone, I couldn't assume I would see them again. It taught me that life was precious and could all be over in the blink of an eye!

In the days that followed, I had to go back to school. I had to return to class and try to live a normal life in the same building where it had all taken place. Every day was a struggle. Every day I walked past the spot Dan was murdered. I knew there was a plan for my life, I just didn't know what that was, and I was scared. I still hadn't really dealt with my feelings of my sexuality and I hadn't talked again to that friend I had confided in.

By senior year, I was a peer counselor and learned a lot of ways to be there for other students going through hard times. I took these lessons to heart and was slowly learning to love myself for who I was. I don't know where it came from or how, but this courage started growing inside me. I had planned to wait for college to come out. That way I could gain new experiences, meet new friends, and hopefully have a new life free of that fear.

In the end, I couldn't wait. I had to talk to somebody quick. I chose a friend named Julie who had already graduated. She wasn't in my direct circle of friend and didn't go to my church. Most importantly, I trusted her. She was so accepting, encouraging, loving, and nonjudgmental. She told me that she loved me no matter what. Her continuing support has given me the courage to open up to my family and other friends throughout the years. I have been so lucky to have the most amazing and supportive parents and brother.

My initial coming out happened over the course of a weekend, though, and before I knew it, the entire school knew. But with the love of my family and newly found love for myself, nothing kept me down. I was teased and called names at school and harassed in the locker room, but I didn't let it get to me. I no longer wanted to hate myself for something that I couldn't control. I either ignored the comments or took action. If I was offended, I would go to authority figures, tell them about the bullying, and an administrator would contact that student and call them into their office to explain the school's "zero tolerance" policy to them. Since I was a peer counselor, I got plenty of support from some staff members and several classmates.

I decided action felt better than inaction so I created a Gay-Straight Alliance at Columbine. It was a little difficult to get the alliance going, especially since there weren't many out students. The posters we put up in the halls were torn to shreds during passing periods but we just taped them back together and hung them back up until they were unsalvageable, and then we made new ones. The GSA didn't really get up and running during my time there. Yet, in that short time, there were accomplishments. We were able to expose our school, students, and staff alike to the idea of tolerance. We created posters that defined words like "hate crimes," "flaming," and "tolerance" for readers. And our biggest achievement: a very successful Day of Silence. On this day students remain silent to honor victims of hate crimes.

At college, I started working through a speaker's bureau, volunteering my time in different classes on campus, or at high schools in the area, to speak about LGBTQ experience. I'd tell my story and talk about coming out and my life since, as well as educating people on tolerance. I eventually changed my major to communication, drafting an independent study from my speaking experiences. I surveyed students before and after my speaking engagements to see if I changed attitudes. If I found even one person who thought differently, or opened their minds up just a little to see what it's like to struggle as a gay person in a straight world, than it was all worth it.

Coming out when I did was the best decision I have ever made. I was able to make an impact at my school and hopefully leave a valuable legacy. I never could have imagined myself where I am today. I live in beautiful Hawaii with my beautiful man. It does get better and we need you to fight this battle for equality with us. High school and the closet are scary places. It seems like the whole world when you are in it, but there is so much opportunity out there. There is a light at the end of the tunnel and people who care about you. We need you to stick around. This life is amazing and I promise you that it is worth it!

Matthew Anthony Houck was born and raised in Littleton, Colorado. He graduated from Columbine High School and from the University of Colorado at Denver with a bachelor's degree in communication. Matt moved to the island of Kauai, Hawaii, with longtime boyfriend, Kevin, early in 2007 and currently resides in the small town of Kalaheo. He is an activist for equal rights and has volunteered at Rainbow Alley for LGBTQ youth in Denver and speaks throughout the state on tolerance and LGBTQ experiences.

PATIENCE MAKES PERFECT . . . SENSE

by Angelo D'Agostino

BROOKLYN, NY

"Be patient and tough; someday this pain will be useful to you."

—OVID

I like to use these words from the Roman poet, Ovid, as a kind of mantra to help me when things are hard. They remind me that no matter what I am going through, someone else has gone through the same thing, or worse. Because one thing I know for sure, if I know anything at all, is that there is nothing that you are feeling, there's no experience that you are having, that someone, somewhere in the world, hasn't had before. You might be thinking, "Terrific, how does that help me now?" Well, think of it this way: There's great comfort and security in knowing that you have an army of people behind you saying, "You know what? I felt that way. Somebody called me that name. Somebody made me feel bad. And I got through it."

There's nothing that you're fearing, or facing, or enduring, that someone, somewhere hasn't feared, or faced, or endured before. There's great comfort and security in knowing that there is an entire community out there waiting for you and welcoming you if you can just push through and persevere.

The technology that enabled this project to reach millions of people via YouTube is amazing. As a creative, I believe in the power of research and, more importantly, the power of educating oneself. I have had the great fortune through my research (working as both an actor and musician) to dive deeply into our community's history. From the riots at Stonewall, to lesbian jazz hero Frances Faye, or the fabled green carnation, our stories of survival are just a click away!

It allows each of us to reach outside of ourselves into someone's living room, into someone else's city, and it also allows you to reach out to resources that may not be available to you where you live. Maybe the town you live in doesn't have any LGBT resources—a library, a center, a drop-in shelter. Maybe you're in a place where you don't feel secure enough to talk to other people. But you can talk to people online, through the It Gets Better Project. You can get in touch with people at the Trevor Project, PFLAG, and GLAAD. You have an entire history, a rich history built brick-by-brick by people who felt just like you do today. And they survived it, and you can, too.

It gets better. It gets really good. In fact, it gets so much better that you might forget how bad it was. That's how good it gets.

•••

Angelo D'Agostino is a singer/songwriter living in New York City.

CHRISTIAN LGBT KIDS: YOU'RE PART OF THE PLAN

· ·

by Raven Mardirosian

CHESTER, VT

I am walking proof that you can make it through this struggle and that life can be good. I grew up in a very strict Christian family. And by my own choosing, I went to Christian schools from seventh grade through college. When I was a sophomore in college, I fell passionately in love with a woman. Not the greatest place to be in love with someone of the same gender, and we were found out. Our relationship was discovered three weeks before graduation and I was nearly kicked out. They ostracized us. It was devastating.

I was so ashamed of being gay that I went though "reparative therapy." In other words, I tried to make myself straight. Needless to say, that was a failed experiment, but I went so far as to have what is called a "deliverance session." That's Christian terminology for an exorcism. I tried to cast out the demon of homosexuality. I was just so afraid of going to hell, and so afraid of displeasing God, that I did whatever I could to be straight. It didn't work. It took me ten more years to really become comfortable in my skin and to really understand that being gay is a gift. It's part of the wondrous diversity of this planet.

I believe we're here to help people expand past their own limitations of what they think life should be like or look like. We can be here. We have always been here, and we will always be here. No one can take away our freedom. That's the freedom of the spirit—the freedom that says we can live life any way we choose.

Don't spend a lot of time trying to convince people that it's okay to be gay. If they believe that you're going to hell, that's their choice. It's better to just follow your truth and follow your bliss. Because life can be whatever you want it to be. If you feel trapped, know that when you turn eighteen you can leave. And you can be anyone you want and go anywhere you want.

It may take time for you to be comfortable being gay. That's okay; life is long. Spend time exploring what it means to be gay. Talk to people who are supportive and find your family, find your community. It took me a long time. When I was your age, I didn't have the support and the community that you have on the Internet now. Today it's possible for people like me, who you have never met, to let you know you have our support.

I used to be a teacher in Manhattan, and I knew which of my students was gay or bisexual. And though we didn't talk about it, my classroom was a safe space for them. They knew that. So keep in mind that there are teachers who support you. They may not say anything but they have your back, just like I had my students' back. Know that you're not alone. And know that you are so courageous and strong to go through this. Life will change for the better. It does get better. I guarantee it.

....

Raven Mardirosian of Shivaya Wellness is a self-taught healer who believes that everyone is blessed with the gift of intuition. Her passion is empowering women and her specialty is "healing the healer." Raven hosted the popular radio show *Tarot Talk* in 2009. She holds an MA in English from CUNY and is a published writer, teacher, and artist. She lives in southern Vermont and happily offers sessions to U.S. and international clients, LGBT-family welcome.

TERRIBLE DAY

· ·

by Patrick Murphy

BROOKLYN, NY

I t was one of those terrible days, shitty thing on top of shitty thing, a dreary Monday this past fall—cold and nasty like my mood. Over the weekend, I was rejected for an apartment I wanted and a guy I was dating told me, "I'm getting a friend vibe rather than a dating vibe," and then promptly disappeared. When I got to my desk that morning, two of my projects were completely screwed up. I fixed what I could and prepared for a day of hiding in my cubicle and grumbling into my coffee.

I went out at lunchtime, hoping to shake off my crappy mood. Not feeling much better despite the break, I headed back to my office for more cubicle hiding and coffee grumbling. I was about to get on the subway at Christopher Street when a guy intentionally walked into me, knocking me into a store window. Speeding around him, I started down the subway steps. "Hey!" he yelled after me. Leaning down to pick up a very old pair of glasses, "They're cracked," he said angrily. Instinct told me that he was messing with me, and I had heard of a con like this before. "Yeah, because you knocked into me on purpose and dropped a pair of cracked glasses. I'm not giving you any money," I responded. "Fuck you, faggot!" he yelled. "I'm not giving you anything," I repeated as I hurried down the steps to the platform.

When I got back to my desk, I had a huge grin on my face that I couldn't wipe off. I felt great. I realized that being called a faggot can't hurt me anymore. I said to myself, "Fuck that guy. Why would I care what a con man bigot thinks? He only called me a slur for what I'm proud to be." That would *not* have been my reaction if the run-in had happened a few years ago. A depressive spiral would have been a much more likely outcome.

I wasn't bullied a lot in school. I was taller than almost everyone my class and I guess it's hard for bullies to look down on someone they have to stare up at. I was still called gay and fag. Like at all American high schools, any guy who's quiet, nonathletic, or awkward is called gay, but I kept my head down and learned to conform. My need to feel "normal" was so intense that I was in the closet even to myself. Fear sent me into complete denial. I couldn't even think about my sexuality long enough to question it.

I was my bully. *I* was the tormenter trying to ruin my life. I almost succeeded, too. I isolated myself from my friends and family, gained excessive weight, and nearly failed out of college. I felt like something was broken in me; I hated myself completely. The bullies may have left me alone, but I continued to torture myself. At my lowest, I felt like I wasn't even human, just a thing.

Just saying "I'm gay," out loud once, I felt like every muscle in my body unclenched. The relief of finally accepting what I had been running from was like nothing I'd ever felt. Still, I was terrified. I thought people were going to cut me off completely. I thought they'd be furious at me for lying to them. I thought coming out would ruin every relationship in my life, but the exact opposite happened.

I told my family and all my friends that same week. I think I needed to tell people right away so I couldn't try to take it back. Initially my parents worried that being gay would only add to my depression. They couldn't understand that coming out was going to let me fix it. They joined PFLAG and it really helped them. Today I'm close to them in a way I hadn't been since middle school. A few months ago, my dad, a man I worried would hate me like I had hated myself, became a PFLAG chapter president. My sister has been there for me from day one, becoming one of my best friends. And I'm closer to all of my friends. More than one has told me that they feel like only now do they know the real me.

It's been three years since I came out and my life is completely different. I'm completely different. I moved to New York City. I have a great job and get to work with some of my best friends. And I lost over eighty pounds, which feels minor compared to the weight I've taken off of my soul. I've made great friends: gay, straight, and otherwise. I've been in love and had my heart broken. I've listened to more dance remixes then I would wish upon anyone. I've grown up, caught up, and started my life. All of that is amazing but the best of it is so small. It's the feeling that I can "just be." That who I am is right. It didn't matter that the reasons why accepting I am gay was so difficult. Once I stopped trying to destroy that part of myself, I started finding the better version of the man I'm supposed to be. And I like that guy.

So a stranger on the street called me a faggot and it made me feel better. The fact that it happened across the street from Stonewall Inn (the place where the modern gay rights movement started) somehow made it funnier. I'm so much happier now; hate like that can't get to me anymore. It really and truly does get better.

Patrick Murphy grew up in central New Jersey. It took him twenty-five years to escape to New York City. He lives in Brooklyn and works in children's publishing. This is his first time being published.

THE WORST OF BOTH WORLDS

by Michelle Faid

KEENE, NH

High school sucked. And being a bisexual kid in high school really, really sucked. Not only was I hitting on girls but I was also competing with them for the same boys. So I was pretty much the most hated girl in my school for both causing their homophobia and at the same time adding to their insecurity. It was the worst of both worlds.

The worst part of high school for me was my senior prom, and the aftermath. I brought a girl as my date and that turned out to be a bit of a problem. I'd bought my tickets the week before from the prom committee, at the little table they'd set up in the cafeteria to purchase them and sign up. They had put out a note pad where you could write down the name of your date and get your tickets. So I put down the gender-ambiguous version of my date's name and then on prom night showed up with a girl in a tux. Honestly, she was probably the best date I have ever had in my life. She took me out to dinner, and we had a nice little sports car and everything. It was really great and she was really awesome but I don't think I was ready for the backlash. I don't think I was quite prepared for how much I was going to suffer for that night.

I really wish that I could say I learned something from that experience that would help you, but the best thing I learned was to keep my head down. I don't want you to have to do that. Maybe you're stronger than I am and maybe you're braver than I am. Maybe you can take them on the way that I couldn't.

After my senior prom, life was hell. I would come in every day and find the typical sort of bullying stuff written on my locker. Not queer, or lesbo, or that kind of thing, because I insisted I wasn't gay. Not that I thought that being gay was wrong, it's just I didn't like being labeled something I wasn't. Instead, I told them that I was bi. Apparently "bi" means whore or slut in seventeen-year-old-girl lingo.

In the end, the thing I came to realize is that high school isn't good for anybody. It was a miserable place for me and it was a miserable place for most of the people tormenting me. It was full of a lot of pain and a lot of ruined expectations. It was a place where a lot of them realized all the things that they wanted to do but couldn't. And more often than not, they were more influenced by what their parents thought they should think than they were by what they thought they should think.

I really wish that I could tell you that it was easy to turn the other cheek, but it wasn't. I got in my fair share of fights. The best thing I can offer is that it does go away. My life has changed quite a bit since I moved on from high school. I am in a better place—in a world where what you do and who you are and what happened in high school just doesn't matter all that much. High school is this weird microcosm where people care about how expensive your shoes are and who you're dating and if you're gay or straight or bi. I found that once I got out of school most people were more worried about whether I could make deadlines, or type fast enough, or knew how to use Photoshop.

So it does get better. People stop caring so much and that's really the best we can ask for in some ways. They say that the real homosexual agenda amounts to us wanting to be left alone and having a normal life. Nefarious, isn't it? The thing is, once you get out of that place—that heinously, socially incestuous place where everybody knows everybody, and everybody has secrets that they're all telling each other behind their backs—once you get out of there, it just really doesn't matter anymore.

Michelle Faid is a twenty-nine-year-old bisexual woman living in New Hampshire. She has two cats, a love of knitting and crafts, and a fondness for blogging, which led her to the It Gets Better Project. An avid creator, she is active in singing, medieval reenactment, and runs an Etsy store. She runs Cooter Space, a blog for awareness on many issues, particularly gay rights and feminist perspectives: www.cooterspace.blogspot.com.

CLOSETS ON FIRE

● ●

by Anthony Antoine

ATLANTA, GA

M y everyday prayer when I was six years old—because I had
already been taught the power of God, and taught the power
of church, and taught the power of prayer—was "God, take
this away from me or take me away." I didn't know then to call it "homosexual" or "gay." I didn't have those words at six years old. I just knew
that I was different, and that I wasn't like other boys. I had all of these
feelings and I had already learned that it was not going to be an easy
road ahead for me. So I got down on my knees and I prayed, "God, take
this away or take me away."

I didn't know then that it was going to get better.

But today, when I think about the best evidence in my life of it getting better, I think about recording my first full-length CD five years
ago. I'm a musician. I love music. Music is my passion and I wanted the
freedom to be able to record the truth about what I was living.

Now, my first few CDs were about the girls this and hip-hop that,
I was putting on a front. But I was in love with Chanté Moore's song,
"Chanté's Got a Man," and I thought, okay, well what if I had the free-
dom to sing about having a man, too? So I recorded "Dante's Got a Man
Too," and soon after that, in 2005, I recorded my first full-length CD,

Closets on Fire. I wanted to depict my real life, to tell the truth about who I am, what I have learned, and who I have grown into. I wanted to record the truth about it getting better, all up in song that you could hear over and over and dance to and sing to and fall in love to. That's the best evidence I can offer from my life that it gets better.

In my dedication for *Closets on Fire*, there's a picture of my four-year-old brother, Eric, and my five-year-old self, standing in the fiercest, queerest, gayest pose. And next to that photo, I wrote:

> "To my brother and me at age four and five, if I could go back and visit these boys in ghetto Newark, I would tell them both to always embrace your specialness and that you're both beautiful little black boys worthy of unconditional love."

'Cause at age four and five I didn't know that, I didn't know that I was even worthy of that. And I didn't know that there was a pathway to understanding that even in your specialness you are still worthy of unconditional love. The dedication continues:

> "I would whisper in my ear, 'there will be brighter days after your struggle with your sexuality and as fierce as your pose is right now, so you will be.' For us at four and five, and for other kids needing examples of gay and okay, I offer you *Closets on Fire*."

Today, when people ask me if I'm gay, often times I'll tell them no. "No. I'm gay gay. I'm double gay. I'm gay to the tenth power. I'm all of that *and* gay." I'll walk in it. I'll walk in the truth and that's okay. I've learned to live a life of freedom and I've found happiness. I'm no longer that six-year-old boy praying to be different, praying to die. It gets better, baby. It gets better.

....

Independent recording artist and activist **Anthony Antoine** is originally from Newark, New Jersey, and has been in the Atlanta area since 1998. Currently he is prevention and testing program director for ARCA (AIDS Research Consortium of Atlanta) and has been coordinating HIV/STI prevention efforts for the Atlanta area for eleven years. You can visit Anthony Antoine online at www .anthonyantoine.com.

THE KING BROTHERS

by Dick and Mark S. King

SHREVEPORT, LA, AND FORT LAUDERDALE, FL

Mark: Hi. I'm Mark King and I am a gay man. My brother's name is Dick. And he's gay, too. Yes, I have a gay brother and his name is *Dick King*.

Dick: Trust me, I've heard them all.

Mark: What do you like to say in bars?

Dick: "Oh, you like my first name? Wait until you hear my last name."

Mark: But this is a family show, so we're going to move on. This is for young gay guys out there who are wondering if life gets better.

Dick: It does. It gets better.

Mark: It gets a lot better. And it gets better for a long time; my brother can tell you that. Dick's been gay for a *really* long time. There's a big age difference between us, almost twenty years, and he grew up in a different time than I did.

Dick: Almost a different generation.

Mark: I came out in high school and everybody knew in my high school—in Shreveport, Louisiana. Not a big town—and everybody knew. It was hard. When I was in sixth grade, before I even came out, I was called a "sissy" and I was bullied a lot. I remember getting kicked on the playground by this one guy, who shall remain nameless. He wore cowboy boots and he would kick me in the shins so hard that blood would run down my leg. I would have blood in my socks. I remember coming home after school and taking my socks off and throwing them away because I didn't want my mother to see the blood. I didn't want her to know.

Dick: Because then you'd have to explain.

Mark: I would have to explain that I was getting kicked on the playground for being a big sissy. And I was ashamed. I was ashamed of myself then.

Dick: Not to mention the fact that your older brother was a star football player.

Mark: We have another brother who is a year older than me and he was the big jock on campus. I was drum major of the band.

Dick: And in the drama club.

Mark: Yes, I was in the drama club.

Dick: So there you go.

Mark: So there you go. Now, Dick, on the other hand, did not come out when he was a kid.

Dick: No, but like Mark, I always knew that I was gay. Growing up I always knew that I was who I was. It wasn't like it changed at some point when I became pubescent. I just always knew. And I grew up in a different place than Mark. I grew up on an air force base.

Mark: Actually, Dick grew up in fantasyland. By age ten, he wanted to be Liberace. Now, for you youngsters reading this, Liberace was a big, big queen. And basically my brother was Liberace by the age of ten.

Dick: I pantomimed Liberace all the time.

Mark: As you can see, there are various levels of talent in our family. And that's okay. And it's also okay that he didn't come out until he was in his mid-twenties. It doesn't matter when you come out or how you do it. Sometimes you don't feel safe coming out until you're a little older. Sometimes it just happens and you can't help it.

Dick: Sometimes it depends on where you are. When I came out I was in New York, so I was in a place where I felt a lot safer.

Mark: And I was in Shreveport, Louisiana. I felt like the town needed a little gaying up. So that's what I did. But it doesn't matter when you do it or how you do it, but when you finally do, it gets better.

Dick: It gets better.

Mark: It gets a lot better.

Dick and **Mark S. King** were raised in a family of six children (two boys, two girls, two gays). Dick, the elder, is haunted by memories of babysitting and diaper duty for Mark. Today Dick is a custom picture-framer and performs in community theater. Mark is a long-time HIV/AIDS activist and writer, best known for his popular blog, myfabulousdisease.com.

COMMUNITY FOUND

· ·

by Taylor Bailey

DALLAS, TX

I had a pretty terrible time in middle school. A lot of bad things happened. I was one of only nine boys in my class. I went to an incredibly small school, in an incredibly small town in Texas, so you can only imagine how accepting these people were. Even though I didn't play football, I was lumped into athletics class with all the jocks. A lot of really terrible things happened in that locker room.

The other boys were ruthless in their torments. At first, it was simply name calling and group mockery. This evolved into physical bullying and harassment. They would touch me and press their bodies up against me while we were changing, and then run around claiming that I had been aroused by their actions. At one point, I attempted to hide in a separate bathroom to change before athletics and they actually hunted me down, barged in, and harassed me there. One Monday, when I was changing for athletics, I put on my gym clothes and was suddenly in an incredible amount of pain. Apparently, a lot of sweet food had been thrown into the bottom of my locker in a locker room with a terrible ant problem. Before I knew it, I was covered in ants. They were on my chest, my arms, my hair, my face. I was standing in the middle of the room screaming, being bitten all over, and everyone was just laughing. Nobody would help me. I kept turning around begging for help and nobody would help me. Even the guys who weren't usually mean were too afraid of the bullies to do anything. I was told later that the food was stashed there with the hopes of this exact thing occurring. The worst part? Nothing was done about it. The coaches turned a blind eye toward it, and I was too afraid to tell anyone it had been intentional.

I hit my lowest point in seventh grade. I was lying a lot to my family then. I would make up stories about interactions I had so they thought I had friends and I was happy, when really I was spending a lot of time alone. Or if I wanted them to think I was spending time with friends, I would hide somewhere and then come home and say, "Oh, I was just with friends." I very strongly considered taking my own life during that time. I was only in the seventh grade! It amazes me to even think about that now. I write these words and I think, "No. Surely not." But it's true. I was so miserable.

The thing that really saved me was my sister—my little sister. She was only about two or three at the time and I loved her so much. She was my biggest fan. And she's who I would think about when I thought about killing myself. I realized I couldn't do that to her. Thank God, because I couldn't have seen then where I would end up now. If I could have, I would have understood that I just needed to get through these few years because much better things were waiting for me. I would have realized that I was going to do much better things than these assholes who are making my life so miserable.

I think that's the key. You have to start thinking, "These guys, they're just miserable people. They're making my life miserable but they're not going to amount to anything. Whereas I can. And I will."

And I did.

It was a rough path. But I am happy to say that I am twenty-three years old and I am a very happy gay man. I've had several really loving relationships with other men, and my family's very accepting of me. At first they were a little uncomfortable with it but now my mom and I actually joke around about it. She'll make gay jokes, and my nanny's the same way. She actually watched the YouTube videos and told me how amazing she thought it was. My mother now always says, "When I hear people talking about their views on homosexuality, I just want to say 'Well you have clearly never loved anyone who was gay.'" My sister, Jordan, is a teacher who advocates strongly against bullying in schools, especially where it pertains to LGBT youth. My father, who died in 2005 at his own hand, was also a gay man who had struggled his entire life with his sexuality. Though he never fully recovered from the traumas of his life, he gave me the strength and courage he didn't always have to make it through mine. Strength and courage I needed to survive losing him to the battle against the horrific tenets of the ignorant. I wouldn't be here without him.

If I could make any suggestion, it would be to involve yourself in something like theater or art or music, or one of these areas where people are more accepting and open-minded. I mean, you don't really find a lot of bigots doing theater. That's what ended up saving me. I transferred to a large high school where my being gay wasn't a big deal. I'd say, "Well, uh, I'm gay." And my classmates' response would generally be, "Oh, yeah . . . we know, dude."

I thrived doing theater. I was able to take the terrible experiences I had in my youth and turn them into an explosive fuel behind my work as a performer. I was surrounded by passionate, artistic, and intelligent friends who would have torn apart anyone who dared hurt me. This community of love thrust me forward into studying performance at a top-ranked school for theater where I earned my degree alongside some of the most talented people in the country.

So find something. Find a group, an organization, or just friends who are like you. Whether it's your family or your day-to-day life, just know that it gets so much better. You will be happy and you will be well-adjusted and you will have the life that you want.

Taylor Bailey holds a bachelor of fine arts in theater performance from the University of Evansville in Indiana and is now a professional director and actor working in Dallas. In addition to his career in the theater, and inspired by the events of his childhood, the life of his father and the It Gets Better Project, he plans to attend graduate school in the fall to obtain his master's degree in social work so he can become a licensed clinical therapist, working with LGBT youth and their families.

FROM SCARED TO PROUD: THE JOURNEY OF A GAY MEDICAL STUDENT

by Jake Kleinman

NEW ORLEANS, LA

'm proud to say that I'm about to graduate from medical school and enter my residency as a physician, but just a few years ago I was in a much darker place.

I'd been a jock growing up and had few interactions with gay people, but during college I began experimenting with my sexual orientation. I didn't know if friends and family would support me. I envisioned losing all of my friends and missing out on opportunities that I deserved because of my sexual orientation. I was worried about hanging out and meeting girls, fearing they'd read my interest in them as romantic. And I was scared to tell my guy friends. The last thing I wanted them to think then was that I was gay.

I also knew I wanted to be a doctor and worried that being gay would make it hard for me to be accepted at the southern medical school I had chosen. I was also concerned it might be a problem in the medical profession I later hoped to enter. I wanted to live my life as an open gay man but was afraid it would end my medical career before it even started.

When I finally did come out to my closest friends, near the end of my senior year of college, my heart dropped when they laughed in my face. I demanded they tell me why they were laughing at such a "serious" issue. They responded, "Jake, we're laughing because the way you told us, we thought you had terminal cancer. Your being gay is just funny compared to that."

Shortly after starting med school, I realized that I was just as guilty of being ignorant about the south as I assumed people were about me being gay. Not only was I accepted at my new school for being gay, I was asked by the dean's office to help welcome the new students each year. They wanted someone who could explain that being gay or being different was actually applauded here and, importantly, that we can use our experiences as gay people to educate and relate to our patients in the future. Standing up in front of a roomful of new medical students was daunting but I have rarely received so much positive feedback in my life.

In my four years here, I've developed a great network of friends, and a number of the best people I've met have been gay. They are some of the most talented, successful, and supportive people I know. We've all had to find ourselves in the realest sense of the word, and that experience has created a solid community here. This hit home to me about two years ago when I was eating dinner with my boyfriend at one of our favorite restaurants. This guy, Mark, came over to our table from the group of about twenty guys he was sitting with. He introduced himself and told us that every Wednesday is Friends and Family night at the restaurant. He invited us to join his "family" next week. We've been going almost every week since then and Mark remains one of our closest friends. Far from my fears in high school, being openly gay has only added to my life thus far.

If you are feeling in a dark place right now, I want you to know I understand. You have to believe in yourself—believe in your potential—and realize it will get better and there are people out there who care about you. Look to friends and family who are supportive, or to organizations like the Trevor Project, working to make this place better for you and me.

Jake Kleinman was born in Westchester, New York, and went to college at Colgate University, where he majored in Spanish literature and pre-medical studies. He is currently finishing up medical school at Tulane University in New Orleans and will be starting a residency in pediatrics in the summer. He lives with his partner of two years, who is also a physician, and the two of them hope to start a family.

AUTHENTIC SELF

· ·

by Sara Sperling

SAN JOSE, CA

was the typical straight girl. I had the boyfriend. I was president of my high school. I played sports. I was in a sorority in college. But I knew I was different. There was something huge missing from my world. I wanted that "butterfly-in-my-stomach" feeling when you like someone and they like you back.

Even though I had friends who were gay, and people who were open around me, I still thought I was the only one going through exactly what I was going through. I thought I was going to lose my friends and my family. I thought nobody from high school would like me again, and later I worried that I'd get kicked out of my sorority.

I decided that I couldn't keep the secret any longer. I told my parents. My closest friends and I even stood in front of my sorority (140 members strong) and told them I was gay. At this point I wasn't concerned anymore if I was going to lose anyone's friendship, I just didn't want to lose me. To my utter surprise those closest to me already knew and didn't show any disappointment when I finally told them. Maybe it was because I wore 501 jeans and listened to the Indigo Girls. My friendships were different going forward. I was able to show my true self to others. There were a handful of my sorority sisters that I didn't hear from after that but I was totally okay with it. I can only hope that their reaction will be different today, especially if their own child comes out to them.

So if you're a parent reading this, talk to your kid. Just love them. Just tell them every day that you love them; that's why I was able to come out. I knew my parents might have been disappointed, which they were at first, but they *loved* me.

When I was in high school I dreamed of having a family but I never thought it was possible. I met my partner ten years ago at San Francisco Pride. We now have a dog, a mortgage, and a little baby girl.

I need you young people, those of you in junior high and high school, I need you to stay around. I need you to make this world a better place for my daughter. I don't want her to ever, ever think twice about telling people that she has two moms. So if you're out there and you're struggling, I need you to stay around. I need your help. I need you to be your authentic self and make this world better for my little girl.

Sara Sperling works for Facebook in Palo Alto, California. She lives in the Bay Area with her wife, her big ole Rotti, and her little princess. Her story of coming out to her sorority can be found in the book *Secret Sisters: Stories of Being Lesbian and Bisexual in a College Sorority.*

YOU CAN LIVE A LIFE THAT'S WORTH LIVING

•••

by Kate Bornstein

NEW YORK, NY

I don't always think it is going to get better. Sometimes it gets worse, a whole lot worse than I ever thought it could. And on those days I don't think it's going to get better. So I had to wait to write this 'til I thought it would. And this is a day I think it's going to get better. It took me about a week to get to this day. So what do you know, it got better! Here's the deal. I'm sixty-two years old. I've led a freaky, geeky life. I've messed around with sex and gender. I've done a lot of things in the world that make people laugh at me, make people want to hurt me, to the point where I've wanted to kill myself. I can remember six times in my life that I've planned it all out, ready to kill myself. Fuck it. Why go on? It's not going to get better. And each time, I managed to find something else to do instead. I've found lots of reasons to go on living, lots of ways to make life more worth living. And that's all I'm asking you to do.

I wrote a whole book about it. It's called *Hello, Cruel World: 101 Alternatives to Suicide for Teens, Freaks, and Other Outlaws.* There are a hundred and one things in there that are better than killing yourself. Some of them are illegal and immoral, unethical and self-destructive. They're all in the book. You don't have to buy the book or buy it for laughs when you've got some extra cash. Great. Help me pay the rent but that's not the deal.

The deal is this. Here's all you need to remember to know that life gets better: You can do whatever it takes to make your life more worth living. Really. You can do anything it takes to make your life more worth living. Anything, baby. There's only one rule you need to follow in order to make that kind of blanket permission work. Only one rule in the whole frickin' book. *Don't be mean.* As long as you're not mean, you can do whatever you want that makes your life more worth living. Now, if you do the illegal stuff and you get caught, I can't help you. That's the justice system. It's a risk. Sometimes all that I can think of to make my life more worth living is the illegal stuff. And if I get caught, you couldn't help me, either.

But if that's what you have to do, if you think that's what it takes to make your life more worth living, do it. Take the risk. Just don't be mean.

Now, the trouble with this kind of permission, this kind of, "Oh, I can do whatever it takes," is that it can get you in trouble with God, especially the sex and gender stuff. That can get you in big trouble with most anybodies God you can think of. You can get sent to hell. Well, I can't get you out of jail.

But I can get you out of hell.

Go to my blog and download a copy of my Get Out of Hell Free card. You can print it out and give it to your friends. You don't even need the card. Here, I'm going to give you one from my heart—this is a Get Out of Hell Free card coming at ya. Take it if you want to. Put it in your heart.

So if what it takes to make your life more worth living—and you weren't mean—gets you sent to hell, take the card out of your heart and give it to Satan. I'll do your time for you. Yeah, ain't that a deal? It's a deal I made with the devil. Satan and I agreed on that one. So, you get to do whatever it takes to make your life more worth living. Anything, baby. Anything at all.

And that's how you can make your life get better. That's how you can look back on life and say, "You know, it did get better."

I love you. I love you for the courage it takes to explore this stuff.

Kiss kiss, my darling.

Kate Bornstein is an author, playwright, and performance artist whose work to date has been in service to sex positivity, gender anarchy, and to building a coalition of those who live on cultural margins. Her work recently earned her an award from the Stonewall Democrats of New York City and two citations from New York city council members. Kate's latest book, *Hello, Cruel World: 101 Alternatives to Suicide for Teens, Freaks, and Other Outlaws*, was published in 2007. According to daily e-mail and Twitter, the book is still helping people stay alive. Other published works include the books *Gender Outlaw: On Men, Women, and the Rest of Us* and *My Gender Workbook*. Kate's books are taught in more than 150 colleges around the world. Her memoir, *Queer and Pleasant Danger*, is due out in 2012.

EPILOGUE

. . . .

My mother made me come out to her.

"I understand if you're gay," she said to me one day. I was twenty-one, and I had known I was gay since I was thirteen, but I was afraid to come out to my conservative Christian parents. When I told her, yes, I was gay, she said, "It doesn't change anything. I still love you."

Then she added: "But don't tell your father."

My father was dying of cancer and my mother didn't want to worry him. I didn't want to upset my father either, or my mother, so I never came out to him. But he would sometimes say things that led me to believe he knew. Once, after he got sick, I drove from Seattle to Spokane in a car I borrowed from my "friend," actually my boyfriend, to visit my dad.

"What kind of car is it?" my dad asked. "A pink Cadillac?"

Dad laughed, kindly, and gave me a paternal wink.

I believe he was trying to tell me, in his own gentle way, that *I* was okay, that *it* was okay, that *we* were okay.

If the It Gets Better Project had existed back when I was a teenager, if there were thousands of online messages of hope for bullied LGBT kids back when I was being brutally harassed in my high school, I like to think my dad would've let me know about the videos. He wouldn't have said anything directly; that wasn't his way. I imagine my dad would have mentioned the videos over dinner.

"Did you hear that the President made one of those 'It Gets Better' YouTubing video things for gay kids getting bullied at school?" he would've said . . . to my mother, but while I was sitting there at the table, listening.

Wink.

And if I'd gone to the It Gets Better website when I was in high school, or read this book, and found these messages of hope and all this good advice from all different kinds of people—gay, lesbian, bi, trans, straight, rural, urban, famous, unknown, *even the freaking President*—it would've made a huge difference for me.

And not just for me. I had one gay friend at school. We didn't know any gay or lesbian adults who could, by sharing their stories, help us see that life could get better. Both of us desperately needed to know that life after high school wasn't going to be more of the same—that the bullying wasn't going to last forever—and we needed to know that there were straight people out there who valued their gay friends and family members. If I had found my way to the It Gets Better Project, I would've made sure my gay friend found his way there, too.

Then we both would've helped spread the word.

When Dan called me from New York City in early September of last year to tell me about this idea he'd just had—to make a video, and post it on YouTube, to call it It Gets Better, to reach out to bullied LGBT kids who might be thinking about killing themselves—I told him I thought it was a great idea, and told him to do it.

There was a catch, he said: He didn't want to do it without me. He wanted us to do this together.

Dan had written a couple of books about our life together; one about our efforts to adopt our son, D.J., and one about our decision to get married, in Canada, on our tenth anniversary. My rule has always been that Dan could write whatever he wanted to about us, and say whatever he wanted to say on TV, so long as I didn't have to go on TV or do any interviews or pose for any photographs.

But I agreed to make this video. I wanted to reach out to the kids I was reading about—kids who were being bullied, sometimes to death, because they were gay or perceived to be gay—because I knew that not every LGBT kid is lucky enough to have parents as loving and supportive as mine would turn out to be.

I don't need to tell anyone reading this book what happened next. There were thousands of people out there who had the same reaction I did to Dan's idea: People wanted to help; people wanted to reach out to bullied and hurting LGBT kids with messages of hope, love, and support. People wanted to share their stories, and their joy, and their advice for getting through it and, if possible, making it better.

So what's next for the It Gets Better Project?

In a way, the messages in this book and the videos online are a little like those red ribbons for AIDS awareness that everyone was wearing to the Oscars in the 1990s. Red ribbons did an important job of raising awareness and giving comfort. But here's the crucial difference between the It Gets Better videos and red ribbons: Those ribbons are gone now, moldering away in dresser drawers and landfills, no longer doing the job they were designed to do. But these videos will continue to exist online. Fifteen-year-old kids who need to see them now can watch them now, and five-year-old kids who will need to see them in ten years will be able to watch them then.

Which is why we've created—with the help of the folks at Blue State Digital—a stand-alone website. These videos will always be archived at itgetsbetter.org. So the same videos that are today giving hope to LGBT adolescents will be giving hope to LGBT adolescents for years to come.

I want to say a few words to LGBT kids who've just finished reading this book.

Middle school and high school can be hard. Believe me, I know. When I was in school I was pushed into lockers, shoved to the floor, punched, slapped—and that was just the physical abuse. I probably don't need to tell you about all the times I was called names. When my parents went to the school to complain, the principal told them that I was bringing the harassment on myself by "acting that way."

There's so much coming at you right now: new feelings, new people, new experiences. Not all of those feelings are positive, not all of those people are kind, and not all of those experiences are pleasant. Sometimes you can feel lost and alone. I did. Kids can be cruel, parents can be hurtful, and preachers can be particularly hateful, quoting certain verses from the Bible while ignoring others. And there are still teachers and school administrators out there who ignore or excuse bullying.

But, after reading this book, you know that there are people out there who went through what you're going through. You've heard from parents who love their gay kids and religious leaders who want you to know that not all faiths reject you. You've heard from teachers and educators who are working to make schools safer and more welcoming for you and other kids who are different. And you've heard from politicians who are committed to standing up for you and your rights.

And there are thousands of more messages like these online—go to itgetsbetter.org to watch them—and there are more coming in every day. You don't have to sift through the clues like I did when my dad tried to reassure me, as best he could. The message you're receiving today is much simpler, much louder, and much clearer.

It gets better.

TERRY MILLER
SEATTLE, WASHINGTON

ACKNOWLEDGMENTS

• •

We'd like to thank all the contributors to this book first and foremost, who gave so generously of their time and talent, as well as their representatives, working long into the night; Ingrid Emerick at Girl Friday Productions for collecting these essays, hunting down releases, and gently bossing us around; Elizabeth Wales for her support, advice, and nudging; Kristen Legg for transcribing the videos; and—as ever—Brian Tart, Jessica Horvath, Susan Schwartz, Julia Gilroy, Daniel Lagin and everyone at Dutton for their patience. Christine Ball, Amanda Walker, and Carrie Swetonic in publicity for their assistance and understanding. A huge thank you to Blue State Digital for creating the It Gets Better Project's amazing website, itgetsbetter.org. Thanks to Brian Pines and Seth Levy for their organizational and legal support; Randy Phillips for his personal assistance; Joe Jervis, Andy Towle, Andrew Sullivan, and John Aravosis for their advice and moral support; Charles Robbins, Eliza Byard, and Chris Hampton and the staffs of the Trevor Project, GLSEN, and the ACLU for all they do every day; Jonathan Finney at Stonewall UK and Shin Inouye at the White House for going above and beyond the call of duty; to all the volunteers in Washington, DC, who have spent countless hours viewing and uploading videos: Scott Zumwalt, Colin Bishop, JP Brandt, Alex Levy, Christopher Nulty,

Jason Rahlan, and Trevor Thomas. And Jake Stigers and Justin Skok went out of their way to keep a flu-sickened Dan alive, hydrated, and propped up in front of his computer when the project went viral. Thanks again, guys. Thank you to the incredible Carol Chen at Google/ YouTube who made it possible to post the thousands of videos that have come in. And a very special thanks to our good friend Kelly O and our son, D.J, who is himself living proof that it gets better.

Thanks also to Tim Keck, Laurie Saito, Anthony Hecht, and everyone at *The Stranger* who pitched in during the hectic first month of the It Gets Better Project's life.

Most importantly, we want to thank everyone who has made an It Gets Better video. We wish would could thank you all by name.

Thousands of amazing and touching and heartbreaking and uplifting videos have been submitted since we started to work on this collection. We're sorry that we couldn't include more of them in this book. Please go to itgetsbetter.org to watch all the videos.

To the LGBT youth reading this: Thank you for being you, thank you for sticking around, thank you for inspiring us. We can't wait to meet you.

RESOURCES

· · · · · · · · · · · · · · · · ·

Some Curriculum Guidelines for Schools and Teachers

Schools are a primary social structure for children, and social relationships with peers are a central part of students' lives. Research shows that school, and the social interactions that take place there, can play a stabilizing or destructive role for young people, particularly if they are experiencing emotional stress. Professor Robert Blum, MD, MPH, PhD, of Johns Hopkins Bloomberg School of Public Health, noted in his monograph "Best Practices for Enhancing School Environment" that "school environment and school connectedness can be determining factors in a young person's educational experience. When students believe that adults in the school care about them, have high expectations for their education, and will provide the support essential to their success, they thrive. When teachers and staff are deeply engaged in creating a safe, nurturing, challenging school environment their job satisfaction increases. A positive school environment is a product of a collective effort."

We also know that, according to the Harris Interactive Study conducted in 2005 titled, "From Teasing to Torment: School Climate in America, A Survey of Students and Teachers," 65 percent of teens report that they have been verbally or physically harassed or assaulted during the past year because of their perceived or actual appearance, gender, sexual orientation, gender expression, race/ethnicity, disability, or religion. The most common reasons cited for being harassed frequently is a student's appearance. The next most common reason is sexual orientation. In this survey, a stunning 90 percent of LGBT students reported having been bullied in the past year, and almost a quarter of these students do not report the incident because they do not believe the school staff will do anything or be able to stop it.

The survey shows how schools need to "bridge the gap between the support that teachers say they provide to students and students' perceptions of teachers' willingness to take action." Cited are measures such as strong anti-bullying policies that prohibit harassment based on sexual orientation and gender identity; student and staff education on bullying prevention and intervention; and a deliberate effort by school administration to create a safe, nonbiased, and supportive environment for all students to reduce the risks and stresses for LGBT youth.

There are several things that teachers and administrators can do in the classroom and school to promote understanding and tolerance and to create a safe and supportive environment for LGBT students:

- Show your support of LGBT youth through modeling inclusive language and behavior. Use gender- and orientation-neutral language and examples in your lessons.
- Create a safe space for students by working with them to set norms and expectations to ensure respect. Lead a discussion where students create ground rules for themselves that are fair, inclusive, and involve respect for all.

- Work with students to create a system of accountability to remind each other when those norms are broken and how to make amends.
- Do not let phrases like "that's so gay," etc., go without immediately acknowledging it and addressing how it affects LGBT students. Glsen.org has specifics on how to respond to anti-LGBT language and behavior.
- Set aside class time every week, as little as twenty minutes, to have students participate in a group discussion or activity where trust, empathy, and acceptance are fostered. You can use activities and lessons from our diversity curriculum, Embracing Differences, which builds communication skills and understanding of how our beliefs and actions about difference can positively or negatively affect how we relate to one another.
- Include gay and lesbian leaders and writers and historical figures as examples in your teaching to create greater awareness and acceptance and establish an environment of inclusiveness.
- Be a caring and supportive adult for young people. One of the most important factors for student success now and later is the number of caring adults in their life.
- Connect with resources from community-based organizations in your neighborhood for information, training, support, and materials.

In your school:

- Assess your school's anti-discrimination policies to ensure that they include protection against harassment and discrimination based on sexual and gender orientation.
- Advocate with your principal or administrator for professional development training on school LGBT issues, including training to recognize and effectively address anti-LGBT bullying.
- Share information and encourage others staff to model LGBT support in classrooms and throughout the school to ensure student safety, emotional well-being, and academic success.

- Ensure that school events and celebrations are inclusive of LGBT students. Support students' measures to address LGBT issues such as the formation of a Gay-Straight Alliance.
- Ensure that the school library and publications include resources that cover LGBT people and issues.

The Leadership Program, a youth development organization with more than twenty years of experience working with teachers, youth, and their families in the New York City public schools in violence prevention, character education, and social-emotional learning, believes that creating time in the classroom to talk about difference and understanding is an important part of empowering teachers and students to proactively create a positive school environment that embraces difference and cultivates respect. Giving students the opportunity in a safe and supportive structure to explore their ideas of difference, how these ideas influence their actions, and how their actions affect others' feelings enables them to relate to one another with increased empathy and understanding. These sample lessons can be used in high school classes where teachers are looking for ways to foster discussion and exploration to create a classroom learning environment that supports students' self-identity, self-esteem, and mutual respect.

For more information go to www.theleadershipprogram.com.

SAVING YOUNG LIVES

The Trevor Project

Each one of us deserves a future where we can dream big and achieve big, no matter who we love or how we express our gender. The Trevor Project is here for young lesbian, gay, bisexual, transgender, queer, and questioning people to help whenever you or a friend might need to talk to someone. Through our lifesaving programs and information, we work every day to help make the future better for all LGBTQ youth.

In 1998, the Academy Award®-winning film *Trevor* appeared on HBO; in the story, thirteen-year-old Trevor attempts suicide after his crush on another boy is revealed and his "friends" reject him. The film-makers wanted to make sure that if anyone watching the film felt like Trevor, they could call an LGBTQ-friendly resource and get help. Since at the time there wasn't a suicide or crisis lifeline for LGBTQ youth, James Lecesne, Peggy Rajski, and Randy Stone founded the Trevor Project.

Now the Trevor Project operates the twenty-four-hour Trevor Lifeline as well as the TrevorChat online messaging service, both connecting young LGBTQ people to open and accepting counselors, free of charge. Plus there is trevorspace.org, where thousands of young LGBTQ people from all over the world can connect in a safe and accepting social space. Trevor is also on Facebook, Twitter, and YouTube connecting young people with positive messages every day.

If you or someone you care about feels depressed or is considering taking their own life, please call the Trevor Lifeline at: 866-4-U-TREVOR (866-488-7386). The call is free and confidential. Visit thetrevorproject.org to learn more.

GLSEN (Gay, Lesbian and Straight Education Network)

Every student deserves a safe space at school and an equal opportunity to get an education. GLSEN's work clears a path to well-being, opportunity, and achievement for any student facing anti-LGBT bias and behavior in schools.

As a national education organization that addresses LGBT issues in K–12 schools, GLSEN is primarily focused on an urgent daily reality: More than four out of five LGBT students have experienced physical, verbal, or sexual harassment at school. One in five has been assaulted on school grounds. And the vast majority never report what happens to them, because they do not believe that school officials will do anything to help. Students who face this kind of victimization do less well in school, are less likely to plan to graduate, and can suffer greatly in terms of their individual well-being and their prospects for success in life.

All of our work is designed to ensure student safety and champion students' success. Our programs include:

- Leadership development training and support to individual student leaders and more than four thousand Gay-Straight Alliances (GSAs)
- National sponsorship of the Day of Silence, a student-led day of action that has reached hundreds of thousands of students
- Federal- and state-level legislative and policy advocacy for effective measures to reduce bullying and bias in schools
- Professional development trainings on LGBT issues for thousands of teachers, administrators, and other school staff
- The Safe Space Campaign to place critical information in all one hundred thousand middle and high schools nationwide

These are just a few of the ways that GLSEN works to improve school climate on LGBT issues nationwide, and contribute to the creation of great schools that serve all of their students. To learn more about GLSEN and our work, visit www.glsen.org.

GLSEN is grateful to Dan Savage and the It Gets Better Project for selecting GLSEN as an official beneficiary.

ACLU LGBT Project

America's foremost advocate of individual rights, the American Civil Liberties Union, is a nonpartisan organization founded in 1920. With national headquarters in New York and Washington and fifty-three affiliates throughout the country, the ACLU has played a major role in nearly every critical civil liberties battle of the last century.

The ACLU has advocated on behalf of lesbian, gay, bisexual, and transgender people for more than seventy years and in 1986 founded its LGBT Project, a division of the national ACLU Foundation. Today, the ACLU does more court cases, legislative lobbying, and grassroots policy advocacy on LGBT matters than any other national civil rights organization. The ACLU also works in the media to change public attitudes and provide advocacy tools to help people take action in their own communities.

The LGBT Project's Youth & Schools program works to make public schools safe and bias-free for LGBTQ students and teachers and helps students stand up to discrimination, harassment, and censorship.

The project's website provides several resources for young people, including information on their legal rights in school and printable letters that students and parents can give to their schools about LGBTQ students' free speech rights and their right to attend school without fear of harassment, to bring same-sex dates to the prom, to have Internet access that doesn't illegally censor pro-LGBT content, to form Gay-Straight Alliance clubs, and other such issues. We promise that every young person who writes or calls the ACLU LGBT Project will get a response.

For more information on the project's work on behalf of LGBTQ youth, visit http://www.aclu.org/safeschools.

To donate to the ACLU's LGBT work, visit http://www.aclu.org/lgbtdonate.

WRITE TO US

American Civil Liberties Union Foundation LGBT Project, 125 Broad Street, 18th Floor, New York, NY 10004-2400

PHOTO AND COMIC CREDITS

FEATURED COMIC ARTISTS

Alison Bechdel wrote the comic strip *Dykes to Watch Out For* from 1983 to 2008. Her graphic memoir about her closeted-gay dad, *Fun Home: A Family Tragicomic*, was nominated for a 2006 National Book Critics Circle Award. She lives in Vermont.

Seattle cartoonist **Ellen Forney** created several Eisner-nominated comic books, including *I Love Led Zeppelin* and *Monkey Food*, and collaborated with Sherman Alexie on National Book Award–winning novel *The Absolutely True Diary of a Part-Time Indian*. She teaches comics studio and graphic novels lit at Cornish College of the Arts in Seattle, and is currently working on her first graphic novel for Gotham/Penguin Books.

PHOTO CREDITS

Taylor Bailey, photo by Annette Haynes
Kate Bornstein, photo by Maxwell Ander
Agustín Cepeda, photo by Angela Hsieh
Andy Cohen, photo courtesy of Bravo Media

PERMISSIONS

· · · · · · · · · · · · · · · · · · ·

YOUTH RESOURCE CARD

OK. You're Lesbian, Gay, Bisexual, or Transgendered—what do you do now?

IF YOU ARE IN CRISIS:
The Trevor Project (1-866-4-U-TREVOR) (thetrevorproject.org)

IF YOU ARE READY TO TALK WITH YOUR PEERS:
Youth Resource (amplifyyourvoice.org)

IF YOU WANT TO MAKE A DIFFERENCE IN YOUR SCHOOL:
GLSEN-Gay, Lesbian, and Straight Education Network
(glsen.org)

IF YOU ARE READY TO LEAD:
GSA Network—The Gay Straight Alliance Network
(gsanetwork.org)
GLSEN Student Organizing (studentorganizing.org)

REACH OUT. GET HELP. IT GETS BETTER.

PARENTS RESOURCE CARD

OK. Your child is Lesbian, Gay, Bisexual, or Transgendered—what do you do now? If you need support or have questions, it can help to talk with other parents of LGBT children about their experiences. Reach out to **PFLAG (Parents, Families, and Friends of Lesbians and Gays)**. You can find the chapter nearest you at **pflag.org**.

YOU ALSO HAVE A CONFIDENTIAL HELP LINE:
Families Matter (familiesmatterusa.org) (1-646-827-3622)

IT GETS BETTER FOR YOU TOO.

Also by Dan Savage

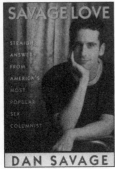

978-0-452-27815-8

978-0-452-28416-6

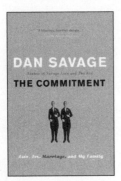

978-0-452-28763-1

978-0-452-28176-9

Available wherever books are sold.

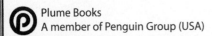

Plume Books
A member of Penguin Group (USA)